WHITE-COLLAR BLUES

658.4095
H356w

White-Collar Blues

Management Loyalties in an Age of Corporate Restructuring

CHARLES HECKSCHER

BasicBooks
A Division of HarperCollins*Publishers*

Designed by Ellen Levine

LIBRARY OF CONGRESS CATALOGING-IN-PUBLICATION DATA
Heckscher, Charles C., 1949–
    White-collar blues: management loyalties in an age of corporate restructur-
ing / Charles Heckscher.
        p. cm.
    Includes index.
    ISBN 0-465-04368-2
    1. Corporate reorganizations. 2. Employee loyalty. I. Title.
HD2746.5.H43 1994
658.4'095—dc20   94–23620
                                                                          CIP

95 96 97 98 ❖/RRD 9 8 7 6 5 4 3 2 1

For Lavinia

CONTENTS

Acknowledgments   ix

PART I. CHANGING THE RULES

1. The Assault on Middle Management   3

    The Decline of Paternalism and the Rise of the Professional Manager;
    The Research

2. The Meaning of Loyalty   13

    The Trouble with Rationalist Management; Beyond Rationalism:
    Patterns of Loyalty; Corporate Loyalty; Forging Corporate Loyalty;
    The Practical Benefits of Loyalty and Corporate Community;
    Loyalty's Limits: The Failings of Informal Trust; The Moral
    Dimension; Conclusion

PART II. THE TRADITIONAL COMMUNITY IN CRISIS

3. The First Shock   39

    Nadir; Patterns of Culture in Shock; Cushioning the Blow:
    The Failure of the "Human Relations Approach"; Conclusion:
    The Flight from Conflict

4. The Retreat to Autonomy   57
       Glover; The Revival of Bureaucracy; Conclusion

5. The Walls of the Box: The Failure of Participatory Management   77
       *Increasing Participation and Voice; Why Problems Can't Be
       Discussed; Conclusion*

6. The Loyalty Trap   95
       *Introduction; The Fundamental Failings of Corporate Loyalty; The
       Dynamics of Organizational Loyalty; Warding Off Change; Limits to
       Change; A Brief Case Study of Managerial Loyalty; Conclusion*

PART III. THE NEW RELATIONSHIPS

7. Breaking Through: Creating the Community of Purpose   121
       *The Four Dynamic Organizations; The "Professional" Manager;
       Conclusion*

8. The Emerging Employment Relation   145
       *The Key Elements; The Potential Strengths of a Community of
       Purpose; Problems and Cautions: The Limitations of the Best Cases;
       What Is Still Needed for It to Work?; Conclusion*

9. Conclusion: Managers as Professionals   171
       Why Change?; Practical Implications; Close

Appendix   185
Notes   201
Bibliography   213
Index   219

ACKNOWLEDGMENTS

THE DATA FOR THIS BOOK were gathered primarily during my years at the Harvard Business School, which provided generous support; many of my colleagues there gave me valuable help from the initial phase through early attempts to pull it together. Richard Walton was always both a friendly and a tough critic. Mike Beer helped me in many ways, not only through critiques but also in making contacts in some of the companies studied, and in setting me up in forums to test the concepts. Richard Hackman, Anne Donnellon, and Russ Eisenstat were among those whose feedback helped shape the final product.

Comments also came from many others with whom I have worked or talked in developing my ideas. Lavinia Hall was a careful commentator who probably more than anyone else affected the tone and presentation of the work. I was blessed with good editors: Martin Kessler initially pushed me to put loyalty at the center of the inquiry, and Kermit Hummel helped me to sort out the central points. Kathy Cannings, Bob McKersie, Myron Roomkin, Nikki Steckler, Fred Gordon, and Sue Schurman also enhanced the concepts a great deal.

The bulk of the credit must, however, go to the men and women in middle management whom I interviewed. My method was largely to talk to them about my evolving understanding of the world of middle management, and to debate or discuss with them whether it made sense of their experience. Academics hold no monopoly on conceptual discourse, and I found many managers whose struggles to make sense of their situation pushed me forward along my path.

I promised confidentiality to those I interviewed. To preserve it, I have sometimes changed details or used pseudonyms in the descriptions that follow.

WHITE-COLLAR BLUES

PART I

Changing the
Rules

1

The Assault on Middle Management

For two decades middle managers have been under attack—widely condemned as bureaucratic deadwood and unproductive overhead, criticized for lack of entrepreneurship, and, most telling of all, subject for the first time to mass layoffs. This is a deep change in fortunes, and it manifests an equally deep change under way in the organization of business enterprises. As middle managers were the frontline troops in the expansion of industrial bureaucracy during the early years of this century, so they now take the fire as bureaucracy has come under attack from all quarters.

The steady reports of layoffs from the largest corporations, for those who keep even a casual eye on the headlines, have become numbing. It is not just General Electric, whose CEO advocates a fierce new performance culture; it is also IBM, which long stood as an exemplar of the virtues of loyalty and commitment. It is not just General Motors, which in some recent years has bled red ink at a terrifying rate; it is also Xerox, to all appearances healthy and highly profitable. Annual surveys by the American Management Association show that over two-thirds of their member firms downsized between 1988 and 1993, and that while middle managers make up 8 percent of the workforce, they have accounted for 19 percent of the cuts.[1]

Their fate is closely bound up with that of the larger society. This is the group that more than any other anchored the middle class, shaped the suburbs, and defined the "good life" for mainstream American culture. Blue-collar workers, who always experienced cycles of layoffs and uncertainty, once looked enviously to the stability and the perquisites of the middle managers and hoped that their children could penetrate those ranks. The image of movement into the safe zones of corporate bureaucracies has been an important component of social mythology for millions outside the middle class.

Until roughly a decade ago the myth had a strong base in reality. Middle managers were among the most favored groups of our society. In most large companies they were virtually guaranteed lifetime employment security: when cost pressures arose, cuts were made in the blue-collar force, but never among managers. They were treated as permanent members of permanent enter- prises. They were paid well and could confidently expect careers of steadily increasing responsibility and rewards. Their jobs, unlike those at the highest levels, were not very stressful: they generally worked 9 to 5 and within clearly delimited boundaries. As a class they expressed great contentment with the state of their lives, and as a class they grew steadily during the postwar period.[2]

It might be said that they deserved this place of honor because they were the key to the development of the large corporate organizations that drove economic expansion during this century. Alfred Chandler, the leading histo- rian of the modern business enterprise, treats as a critical event the separa- tion of middle layers, responsible for allocation and coordination, from a top layer responsible for policy and strategy; this innovation, perfected at General Motors and Dupont in the interwar period, created enormous competitive advantages and increased productivity. The power of the "decentralized bureaucracy" developed by Alfred Sloan rested on the administrative skills of the organization men.[3]

The recent waves of layoffs have shattered the pattern. The current restruc- turing cuts managers adrift from the stable communities that formerly framed their career prospects and threatens to throw them into a world of fierce com- petition. The reduction of security, the threat to poor performers, and the gen- eral diminution in numbers have raised the stakes for those who remain. There is great pressure for harder work, higher productivity, and beating out fellow workers. As the ranks of management have thinned, opportunities for advance- ment have necessarily declined; thus promotion is no longer a predictable reward for steady work. Indeed, the downsizing trend has begun to erase the key distinction between managers and workers: for the first time managers are being treated as a variable cost rather than a part of the fixed base.

Why is this happening?

To begin with, I find the usual explanations thoroughly inadequate. Two fac- tors are widely cited: international competition and technological change. These make the transformation of middle-management roles sound like a rela- tively simple reaction to external pressures; they fail to account for the deeper shifts that have been going on in corporations for several decades.

It is of course true that international competition, from the Japanese and increasingly from the rest of the world, has greatly increased in the last two decades. The United States no longer dominates the world economy: growth in productivity and incomes has slowed dramatically since the 1970s. Many com- panies and industries that had worked out relatively comfortable "live and let live" accommodations with their domestic competitors in the 1950s were deeply shaken when companies from outside the party showed an ability to break in. Cost-cutting is in part a reaction to this pressure.

Yet despite the drumbeat of press reports, international competition doesn't begin to explain the extent of the change: it fails to deal with a whole set of crucial facts.

- Management layoffs and corporate restructuring are not limited to companies in competitive crisis; by now they have grown to a wave sweeping through all sectors of the economy, even the healthiest.
- There have always been companies and industries in trouble, yet almost none of them used management layoffs before the mid-1970s. When Chrysler (to take a celebrated example) came to the federal government in 1979 claiming a danger of imminent collapse, it did not start by cutting its middle-management force. Something happened after that time that made such previously unheard-of actions seem legitimate.
- The focus on international competition does not explain why the only major industrial country *not* to share in management downsizing in the eighties was our most feared competitor, Japan.[4] The Japanese, at least in the corporate sector, are particularly fervent advocates of stability and loyalty—indeed, unlike businesses in the United States, they have extended this approach down to the blue-collar ranks. They have been extremely reluctant to lay off anyone. Although I have been unable to get reliable comparisons of the number of managers,[5] there is a general belief among American executives that the Japanese middle ranks are bloated. This belief does not square with the notion that the revolution in treatment of our own managers is a response to the competition.
- By their own account, many of the companies leading the revolution are not doing so from a sense of crisis. Going back to 1988, for example, less than half the American Management Association members who had downsized that year cited a business downturn as even a contributing factor. Since then the proportion has gone up, but a sizable majority continues to say that business pressure is not the sole determinant. At least equal numbers cite a positive rationale for the cuts: the opportunity for "improved staff utilization (productivity)," as distinct from a pressing demand for such improvement.[6]

In short, most of the turnabout in the treatment of middle managers has nothing directly to do with international competition. The competitive situation may have created a climate more open to change, or it may simply have provided a convenient rationale; but the unprecedented willingness to break long-standing expectations of security goes deeper than a crisis response.

As for new information technologies, these certainly present a theoretical opportunity for a revolution in the way managerial work is done—but this theory is still far from realization. Significant use of computers among managers dates back no further than about 1985—a quantum leap did not occur in most companies until the 1990s, far too late to explain the transformation of attitudes beginning fifteen years before. Nor does computerization in itself set a direction: it can be used to strengthen the hand of middle managers as well as to weaken it.[7] Many of the early visions about the advent of computers involved armies of bureaucrats amplifying their powers through the reach of electronic networks.

None of these immediate explanations, in short, accounts for the turnabout in the relation of managers to their firms. As one digs deeper into the roots of the transformation, moreover, there is evidence that the change in the job of middle managers goes back well before the recent sense of crisis. The classic image of the job is a desk-bound, paper-based one, that of reviewing reports and sending them forward or backward along the chain of command. As far as we can tell from research in the 1940s and 1950s (we will review this evidence later), the classic image was not too far from the truth. But those who have been in management for a long time agree that starting in the 1960s there was an increase in the amount of time spent in meetings, managing problems by committee and consensus. The dramatic fads of recent years—empowerment, involvement, cross-functional task forces, and so on—are experienced by managers not as radically discontinuous with the past, but as extensions of a development that has been under way a long time.

These are strands of evidence which lead us to look beyond simple connections between competitive pressure or technology and downsizing. External threats have served primarily to accelerate a movement already under way. The response has taken as a model neither the Japanese nor our own traditions, but moved in a new direction. In the process it has violated deep values and expectations, and it is struggling to define a new set of beliefs.

The Decline of Paternalism and the Rise of the Professional Manager

The central problem we will be examining is the nature of the change in the employment relationship. My thesis is that we are moving beyond the ethic of paternalism, which had marked large corporations for the last century. At the moment, companies and their managers are struggling to define a new ethic that validates the needs of diverse individuals but preserves a sense of community and commitment.

By *paternalism* I mean a relation in which an organization offers protection and security in exchange for undivided loyalty. Until the 1960s this relation was omnipresent. Corporations implicitly pledged that they would take care of their employees if employees would subordinate their needs to those of the company.

The paternalistic ethic was central to the growth of the large bureaucracies that dominated the corporate world. Bureaucracy is founded on obedience, each level carrying out the instructions of those above. Loyalty is the motivational base of obedience: it sets the conditions under which people will agree to carry out orders and submit themselves to the organization.[8]

This complex of paternalism and bureaucracy defined the shape not only of corporate organization but of much of the rest of modern society as well. The economic structure of the past century can be called "bureaucratic capitalism": it has involved the development of large bureaucracies that manage relationships among the key social stakeholders. Corporatism, which became after World War II the dominant social form in every advanced economy including our own, is essentially a balancing of three major formal systems: business, labor, and government. The events within large companies therefore have wide implications not only because of the key role of middle managers but also because of the key role of paternalistic systems.

Over the past thirty years this complex has been under attack in all spheres of society; the assault on middle managers is only one manifestation. Bureaucracy and hierarchy, which were once symbols of efficiency and strength, are now scorned in government as well as industry throughout the industrial world. The idea of organizations taking care of people has lost its attraction. Entrepreneurship has risen in the scale of values above size and power. Excluded social groups—women, minorities, the disabled—who used to try to demonstrate their loyalty in order to get ahead are now demanding recognition of their independence.

Businesses, moreover, are increasingly looking for more than obedience. Instead of encouraging subordination, they are promoting "empowerment." They are searching for ways to motivate people to invent new things, to make the old rules obsolete. This demands a less hierarchical relationship than traditional loyalty.

Middle managers are at the center of the investigation because they were at the center of the old order: by understanding their experience we can get quickly to the heart of events. Their insight on the future is no more privileged than anyone else's, but theirs is a perspective that has often been ignored, and one that by virtue of their deep feeling for the needs of bureaucracy can contribute importantly to our understanding.

As these managers have suffered through the upheavals of the last decades, they have taken two major routes. On the one hand are those I will call "loyalists"—the bulk of my sample—who have held on to familiar expectations in the face of mounting disruption. They have "put their heads down," focusing more and more narrowly on their jobs, and trying to block out the seeming chaos around them. On the other are those who have embraced a new identity: instead of "loyal servants," they have defined themselves as "professionals," whose commitment is to a mission or task rather than to a company. The relation to the company then becomes contingent, valuable only as long as the employee feels challenged and respected.

The ethical dimension of this shift—the mutual obligation between employee and company—is particularly significant. Within corporate bureau-cracies there was almost always an assumption of reciprocal loyalty. Companies became for their managerial employees a kind of supplementary welfare state, offering lifelong security and many forms of support, both emotional and finan-cial. In return, managers were expected to devote themselves unreservedly to the company.

There are many reasons to criticize this moral compact, which we will exam-ine more closely in chapter 2. "Paternalism" has a negative ring to it—one might describe it as a matter of selling one's soul to buy security. Yet the man-agers themselves rarely experienced it that way; as they look back today they stress the positive qualities of mutual caring and support. They characterize the old corporation, in fact, as a form of community, with values in which they believed deeply. Its loss, then, leaves them adrift—not merely hurt in an objec-tive or material sense by the inability to plan for the future but also morally con-fused and often outraged. They feel that loyalty is a good that is being lost.

This is why the reaction of those involved in downsizing and restructuring carries a load of pain far beyond the "rational" fear of individual injury. It quickly became evident as I spoke with middle managers that most were not simply cal-culating personal risks and rewards. They were expressing feelings of affection, of betrayal, of sorrow; they spoke with moral fervor and passionate sensibility. The world that was threatened was far larger than their personal one:

> Loyalty comes with trust and believing, and this has been cast out across the whole company as being not the way to run things. And then when you look around you see takeovers and the crumbling of everything in the whole economy.

The sense of anguish is matched by many of those who are leading the down-sizing efforts: the loss of loyalty is for them a sadness—perhaps the loss was necessary, but it nevertheless was greatly to be regretted.

The undermining of communal ties is a theme that resonates throughout our society. There seem to be few bastions of security and unconditional caring left. The problem has come to the surface many times before: capitalism always breaks down communal barriers in its periods of growth and change. But that does not make it any less painful or serious for those cut off from traditional sources of support. And although there have been many cries of "Wolf!" going all the way back to Adam Smith, the erosion of community must still be of seri-ous concern for the society as a whole. Without that stabilizing influence nations become fragmented and lawless. We seem currently to be moving in that disturbing direction, and our media and political discourse are therefore full of efforts to identify points of moral stability.

It is of some interest to trace the breakdown of the ethic of loyalty, to under-stand the dynamics it sets in motion and the problems it creates for corporations. That is one major theme of the pages that follow. But it is of even greater interest to notice that some companies seem to be doing rather well without loyalty—not because they have managed to create a successful organization with no community at all, but because they have developed the beginnings of a different ethic. As they abandon the community of loyalty, they are starting to sketch something I will call a *community of purpose.* I am guarded about it because it seems to me to be genuinely novel and largely unformed, but there are, in a few of these downsizing companies, signs of a new way of working together. This represents, in my view, the first major shift in practical ethics since the development of modern individualism, and it carries the potential of resolving the long-running conflict between individualism and the essentially precapitalist structure of traditional community.

The Research

My argument is founded on a set of loosely structured interviews with about 250 middle managers in 14 units—divisions, headquarters, or plants—spread across 8 large industrial companies.[9] All of these organizations were undergoing major changes, and almost all had recently reduced their managerial forces. The companies were Honeywell, General Motors, Pitney-Bowes, Dow Chemical, Figgie International, Wang, Dupont, and AT&T. I chose them, for the most part, because they seemed typical of the current struggles of large manufacturing corporations in this country; I was not generally seeking out "best cases" or exemplars of how to handle restructuring.

In each of these fourteen organizations (with a few exceptions) I interviewed between ten and twenty middle managers. In almost all cases I also interviewed a top officer—at least the senior human resource manager, and frequently the top line manager. In four of the cases on which I will focus most closely in the following pages—for which I use the pseudonyms Apex, Barclay, Glover, and Lyco—I returned one or two years later for follow-up interviews. At Lyco and Fixx I also had ongoing consulting relations that enriched the picture. Finally, I conducted a few focus groups with managers who were attending executive education sessions at Harvard and Northwestern Universities.

These main research sites are described in summary form in the appendix, and will be referred to by pseudonyms to maintain confidentiality, with this memory aid: the pseudonyms are alphabetized in order from Apex, the most dynamic and positive company in the sample, to Nadir, the most angry and troubled.

There is no accepted definition of *middle manager,*[10] and there is enormous variation in titles and structures among companies. But I gradually developed a working definition that seemed to mark off a distinct group: those below the general manager's executive team and above the level of supervisor.

- Marking the upper boundary, the *general manager* is the one responsible for a fairly autonomous organization—most often the head of a division, in a few cases plant managers or company CEOs. Whatever the formal level, these leaders and their immediate team have an integrated and systemic view of their organization that is almost always sharply different from those below them. As soon as I moved down from these, in all but the most successful cases, I found managers who focused only on a small piece of the business, who expressed bewilderment and frustration with the policies of the top, and who saw themselves as clearly separate—as coordinating the day-to-day operations in a way their leaders did not and could not understand.

- At the lower boundary, *supervisors* are generally a breed apart: their identity as managers is fragile because they are required to bridge the gap with nonmanagement. In order to be effective, they need to identify in part with workers. Frequently they have "come up from the ranks," and the supervisory position is the end rather than the beginning of their career path.

- Between these levels, the *middle managers* of several levels shared a common view of themselves as the operational core, holding the business together at a practical level while the top managers thought long-range thoughts and the supervisors dealt with the workers.

THE RANGE OF RESPONSES: TROUBLED AND DYNAMIC COMPANIES

Across the fourteen organizations there was a wide range of responses, or "morale," among middle managers—even in situations that were superficially quite similar. By *morale* I do not mean simple satisfaction or happiness: individuals can be perfectly content when organizations are falling apart. In fact, I encountered a number of people who said, in effect, "My situation is fine, but the business is in terrible shape." These people had withdrawn into a kind of cynical satisfaction, which seemed good neither for the company nor for them. The kind of "morale" that is important involves a sense of confidence in the future, of enthusiasm about the collective mission, and of fully using one's talents.

Though this is in theory a complicated concept, in practice it is not hard to judge: I am confident that other observers would place these companies in about the same rank order. In three organizations managers manifested almost universal anger, bitterness, confusion, and pessimism about the future; in four, they were mixed, with some being angry and others more hopeful; in three, hope outweighed pessimism, and anger was nearly absent; and in four, feelings about both personal and organizational futures were widely positive.[11]

For most purposes I will focus on one broad distinction which seemed to me to mark the most dramatic divide in the group: between ten "troubled" companies and four "dynamic" ones. The former were not only dominant in my study but are probably even more dominant in industry at large: there is a lot of trouble out there. The dynamic group gives some reason for hope: though as models they are incomplete and partial, they seem to point to a new relationship that avoids both the bitterness of fractured loyalty and the cynicism of individualist free agency.

Within the troubled group there was a further distinction. A few companies (which will be represented by Nadir in chapter 3) were shot through with anger and bitterness—which is what most outside analysts expect. But a larger cluster (represented by Glover and Lyco in chapters 4 and 5) showed much subtler reactions; morale was not exactly high, but most managers seemed resigned to what was happening and fairly optimistic about the future. The problem—and the reason I still call them troubled—is that they achieved this optimism by blocking out evidence of competitive problems, and by withdrawing into an ever-narrower focus on their own particular job. Their confidence, I will argue, came from defensiveness, and did no good either for them or their companies.

BASIC FINDINGS: THE PARADOXICAL EFFECTS OF LOYALTY

One of the first things that struck me as I conducted these interviews was that in most cases loyalty to the company remained very strong among managers, even after substantial downsizing and, in some cases, rather brutal layoffs. Managers continued to express a strong emotional attachment to the corporation and an expectation that they would finish their careers there, if at all possible.

The second thing I noticed, however was that this persistent loyalty did not help: the places where it was strongest were neither the happiest nor the most effective organizations. The managers were terribly torn, feeling they were holding on to values that were no longer valued by the system around them. And they did not, by any evidence I could find, work very well together.

These findings seem paradoxical. The usual assumption in current writing on this topic is that loyalty is being destroyed by the downsizing wave, and that this is harmful to managers and their companies. The responses of the managers I talked to, however, suggested that the opposite was closer to the truth: loyalty is not being destroyed, and *that* is harmful. In the few companies that seemed the most positive, the managers by and large rejected traditional loyalty.

So that leads in turn to another question: If companies can in fact function well without loyalty, does this mean that pure untrammeled individualism is the best form of social organization? That view didn't fit the facts, either. Very few of the managers advocated the kind of market-based individualist entrepreneurship that has become popular in much political discourse and journalism, and none of the companies came close to exemplifying it.

None of these organizations was trying to create a culture of individual competitiveness: all were looking for a way to build a sense of unity. The usual approach was to be nice: to preserve a family spirit by softening the blow of downsizing as much as possible, by providing elaborate outplacement and counseling, and by treating survivors well.

Such niceness, however, had little impact—the most caring companies often had the most distressed managers. Instead, what made a dramatic difference was quite a different factor: how well the managers understood the business they were in. To a surprising extent most managers, even in companies that had actively been trying to communicate business imperatives, had a very poor understanding of markets and competitive positioning. They understood their own jobs, but not their context. Those who had attained a wider view, regardless of other objective conditions, were more energized and optimistic than those with a narrower perspective.

The older form of loyalty seemed to be based on a sense of a shared destiny—that we are all in this together through thick or thin. In the organizations more successfully making the transition, there seemed to be a sense not so much of being *in* this together as of *working* together toward a common purpose, one based on a collective definition of a strategy and of the demands of the environment. It is a far more contingent and voluntarist form of community than the old; some might also say it is colder and less fair. But it can also be seen as less paternalistic, more capable of responding to and developing individual capacities. These tensions and ambiguities are today being worked out throughout the corporate world, and in many other arenas as well. The investigation of these downsizing companies will help to clarify some of the parameters of this potential alternative to loyalty.

2

The Meaning of Loyalty

To start with, what is loyalty good for, and why is it such a powerful force? The answers are far from obvious. Much of management theory ignores loyalty or treats it as an annoying complication, instead finding it more convenient to begin with the assumption that employees are rational agents seeking personal gain. The world would be simpler if this hypothesis were correct, but it has proved impractical as a guide to managing organizations.[1]

On the other hand, writings that pay attention to emotional factors such as power and attachment, while they take in a richer slice of reality, don't generally tell us what to make of these phenomena: they are more descriptive than analytic. Certainly strong emotions may motivate people to work hard and think of the greater good, but may equally motivate them to engage in destructive "politics" or resistance to change.

On balance, is it better to rely on the loyalty of a traditional organization or the rational self-interest of a free-agent system? The former has clearly won in practice, though the latter has always had strong advocates. Neither of them, however, fully solves the problem of motivating people to cooperate—especially under the current conditions of rapid change and downsizing.

The Trouble with Rationalist Management

Rationalism is most associated with economists, who see rationality everywhere. "Agency theory" is the branch of economics that has tried to apply the principle to the internal organization of firms. But it is surprising to see that the economists are not alone in this basic assumption. Practical management theorists, influenced by Frederick Taylor, have often worked from the same rationalist principle, at least when they are dealing with blue-collar workers; that is, they have designed systems that rely primarily on motivations of fear and material reward. And even sociologists in the tradition of Max Weber, so quick to criticize economists for ignoring the real play of emotion and politics, have often described bureaucracy in highly rational terms. Agency theory, Taylorism, and the Weberian theory of bureaucracy are, from this perspective, variations on a single theme.

To start at the chronological beginning: Weber, the great sociologist who was the first to define bureaucracy, put enormous emphasis on the concept of rationality. He emphasized the administrative role of bureaucrats, exercised within a framework of technical autonomy: they were supposed to receive general orders from their superiors and apply their expertise to carrying them out. Within this administrative process, according to the conception, they were to have freedom to apply their expertise to the goals; but overall direction came down through the hierarchy:

> The following may be said to be the fundamental categories of rational legal authority:
> 1. A continuous organization of official functions bound by rules.
> 2. A specified sphere of competence. This involves
>   (a) a sphere of obligations to perform functions which have been marked off as part of a systematic division of labor;
>   (b) the provision of the incumbent with the necessary authority to carry out these functions; and
>   (c) that the necessary means of compulsion are clearly defined.[2]

Weber emphasized the power and flexibility of this form of organization, and most classic management theory, at least until the last two decades, has implicitly or explicitly adopted the paradigm. The primary concerns were structure and control: how to specify roles clearly in a way that would produce coordinated organization, and how to make sure that people performed them. Early management theorists—Henry Poor, Daniel McCallum, Henry Metcalfe, and others[3]—elaborated the system of controls needed to make a bureaucracy function: how jobs could best be broken down, how many people could be managed by one supervisor, how to match authority and responsibility, and other basic techniques that remain rules of thumb to this day. They evinced little concern about the motivational issues of interrelations among managers—why they would *want* to cooperate. For in the idea of bureaucracy there is no need for people to want to cooperate: cooperation is an automatic outcome of doing their jobs as defined. All they need to want is to do their jobs well, in the sense of demonstrating technical competence.

Bureaucracy's great success was that it made possible united action on a large and complex scale. Before its invention the scope of action was small; even armies were tiny compared to modern ones, and complicated efforts involving many different tasks could not be managed beyond a small traditional community. But in a bureaucracy the will of the superior could be spread rapidly on a wide scale through the division of labor and the rationality of control.

After a while, however, some began to notice that rationality failed to account for some important things. Sometimes, for example, people refused to carry out the instructions or fit into their slots. Frederick Taylor, a foreman in a machine shop, noticed that workers were "soldiering"—deliberately doing less work than they were capable of. The group frequently held back individual productivity— and reward—in order to keep to a pace that everyone could maintain.[4] This was a recognition of an important breakdown in the rationalist theory of motivation.

The response to this observation might be to try to understand what was really motivating people and then try to draw on it to develop cooperation. But Taylor was a man of the bureaucratic mold. It did not occur to him that workers might have better ideas than he, and he assumed that the only way to organize was to figure out the tasks and get people to do them. So if people were not acting "rationally" by carrying out the correctly defined tasks, he decided, one should take things to the next step: to *make* them act rationally by increasing the level of control.

The result was what Taylor called "scientific management": an effort to make the rules of rationality so specific, and the sanctions so powerful, that they could not be avoided. This is the world of the stopwatch-wielding industrial engineer, of fragmented jobs reduced to their simplest components, which Charlie Chaplin lampooned so memorably in *Modern Times*. Its enormously influential contribution to management was rules worked out so carefully that they could be linked to specific punishments and rewards, so that workers could be pushed and pulled through the precise motions that management had determined to be most effective.

But that never worked as planned, either. Soldiering continued as an intractable management problem: the famous Hawthorne study at Western Electric is just one of many to document continuing underground resistance to management control.[5] Furthermore, it became apparent that the logic of Taylorism could not be indefinitely extended. Trying to beat down the continuing resistance merely created new problems. First, it required an escalation in the managerial hierarchy to develop ever more detailed rules and ever stricter enforcement. Second, the rules became so detailed that they eliminated the flexibility needed for ordinary day-to-day problem solving. Try as they might, the industrial engineers could not anticipate all contingencies or schematize all the workers' knowledge.

In fact, the good will of workers—their willingness actively to contribute their working knowledge to the good of the company—has remained an essential though generally unacknowledged ingredient in the efficiency of production. This has at times been made dramatically evident through the tactic of "working to rule": by actually following all the procedures that have been laid down for them—by acquiescing to the Taylorist logic and refusing to use their own discretion—workers can effectively bring a factory to its knees.[6]

Thus in the last thirty years there has been a growing recognition that production workers should be treated as more than agents to be manipulated with carrots and sticks. "Worker participation" has by now become a widely accepted principle, if less widely implemented in practice; few managers today would support the pure "scientific management" model. This shift is in effect an admission that it is not possible, no matter how logical it seems, to organize people solely through rewards and punishments, or appeals to their rational interests; the eliciting of active cooperation remains vital.

So far I have described blue-collar work. The world of managers has traditionally been different. In the past, managers, in their role as employees, have not themselves been treated in a "scientific" way: workers might need to be controlled, but managers are, after all, the controllers. In order to figure out what needs to be done by the workers, managers must necessarily exercise judgment and discretion. Thus there has always been far more reliance on intangible elements of leadership and motivation in this domain.

But today we have a paradoxical reversal: while there is a widespread effort to draw out the good will of blue-collar workers, middle managers are being treated increasingly as cogs in the machine—a kind of Taylorization of management. Economists have entered the management field with prescriptions drawn from "agency theory"—an approach remarkably continuous with the tradition of Taylorism.

Agency theory begins with the same basic management problem: How can employees be motivated to act in the interest of the whole?[7] It takes Taylorism a step further by assuming that managers, like workers, are oriented to rational rewards and punishments. This produces a breathtaking simplification of the problem of human resources management. All that is necessary, in this view, is to determine—in the pure bureaucratic tradition—what tasks need to be done, and then reward people for doing them. Thus its proponents advocate the extension of pay for performance, linking rewards closely to individual accomplishment of goals.

When agency theorists look at real organizations, they are rather startled and dismayed to find that they do not operate on these apparently obvious principles. True pay for performance remains rare: though there are increasing efforts to introduce it, it is almost always defused in the implementation. Managers simply refuse to make strong performance distinctions among their subordinates, generally rating the vast majority in the above-average category. Pay within groups is therefore far more equal than would be justified by individual performance.[8]

The theorists' response today is much the same as Taylor's ninety years ago: if people won't spontaneously be rational, perhaps they can be forced to be so.

Since managers resist the prescription of distinguishing among subordinates, top management with increasing frequency has tried to compel them to rank their people or place them on a "forced curve," so that some would have to be rated low. Two organizations in my sample (Karet and Glover) had tried such efforts, resulting in major outbreaks of open anger and resistance. Others, according to the stories they tell, have had less trouble; there is to date, however, no hard evidence either way about the effectiveness of such incentives.

The links among these three traditions—bureaucratic theory, Taylorism, and agency theory—are strong, not because they derive from each other, but because they all share key assumptions: that the direction, or purpose, of an organization must be set from a single point (the "top"); that the implementers must focus on specific tasks within that overall purpose; and that these implementers are motivated by utilitarian rationality.[9] They ignore other aspects of motivation, from jealousy and envy to the desire for honor and the pursuit of principles. When such motivations force themselves on their attention, they respond by increasing the power of incentives to try to overwhelm the nonrational aspects.

The two later approaches—Taylorism and agency theory—are in essence variations on the concept of bureaucracy. Now, agency theorists, in particular, would deny this claim: they see themselves as apostles of individual initiative, freeing people from the dead hand of bureaucratic conformity. Unlike Taylor, they advocate reducing the number of detailed rules, specifying only outcomes and rewards and letting people figure out how to get to them. But the question of how detailed the rules are is not central to bureaucracy: Weber's original concept involved highly skilled technical workers with a great deal of autonomy to exercise their expertise. Since then bureaucratic organizations have gone through repeated cycles of centralization and decentralization, tight and loose control; there seems to be a perpetual rhythm to the form, with the pendulum swinging back and forth. But as in an old grandfather clock, both ends of the swing remain within the unchanged casing of the bureaucratic order.

The essence of bureaucracy, that which links the three traditions I have described, is that individuals are conceived of as within a box—a focused, limited task, to which they are expected to devote their whole energy. Whether that box is a small prison cell or a spacious stadium is a matter of management style and policy. But in either case you want to make sure that people do not wander beyond the confines of their box, because if they do they will upset the rest of the system. Taylor said it most clearly: "Any improvement the worker makes upon the system will be fatal to success." Only those hierarchically up the ladder have a broad enough view of the system that they can judge whether an "improvement" is indeed better.

Taylorism and agency theory have emerged in practice when the problem of control within bureaucracy became acute: when for one reason or another people refused to play the parts assigned to them. In the case of blue-collar workers this resistance was quickly apparent and often emerged into open conflict over a century ago. The evident class tension made bureaucratic leaders early on give up most efforts to create a unity of motivation among their employees, and opened the way for the strong appeal of Taylorism, with its promise of predictable control.

But in the case of managerial employees, the problem is much more recent—as recent as the past two decades. Until that time the stability of employment and the underlying class unity made it possible to rely on "informal" modes of motivation: on "leadership," implicit contracts—and loyalty. The restructuring process has shaken that set of tacit principles. The popularity among top management of incentive approaches derived from agency theory is evidence of the resulting strain on the system of control.

In short, theories that try to ignore the emotional aspects of motivation, and to rely exclusively on the logical workings of incentives, have consistently encountered blockages erupting from the very emotions they deny. The response has typically been to increase the power of incentives, through a combination of stronger means of compulsion and larger positive inducements—to try, as it were, to overpower the illogical side of behavior. But rationalist theorists have never succeeded in getting people to act rationally.

Beyond Rationalism: Patterns of Loyalty

Effective managers have always recognized that management is more a psychological business than a logical one. They have therefore never relied primarily on material incentives, but have drawn on emotional connections.

For instance, Chester Barnard—president of New Jersey Bell in the 1930s, whose theories have influenced generations of managers—believed that the creation of an atmosphere of fidelity was among the most important management tasks: "The most important single contribution required of the executive," he wrote, ". . . is loyalty, domination by the organization personality."[10]

Even scientific management, as we have seen, was "scientific" only for blue-collar workers. Embodying classic employment relations, it drew a sharp line between management and labor, and it relied on good will to ensure the cooperation of the managers. "Science for the workers, magic for the managers," one might say. This "magic" is what we mean by loyalty: the force that keeps people using their intelligence in the service of the company even when no one can scientifically measure performance and enforce conformity. This enchantment is not, however, a single phenomenon. It has taken different forms in different social organizations in the past; and it is a central contention of this book that it is transmuting into still another form for the future.

The historical patterns of motivation, at least those identifiable in business organizations, are three: personal dependence, the bureaucratic ethic, and corporate loyalty. The first two have largely been relegated by their limitations to the waste heap of history; but the third remains dominant in most large corporations.

PERSONAL DEPENDENCE

The most basic kind of loyalty is to a person; this goes back to the earliest forms of social life. Before the development of bureaucratic administration, for instance, monarchs gathered people who were tied to the largesse of the crown. The most reliable of these (as Lewis Coser shows in a stimulating study) were those who were most dependent: foreigners, commoners raised above their station, and eunuchs. For these categories, loyalty literally knew no limits: there was no boundary between the private life of the servant and duty to the master. The "greedy institutions" that supported them also demanded their lives.[11]

Such systems were, however, notoriously unstable: internal battles for the master's favor, jealousies and intrigues, continually threatened the fabric of cooperation. And this primitive form of loyalty was also very limited in scope, bound to the personal presence of the ruler. These weaknesses were largely overcome by the bureaucratic form, which stabilized relations into a series of specific roles and relationships.

The personal form of loyalty seems rarer in middle management than I expected. Only one organization—Marks—was clearly structured around attachments to an individual; in addition, Dest had been dominated by its founder until a few years previously. In these cases it was clear that people felt dependent on the individual, not the system—and the leader constantly reminded them of that dependence through arbitrary actions. In both companies there were common stories of the top man appearing unexpectedly, getting deeply involved in the details of someone's job, changing everything around, and then disappearing:[12]

> You could not have imagined the level of detail that [the founder] decided. The managers became uncomfortable with him making all the decisions. He often came down and reversed decisions that had been made at lower levels. So people found it easier to just let him know everything that was going on, including the placement of signs, the colors of the rooms, and the arrangement of the parking lot.

At Marks, similarly, most managers felt that they were directly reliant on the leader for their position in life, and that without his singular favor they would be lost. Several managers told me that they could never duplicate their success in this company, because the leader had favored them far beyond their abilities.

But outside these organizations, no one in my sample admitted to being so personally dependent. To be sure, one hears occasional anecdotal accounts of corporate lords who demand absolute personal loyalty from subordinates—Walter Wriston of Citibank, say, or Harold Geneen of ITT. Perhaps such dependencies are more extreme at the higher reaches of corporations, where leaders may pick favorites for succession,[13] and it seems likely that it was far more common a half century ago, when the true bureaucratic order was still struggling to supplant the rule of "robber barons," than it is now. All I am sure of is that I didn't find it much in my sample.

The example of Marks suggests a reason for the rarity of this type: though it is a powerful way to secure obedience, it has serious side effects. At the top of the company, the autocratic and enormously successful founder, approaching retirement, realized that he had no one below him with enough strength to take over, and failed over several years to develop someone. Lower down, within one of the constituent companies—where the pattern of personal fiefdoms was repeated—I got a rich picture of the way that dependence on the leader was linked to internal jealousy and feuding among his subordinates, very much like the court intrigues of the feudal order. As soon as the founder's dominance began to wane, as he pulled back from day-to-day control, the company fell apart, plunging within a few years from very high returns to bankruptcy.

THE BUREAUCRATIC ETHIC

The development of bureaucracy resulted in part from a recognition by monarchs of the limitations of feudal dependencies, and represented an effort to free themselves from such personal entanglements. It is therefore not surprising that the rationalist conception described above initially received heavy stress. But that conception has not survived the test of reality: indeed, in the last decade bureaucracy has come to be seen as the ultimately *irrational* institution, shot through with politics and special interests. Long before that time, however, it had been recognized that bureaucracy tapped into motivations other than the logical pursuit of self-advantage.

Bureaucracy does involve a form of loyalty, but not to a person: instead, the loyalty demanded is to a job. The ethic, as Weber defined it, is shaped in terms of the performance of a task in a universalistic way—unbiased by passion (sine ira et studio). Robert Merton expanded on this pattern, remarking, "Discipline can be effective only if the ideal patterns are buttressed by strong sentiments which entail devotion to one's duties, a keen sense of the limitations of one's authority and competence, and methodical performance of routine activities."[14]

We can add a few more elements to Merton's definition of this pattern. The "sense of limitations of one's authority" has as a correlate the sense of mastery over one's own domain: though bureaucrats do what they are told, they do not allow anyone to tell them how to do it. Within the boundaries of their tasks, they are the experts and the masters. (The individual incentives advocated by agency theorists add a material base to this motivation, but do not change its form.)

The motivation of bureaucrats therefore takes the form of *autonomy:* their devotion is directed not to the leader but to a conception of duty. It involves a more limited form of obedience than the feudal relationships that it supplanted.

The great advantage of the bureaucratic form of loyalty is that it directs members' attachment not toward an individual, but toward an impersonal task. It therefore allows a great expansion of the scope of coordination. It requires neither emotional reinforcement from the leader—the satisfaction comes from a job well done rather than from personal rewards—nor detailed behavioral dictates. The loyal bureaucrat figures out how to carry out the directions received. There can be, in principle, a network of such bureaucrats from Tehran to Timbuktu, all independently working on the best way to carry out the general mandate.[15]

The realm of individual judgment is substantially larger in this pattern of motivation than in personal loyalty. The values tied to the bureaucratic role give people a general area within which they "know" the right thing to do; they do not need to wait for their superior to tell them. They have the right—indeed, the duty—to interpret those values for a given situation. The bureaucratic ethic, in short, leads the employee to do anything asked by the leader that is *proper* (by the rules), but not anything that is improper. As a further part of this pattern, a sharp line was drawn between the public and private segments of personality. Bureaucrats are dutiful at work, but free at home: unlike servants, they are not expected to put their entire personalities at the disposal of the master.

Weber argued that the bureaucratic structure was superior to every other form of organization. Others have expanded on his fear that the overwhelming power of this depersonalized form would dominate all else in social life.[16] Studies have confirmed that such an ethic works powerfully in government agencies.[17]

The failing of bureaucracy has been that this motivational attachment is still narrow: though it does not restrict one to seeking a superior's approval, it does restrict one to a focus on a single job. Therefore those bureaucracies that are closest to the pure type, especially in governments, are marked by a pattern in which an aggregate of rational actions frequently adds up to an irrational whole: the pieces do not coordinate, rules are applied without an understanding of their intent, and the results of actions stray increasingly far from their purpose.

In the business world this problem has proved so fundamental that true bureaucracies are extremely rare. None of the companies in my sample exhibited the sober logic of the ethic described by Weber and Merton. All of them tried to create a sense of unity as a framework for cooperation—to establish a community among their managers.

Corporate Loyalty

Large corporations in time have overwhelmingly rejected these motivational alternatives—reliance on rational incentives, personal dependence, or the sober bureaucratic ethic—to end with a primary focus on building loyalty to the corporate body. This theme is stressed in all of the previous studies that have explored the perspective of middle managers, and my interviews only further confirm the point. The themes of these studies, dating back to the 1950s, are remarkably consistent:[18]

- They stress the closed, communal nature of the corporation rather than a rational, bureaucratic nature. Whyte describes corporations as "feudal communities"; Rosabeth Kanter, writing in the 1970s, labels them "tribalistic"; C. Wright Mills refers to the "managerial demiurge"; William Ouchi writes of corporate "clans."
- There is a strong emphasis on conformity and suppression of individual style, on "fitting in" in a general social way as well as performing specific duties. Mills describes the "psychology of prestige striving," motivated by "status panic"; his devastating dissection of techniques of self-presentation are picked up by later studies such as Diane Margolis's and Robert Jackall's.
- This pressure for conformity is justified by a language of "teamwork." People, to be promoted and rewarded, need to be "team players," not too abrasive, able to cooperate with their peers. Though the language of "teamwork" is in tension with espoused ideologies of individualism, all these studies in essence demonstrate that individualism is tightly circumscribed in corporate communities.

Corporations, in short, have strong elements of traditional "warm" community, or *Gemeinschaft*. We will see this in more detail in later chapters, but the theme is clear: individuals are expected, and themselves expect, to sacrifice short-term interests for the support of the larger community. They work hard and delay rewards, which involves a belief that the relationship will last long enough for fairness to be reestablished. A manager at Glover noted,

> We're in a war now, the company can't reward people for everything they're doing. People are still working, though. The company is fair in the long run, and people know it.

More than this, they will at times do things that are neither recognized nor appreciated, even in the long run—even, at times, things that are personally damaging in the eyes of their superiors—because they are convinced of its rightness for the company. Of doing unrecognized work I have dozens of stories; of directly subordinating personal to corporate interests, only a few. But these are steps on the same chain, and their relative frequency shows an attitude far from the individualistic calculation of *Gesellschaft*.

In certain respects this pattern of motivation resembles the master-servant form. It invades the private domain: managers in these studies are expected to open their homes and show off their wives to their superiors as part of their proof of fitness for office; they are often required to move families without demur at a moment's notice. They are also expected, like eighteenth-century servants, to maintain the reputation of the master to the outside world. Much of employment law is in fact drawn explicitly from master-servant codes: public criticism of the employer, for example, is treated as an "elemental" violation of the obligation of loyalty.[19]

Yet the pattern is more complex because it is not confined to narrow personal relations; it is intertwined with large bureaucratic structures. It is for the most part oriented neither to an individual nor to a role, but to the organization itself: the managers of these studies are loyal to Dupont or General Motors rather than to the CEO or to their particular jobs.

It is a solution characterized by its vertical focus. Loyalty is directed to a higher body—abstractly to the organization as a whole, and concretely to the higher managers who are its representatives. The mechanisms that create loyalty are, in the main, ways of making managers dependent on their particular company and on the favor of their superiors. These mechanisms, as described by Whyte and Kanter and the others I have cited, include binding managers with company-specific benefits, providing company-specific training, holding out carrots of potential promotions, and requiring frequent moves to prevent competing attachments to local communities. The hoped-for dynamic is that in seeking to please superiors, people will do more than just follow rules and orders: they will use their intelligence to meet the needs of those superiors, even where there are no good rules.

This form of motivation, rather than the bureaucratic ethic or a rationalistic orientation to rewards, seems to be fundamental to the success of large corporations. Every organization in my sample had this form of loyalty in its background; every one was therefore struggling with the emotional fallout caused by downsizing.

Forging Corporate Loyalty

Corporations began from their earliest phases to take steps to ensure the loyalty of their managers. From the mid–nineteenth century one can identify a set of policies designed to link managers more closely to the whole. At least three key mechanisms were developed among the railroads of the 1870s and remained in near-universal use in large companies a century later.[20]

The first of these was the development of internal career tracks—that is, orderly and planned progression through a lifetime of work "up the ladder" of the company. Such a concept was, of course, unheard-of in an economy of small crafts and merchants; it became feasible for the first time with the development of bureaucracy. Its desirability became quickly apparent as employers sought to develop their managers into trusted members of the hierarchy.

In the last two decades a substantial economic literature has documented the strength and pervasiveness of internal labor markets in the corporate sector, and observational studies have stressed the motivational centrality of career opportunity.[21] Orientation to promotion is possibly the most important element holding the structure together. It gives superiors tremendous leverage, since promotion depends on diffuse approval over a long period of time. In my interviews, managers frequently described certain illegitimate actions, such as pushing the rights of minorities or taking time off for child care, as "career-killers": this fear was an extremely effective way of keeping people in line.

The second mechanism introduced in the railroads was stock sharing, which tied the financial fortunes of managers more closely to the performance of the firm. These, too, have remained extremely important, though limited to a higher level of manager than the first.[22]

Most important, perhaps, was the development of near-guarantees of employment security, which were already present in the early railroads. It is not generally realized how widely this phenomenon has characterized the U.S. economy, despite its common image of mobility and individualism. A recent estimate is that, at least through the 1970s, half of the men in the U.S. workforce ended in jobs that effectively offered lifetime security. Amazingly, this percentage is by the best estimates *higher* than the model of loyalty, Japan.[23]

These internal company policies served to link the long-term material interests of managers (in particular) to their employers. Their prevalence is surprising only to those (such as the agency theorists) who deny the importance of loyalty. Over time, moreover, mechanisms began to develop that created a subtler "psychological" dimension of loyalty: cultural patterns that linked the personality to the company, so that one became an "IBM man" or a "General Motors man."[24] These mechanisms have been thoroughly dissected in the observational tradition of research described earlier. They include policies of frequent geographic transfers, which had the effect of weakening competing ties to other communities and friends; codes of presentation that defined the "right" kind of behavior; rituals of passage that reinforced the company image; an ideology of being a good "member of the team." These are the sorts of things that William Whyte identified in *The Organization Man,* and lambasted for their threats to individualism and independence.

At the same time, again starting well back in the last century, societal mechanisms fell quickly into place to reinforce this pattern. Employment law, which one would assume would have no room for sentimentality, has (as mentioned earlier) forcefully taken up the theme. The Supreme Court has, for instance, upheld the right of employers to discharge those who criticize their companies in public, because "there is no more elemental cause for discharge of an employee than disloyalty to his employer. . . . The [law] seeks to strengthen, rather than to weaken, that cooperation, continuity of service and cordial contractual relationship between employer and employee that is born of loyalty to their common enterprise."[25]

In the legal tradition, moreover, loyalty is seen as particularly important for managerial employees. In 1980 the Supreme Court excluded university faculty from the protection of labor laws because of their high level of managerial responsibility; the court sought to avoid "the danger that divided loyalty will lead to those harms that [employment law] traditionally has sought to prevent."[26]

All this makes a potent brew that yields the "magic" of loyalty. It is a compound of self-interest and self-image, of the rational and the emotional; no single factor determines it. In my interviews, when I asked why people felt such continuing loyalty to their companies, all these factors were cited:

1. CAREER ADVANCEMENT:
   "I worked my way up. I always thought of this company as a land of opportunity."

   "People sacrifice with the expectation of eventual rewards."

2. DEPENDENCE AND FEAR:
   "There are fewer positions now but I'm still loyal. I am 47 years old. If I was in my twenties I would be more concerned, but it's hard to move when you are 47."

3. PRIDE IN ASSOCIATION WITH THE COMPANY:
   "We were number one in the market, and you were held in high esteem in the community. It had always been that way."

4. GRATITUDE AND SENSE OF OBLIGATION:
   "I have been described as being very loyal because I feel as though the company has provided everything I needed in terms of my career development, my self-actualization, as a professional."

5. PSYCHOLOGICAL INVESTMENT:
   "This company is a part of me. I feel responsible. I have lost a lot of weight and a lot of hair here."

6. SHARED VALUES:
   "The emphasis there is on people as individuals and we share strong values."

   "We have lost a lot of loyalty because people lost their identity—that is, their identity with the product."

7. PERSONAL FRIENDSHIPS AND CONTACTS:
   "I've been the godfather of many people who work here. We used to be friends here. I don't see that so much anymore."

SECURITY AND EMOTIONAL ATTACHMENT

And what about security? This is, after all, the central problem, the one with which we started.

The issue of security is a complicated one. In discussions before the 1991 recession, despite the job reduction in the corporate ranks, the people I spoke with expressed relatively little fear of losing their jobs. There was good reason for this: headhunters were prowling through their ranks, offering them opportunities at other companies; demand remained strong for managers at smaller companies. People regularly told success stories about those who had left through layoff or early retirement, with the theme that the leavers were better off than those who remained. The tone shifted somewhat in interviews conducted after the start of the recession, as it became genuinely difficult for managers to find new jobs; there was more insecurity and anxiety.

But there was not, even in the later interviews, a decline in expressions of loyalty. This is perhaps the most surprising finding: that despite the destruction of a pillar of the traditional employment relation, the fundamental sense of attachment remained solid, if anguished, among most managers as much as eight years after the start of the layoffs.

It appears that the complexity of the system of loyalty is sufficient to withstand simple shocks. If it were supported merely by mechanisms of self-interest, it would vanish as soon as those mechanisms were undermined. That is indeed what most commentators seem to expect. But the reality is that it is also supported by a deeper psychology: it is internalized in the motivations and self-images of managers, and therefore cannot be easily abandoned even when the conditions change. The connection to these companies is not like the connection to a stock on the market, which can be abandoned when the price drops; it is more like an affection for a favorite singer, which may long outlast his real vocal ability, or even for a parent, which is based even more firmly on moral principles that are not expected to fade even when the parent needs to receive care rather than give it.

Overall, the theme emerging most clearly in company after company was emotional attachment, something one can only call *love for a company:*

> "I care about this company in great depth, because I've given a lot to it and they've given to me." (Nadir)

> [When there are layoffs] "it's like a husband who has an affair on you."

> "You can't suddenly turn around something you lost almost totally or in large part and get it back. It's like a parent deceiving their child and then trying to ask for trust from that child. If it's some major significant issue that affects their life, that is very emotional to the child, you don't get that trust level back in a hurry."

Like all love, this is a complex emotion, often combining resentment and frustration with pride and attraction. It becomes visible in the current period of downsizing, when the love seems to be spurned. It is identifiable by its depth and diffuseness, seeming to touch all aspects of the personality. It is this reaction that most clearly uncovers the power of the managerial community.

It is also much harder to predict than shifts in self-interest. How long will it last? How many will retain the words of attachment while shifting to behaviors of self-interest? These questions involve nonrational dynamics that are crucial to the next chapters.

The Practical Benefits of Loyalty and Corporate Community

Firms have, then, gone to a lot of trouble to secure the loyalty of their managers. Why have they engaged in such an "irrational" practice? It is not so hard to see the attraction from the individual's point of view—the warmth, security, and community which comes from the loyalty bargain. But what is the advantage for the corporation?

From the point of view of the firm, corporate loyalty combines the generalized power of the bureaucratic ethic with the unconditional obedience of the master-servant relationship. It does not require a personal link to the leader, but it creates an emotional bond to the success of the whole. It solves the motivational problem of unifying a large group of managers: it is a powerful practical tool for management.

This practical power accounts for the universality of the phenomenon, not only in my own sample, not only in previous studies, but even in other cultures. Large Japanese companies, for example, are notable for their elaborate reinforcement of company loyalty. What has been somewhat lost in the many discussions of Japan, however, is that their high level of security and loyalty is no different from that in the United States, at least at the management level. Japan is different only in that it extends this culture of loyalty down to the blue-collar ranks, while most American companies draw a sharp line between white- and blue-collar policies. The productive success of the Japanese is often attributed to their ability to mobilize the same kind of commitment from shop-floor workers that they (and we) do for managers.

What loyalty does, and what bureaucracy in its classic form fails to do, is to provide a *motive for cooperation*. It reflects the fact that an atmosphere of good will, of voluntary and intelligent working together, is essential to the functioning of any organization. If that is true of the routinized tasks of the assembly line—as the evidence we have reviewed demonstrates it is—it is even more true of the complex tasks of middle management.[27] The rational division of tasks into predefined offices, if strictly adhered to, would bring any real organization to a halt. Cooperative activity—people doing more than their jobs— makes the wheels turn.

WHAT MANAGERS DO: LOYALTY AND MANAGERIAL "POLITICS"

Collaboration is vital at every level of the organization, but probably more in middle management than anywhere else. That would account for the fact that loyalty is most heavily stressed for this group. Blue-collar workers are often treated as expendable parts, technically focused individual contributors may come and go, but assuring the networks of middle management cooperation is vital to organizational success.

Research on what middle managers actually do has been scarce. One theme has indeed emerged from a series of studies so far: while the traditional picture sees managers as orderly executors of organizational objectives, the reality is that their jobs are disjointed, fragmented, unplanned, and instinctive.[28] What are they actually *doing* in this spontaneous, unplanned, instinctive manner? That is a question no one has satisfactorily answered.

Many of those who have tried have stressed the importance of lateral politics, of building networks of informal contacts. Studies going back to the 1950s show that, contrary to the expectations of those who focus on hierarchical relationships, between one-third and one-half of middle managers' time is spent in lateral contacts, and that amount seems to be increasing.[29] Yet a 1983 compendium of studies on these processes is very thin, consisting largely of laments about the lack of data on the topic. Only a few studies go into any detail at all about how these relationships are built and managed, and fewer still try to develop generalizable concepts or to explain why these patterns develop.[30]

The problem is that because this activity is underground, there is no language for it. Middle managers' descriptions of their technical functions are clear, but when they get to their true "managerial" work their tone becomes vague.[31] They know that they *don't* do what the popular stereotype says they do—as one put it to me, "If what we did was to pass information up and down the chain, you could get rid of us now." But they have a hard time analyzing the networking activity that takes so much of their time.

There are in effect two aspects of middle managers' jobs. The first is how well they do their assigned tasks. This is relatively above-board, tied into the control systems, generally measured and rewarded through some kind of "management by objectives."[32] The second—less visible, less measurable, hard to grasp with the tools of bureaucracy—involves their collaborative relations with others, which extend beyond the parameters of the job. The two aspects are, to be sure, linked: those who focus purely on their assigned tasks and ignore relationships do not usually go far in the long run, because they are not effective in accomplishing that on which they are measured. But the two sides are also frequently in tension, because getting things done in a collaborative way cuts across formal organizational lines and may involve short-term distractions and losses.

Such tensions were very visible in all the organizations I studied that retained the classic culture of loyalty, and gave rise to numerous stories:

> "[In order to develop the new product] we had to develop a peer network to do end runs around the top management. We took a lot of risks and made it work. The executive committee got duly rewarded, because the product was a big success, but we did it in spite of what they were doing." (Karet)

> "We have made inroads on the quality process, but almost in spite of the top. People at the middle on down really want to do it." (Karet)

> "We are collegial, we work with our brothers. We may make less profit in one plant to help the other—though the new compensation system works against cooperation." (Emon)

These managers, and many others, did an amazing thing: they did what they thought was right for the company even when it was not in their self-interest—regardless of what their bosses told them, even regardless of compensation incentives. Their loyalty to the company made them want to solve the problem more than they wanted to gain a personal reward, and it also provided the essential sense of trust that in doing so their peers would probably not take advantage of their resulting vulnerability. Loyalty was not an individual quality, but part of the culture; individuals therefore could be reasonably confident that their fellow managers were also loyal, and so could be trusted to do the right thing.

This phenomenon of working against the hierarchy is, of course, extreme; what was surprising was how many examples of it I found in my sample. The less dramatic phenomenon of building collaborative networks, using the informal organization to get things done, was universal: all recognized it as an essential part of doing their jobs.[33] A Crown manager remarked:

> Whenever you go up the chain it makes things harder. Either they wind you up in red tape or they give you stuff you don't need. What you need to do to get things done is to set it up and then negotiate it with your peers, work it out at the grass-roots level—then you can present them with a *fait accompli.*

As one searches for the characteristic that defines middle managers—that distinguishes them from workers of other layers, yet unites them among themselves—it is this political function, which emerges as a common core. There were a few managers who expressed this idea, one very succinctly:

We are the people that can put the pieces of the puzzle together.

This metaphor has many ramifications. Top management can be seen as design-
ing the puzzle—the overall picture; middle managers, by virtue of their position
closer to the action, are the ones who have to put it together. Each of them has a
piece; in order to create the whole they all need a sense of where their pieces
are located in the overall picture, and the ability to test out fits with other pieces.
They need to wander around, as it were, looking for matches—connections to
other managers that help solve the puzzle, that deal with visible problems.

A Crown manager elaborated:

> Without middle management you get chaos. You need a focusing lens in the
> organization. Otherwise, no one would know who was in charge and it would
> just be too much work. Someone needs to spend full time coordinating. For
> example, there's a piece of hardware that's coming out now and I happen to
> know that the testers need to fix the software. And the production people are
> two days late and they don't even know that they're late—they don't even
> know that the testers are waiting for them. Someone needs to ferret out the
> fact that there are different expectations, and the only people that can do that
> are middle management who coordinate.

This description of the middle-management function has a formal analogue
in the work of general systems theorists. They have found, whether they deal
with biological or artificial cybernetic systems, that a system that learns or
develops cannot be purely hierarchical; it cannot work, for example, like an
orderly computer program with a hierarchy of routines. It is essential that there
be mechanisms of spontaneous, unplanned adjustment to environmental
demands—ways in which subparts of the organization in close contact with the
environment can "work out" tactical innovations, ways for them to "wander
around." These adjustments may then be fed back to contribute to an overall
planning process.[34]

That process of adjustment is what the Crown middle managers claim for
themselves when they reject the interference of top management in details.
That kind of middle management politics is crucial to the functioning of any corporation. I would even argue that it is the defining function of middle managers:
their most important task is facilitating the spontaneous adjustment of the organization to the changing operational environment—making tactical adjustments
within a strategic framework devised by top management. In order to do this,
they need to construct new configurations of relationships as problems change,
seeking out those who have the necessary knowledge and responsibility. No
other group faces quite this issue: top management, production workers, and
technical staff all can function in relatively bounded, small groups. It is only the
middle managers who are constantly scrambling, needing to seek out new con-

nections throughout the organization as environmental demands shift.

This integrative political role does not work automatically. "Politics" has a bad name in many corporations: it becomes synonymous with private deal-making, advancing the interests of the part instead of the whole, with connotations of empire-building, favoritism, cliquishness. An essential characteristic of effective organizations is that their politics are not of this kind.

Good politics are created by loyalty; in its absence, politics turn bad. To the extent that employees, especially middle managers, are oriented emotionally and practically to the whole, they will turn their discretionary activity toward the general good. When loyalty flags, they will turn their attention to shoring up their own positions first.

To put it another way, *an effective organization must be a community:* that is, its members must want to cooperate. Bureaucracy, however, has no theoretical place for such a nonrational dynamic. The culture of loyalty has therefore grown up largely as a pragmatic adaptation to reality rather than as an organized management system. A few companies—IBM, Hewlett-Packard, the Japanese giants—have paid conscious attention to fostering it; more often it has emerged unreflectively. But every large corporation in my experience has recognized its importance in practice.[35]

Loyalty's Limits: The Failings of Informal Trust

Though corporate loyalty provides a context for trust, it is at the same time a relatively crude way of doing it. The basic problem is that it is informal, "hidden" from the formal control systems of bureaucracy. As we have seen, many acts of true loyalty are in tension with the stated responsibilities of the job; though they aim at the good of the company, they have an almost "subversive" air about them. Managers commonly cross lines drawn by their superiors— lines of organizational unit or function—in order to get things done, but their only reward is likely to be a confidence that in the long run favors will be returned. Cooperation works largely on the simple principle of personal logrolling, or "trading of mutual favors."

This can quickly degenerate into "bad politics." The line between trading favors for the good of the whole, and doing it for the good of the individuals involved, is thin; when the whole process is underground, it can vanish entirely. In addition, managers can use their control of the promotion process to build "fiefdoms" of people dependent on them personally. These distorted forms of trust are found to a greater or lesser extent in even the best organizations.

But the problem goes deeper than that: even "good politics," in the classic corporate community, are seriously limited. No matter how strong the desire to cooperate is, lateral relations are restricted from doing the most good:

1. They are built from personal contacts and are dependent on accidents of friendship and personal trust. Thus they do not necessarily involve those with knowledge relevant to a decision; the political network follows paths defined by other, more personal criteria.
2. They generally function only in homogeneous groups, among people who can easily trust each other because of their similarity; this is the source of exclusive "old boys' networks." One of the great problems in integrating minority groups is that they disrupt the personal links that make organizational cooperation possible, thus pushing the structure toward more formal and "bureaucratic" systems.
3. The informal networks are built from series of one-to-one relationships; the building of *group* associations outside the hierarchy is viewed as especially threatening. People may view themselves as part of a category—"the programmers," "the old-timers," and so on—but they do not act in a concerted manner. Thus, achieving a coherent team effort across bureaucratic boundaries is extremely difficult.
4. When conflict among different groupings does emerge, there are few mechanisms for resolving the dispute. Since the groupings themselves are unacknowledged by the formal organization, there is no way to discuss the differences. The conflict remains a matter of water-cooler conversation rather than open dialogue, and it is dealt with through backroom maneuvering and horse-trading.[36]
5. When there are differences in view between levels of the hierarchy, a vicious cycle of power and resistance is easily set up. Middle managers, for example, often disagree with the dictates of the top: sometimes this is for "good" reasons (they know important things that the top does not) and sometimes for "bad" ones (they are resisting changes that might disrupt their domains). But in either case, it is difficult to overcome the misunderstanding.

Despite these weaknesses, for a century loyalty has been essential to the effective operation of bureaucracies, which would otherwise quickly collapse from the inefficiency of formal rules. Its maintenance is therefore a crucial practical issue for corporations. It must either be sustained or be replaced with something better. The emerging "community of purpose," which I will describe later, takes over the functions of loyalty in giving people a reason to cooperate, but within a more developed and flexible framework.

The Moral Dimension

Loyalty is also more than a practical issue, more than a managerial tool whose benefits must be weighed against the costs of maintaining it. It touches on profound moral concerns as well. It is this mix that gives it its peculiar volatility.

Is loyalty a good thing? Most of those I interviewed clearly believed it was:

they equated it with trust, caring, and respect and contrasted it with the "cold," "unfeeling" quality of the modern free-agent mentality. For them, the moral issue was an old-fashioned one of greed against human values. But this was not the only view: there was another perspective, also moral in tone, which was *critical* of the demands of loyalty. Among the people I spoke with, it was best summed up in this way:

If you want loyalty go get a dog.

What is at issue here is the interconnection of the individual and the corporate. For this we have two moral models, one featuring a strong bond, in which individuals sacrifice themselves to a higher good; and one with a weak bond, in which individuals are responsible for their own fate and are obligated to seek a kind of autonomous growth. In familiar sociological language, this is *Gemeinschaft* versus *Gesellschaft,* tight communal bonding versus cosmopolitan liberty.

There is a long tradition of criticisms of capitalism because of its destructive effects on communities. Adam Smith himself was torn between his analysis of the efficiency of the market and that market's erosion of moral bonds.[37] The subject has produced some evocative titles: in recent times, *The Lonely Crowd* captured the dissolution of human linkages by the corrosive force of markets, and *Habits of the Heart* has appealed for a reconstitution of commitment to the collective good.[38]

But there is an equally strong line of criticisms of traditional communities and celebrations of the liberating power of modernity. Communities as we have known them are closed and limiting, intolerant of outsiders and diversity, slow to respond to forces for change. Consider, for example, the current debate about family and feminism: on one side, attractions to the stability and moral power of the family community; on the other, a moral charge by women that this same community oppresses them and limits their freedom to develop.

These debates have endured throughout the modern era because both the individual and the group have retained moral status. In pre-modern writings—from Plato's *Republic* through the medieval theology of Gregory the Great—the hierarchy of privilege diminished as one moved down the chain of being; lower orders had no claims against the higher. But the key distinguishing feature of modernity, brought centrally into political theory by John Locke, is the assertion of independent claims to rights for abstract individuals. In this tradition there is no clear place for the group's claim to loyalty.

Obligations to the community have therefore acquired sentimental quality, as something we may wish for but which cannot be justified in the harsh light of modernity. Images of community are in a sense "left over" from an earlier age. They have had a hard time surviving the pressure of free-market arguments through the 1980s.

Sociological and hortatory writing about community generally shares three characteristics: a belief, or rather an assumption, that community is good; a critique of actual communities as repressive and closed; and a failure to provide any real alternative. One might term this the "Lake Wobegon" pattern: nostalgia for the virtues of small towns, at the same time that those small towns are everywhere dying because no one wants to live in them.[39]

The current struggles of management are played out in this moral matrix: Is it more valuable to reward merit or loyal service? Do the traditions of a company deserve any consideration independent of the immediate competitive pressures? Is it better to open up to outside influences or to maintain a culture of shared commitment?

What the downsizing process reveals, somewhat surprisingly, is that most managers are not ambivalent about this: they long for community and its values, for warmth and close support. They largely reject the individualistic ethic and the "harsher" world of merit and reward, especially if it involves breaking the boundaries of the firm. At times, as in this account by a Nadir manager, they are quite explicit about the tensions I have sketched:

> There was a time when the attitude was, you do your job, and the company will take care of you; it was a situation of trust in the company. Then the word *professionalism* came in, you come in and do your job, you do it in a highly professional manner. Never mind the word *trust*—you're here for this job, you're here for this purpose. And with professionalism came mobility, so loyalty and dedication went with it. The highly skilled professionals didn't care about trust, they didn't care about where the company's been, what kind of a family relationship we've had here. They say, "Hey, I'm a professional, I do my job, and if it works out, fine; if it doesn't work out, hey, I'll go to another company." That's the raw edge of professionalism, as opposed to the soft edge of trust which has gone.

Middle managers in general—the overwhelming majority of my sample—*want to be loyal*.[40] They want a community that goes beyond short-term performance and reward, that nurtures and supports, to which they can devote themselves. Though I myself, like many researchers before me, often felt the demands of the corporation on the individual to be excessive, I rarely heard this complaint from the managers themselves. On the contrary, their lament was that they were being forced to be free agents.

On the whole, they felt they were *morally* a dying breed: not that middle managers would disappear, but that the values that they held important in their relation to the company were in peril. They recognized the power of the "professional" ethic cited above and believed it would triumph. Many of the older managers in my sample had an attitude of "holding on." They felt that they could remain loyal because they didn't have too many more years and the company was unlikely to lay them off. The younger managers more often took a cynical or resigned stance:

I want to feel that the company is loyal to me and I do, to some degree, but I also know intellectually that they will only remain loyal for as long as they need me. When it comes time for them to make a choice, if there is someone better, I'm out and they are in.

The anguish of these managers reverberates through society: *What kind of community do we want?* How do we combine family values and markets, kindness and competitiveness, responsibility and freedom? And what are the relations of the individual to the social group?

There are clearly circumstances in which corporate demands step over a line protecting the individual. We tend to feel today that Henry Ford's investigations of the love lives of his employees stepped over that line—though similar instances still occur today, and the law generally supports this corporate right. Most people feel similarly uneasy with the old IBM requirement that managers wear hats, though required suits seem to be more widely acceptable. Recently a number of lawsuits have challenged companies' right to control the sexual preferences or political views of their employees. What is the boundary of legitimate corporate demands?

The current struggle of the corporations potentially adds to our understanding of these issues, for the human costs and benefits of community are highlighted by the forces at work to change them. If loyalty is untenable—as so many companies are now implying through their actions—we can learn something of the consequences of its dissolution, and perhaps something of the alternatives, through observation of the downsizing process.

Conclusion

Despite the theoretical views of classical economics and Scientific Management, businesses have almost never treated their managers as rational individuals. They have instead built warm communities emphasizing trust and security. Within this context managers have been able to move beyond the formal limits of their jobs, building personal networks that help them in getting their tasks done. This is essential because true bureaucracy is unmanageable: if people ever had to follow all the rules and go only through the proper channels, organizations would come to a grinding halt. Loyalty, as it were, lubricates bureaucracy.

But it is a limited corrective. The informal politics of the corporate community are vulnerable to distortions, including the building of fiefdoms and the corruptions of personal favors. At their best they are limited by the accidents of personal relations. And they depend heavily on the stability and sense of permanence of the whole.

The current downsizing wave brings loyalty from its usual place in the background of organizational life to center stage. Insofar as loyalty is valuable to managers and to companies, its disruption could be profoundly damaging; insofar as it is limited and restrictive, there may be new opportunities to break free of its power. For a moment these issues, usually taken for granted and hidden, are the subject of intense emotions and conflicting visions.

PART II

The Traditional Community in Crisis

3

The First Shock

THE LAST CHAPTER sought to explain the forces generating corporate loyalty—its benefits from the point of view of both the individuals and the organization. The argument should lead us to expect problems in dismantling the traditional relation—and trouble is indeed widespread.

Let us start with the raw end of the spectrum—with cases where emotions are on the surface, and where pain is widely expressed. Such examples make clear the power of the traditional culture of loyalty, and its continuing hold even when it seems to have been brutally tossed out the window.

It may be surprising that there were only a few cases in my sample of such organizations, riddled with anger and distress.[1] That is different from the popular picture, which suggests that drama is the norm. But it seems that people cannot long sustain the intensity of the initial feelings and quickly withdraw to a more "philosophical" perspective (which we will explore in the following chapters). The truly angry organizations were those that were still dealing with the first shock of change—they represented, in short, an early phase of reaction.

Though few, the openly troubled organizations were revealing. Their story is not a simple one. When the break in security comes, middle managers do not just turn against their companies. That, as a matter of fact, is the problem: the company is (from their point of view) treating them wrongly, making mistakes, throwing out all sorts of moral covenants—yet they still depend on it and feel great affection for it. The result is a cauldron of contradictory feelings.

Let me begin by describing the purest case of this kind.

Nadir

Until the early 1980s this old manufacturing organization, now a subsidiary of a larger company, had a near-monopoly on its products. It also had a strong reputation as a "caring" employer: layoffs were unheard-of in the white-collar force, and rare among the blue-collar. Many employees at all levels were second-generation members of the "family."

The 1980s brought competition, particularly from abroad, resulting in new pressure on all dimensions of performance: product innovation, product quality, service quality, and cost. The organization responded sluggishly: as of 1985 there had been no significant new products for several years, and quality was perceived as low.

There followed two major cycles of change. In 1985 the president was removed by a new chairman of the board and replaced with the head of another subsidiary with a reputation for dramatic innovation. The new president lived up to his reputation: he replaced almost all his executive staff with people from outside the company, announced a layoff of about 115 managers, the first in company history, restructured the organization from functional units to business units built around product families, and sharply decentralized the staff functions. He placed a great deal of emphasis on innovation and involvement, with explicit citing of the principles of *In Search of Excellence*.[2] The immediate results were a jump in new product introductions and an improvement in quality—but continued poor results on the bottom line.

In 1987 this president was replaced by the former chief financial officer of another company. The new leader tightened the structure: some recentralization of functions, clarification of controls, and further cost-cutting. There were limitations on hiring, but no further group layoffs. Under his direction the company, by late 1988, had begun to improve its profit figures, though they were still in the red.

When I visited the company in September 1988, the middle managers were in the midst of dealing with the initial trauma of change. Though leadership had been talking of transformation for three years, actual layoffs had only begun to penetrate the middle ranks in the previous six months. I gathered that up to that point everyone had continued to assume that everything would be all right; now it was suddenly clear that it wouldn't be. People were scrambling to readjust.

Those I spoke with were, with few exceptions, fearful, confused, and hostile toward the "outsiders" who threatened their culture.

> "We don't go out at lunch, we're afraid the doors will be locked when we get back. I'm not confident about the future. Not many people are these days."

> "I don't understand why they bring in people from the outside. They come in and say everything stinks. And we say we did OK without you."

> "I'm anxious, I'm fearful, I distrust people now. It's a corporation now, rather than people."

There was a dramatic absence of any shared definition of the problems facing the division. Many were not convinced that there ever had been a problem: they felt that a bunch of outsiders came in with big ideas they had picked up from consultants and just laid them on the existing culture. Others believed that there had been a problem, but now it was over: we have got our house in order, we can lick the competition, and (by implication) we can stop all this disruptive change.

The discontent was blamed on a number of factors. The layoffs were important—indeed, they had an extraordinarily negative impact considering the small number of people who were directly affected. Though over 100 layoffs were announced, only a handful of managers were eventually forced to leave—the rest either took early retirement or found other jobs inside the company. Everyone agreed, moreover, that the company had made exceptional efforts to provide counseling and placement for those who left. Yet the changes had the effect of a neutron bomb. As several said, even those who were not directly affected felt the events very intensely: "The layoff has scarred me. I used to speak out, but now I come and do my job and go home, and probably I'll come back tomorrow. I still love this company, but it has scarred me."

Another focus of complaint was the move toward decentralization, which was criticized by most because it undermined coordination and led to duplication of effort. But the most important criticism—insistently voiced and repeated by many separate individuals—was the feeling that the new division management had failed to make a case for the direction of change:

> "I'm uncertain about the direction and effects of changes and future changes. I haven't seen real changes from the past. I don't know what they were trying to accomplish: maybe just keeping things the same with fewer people, I don't know."

> "I think this company was in desperate need of change, but decentralization was not the needed change. We just grab the fads. I'm amazed our executives aren't out in California doing scream therapy now."

This, then, was a company that had failed to communicate a vision of the business. The upper managers claimed that they had told everyone the problems and the needed solutions, yet these explanations carried no credibility: "Upper management has not blueprinted the future and that causes a lot of insecurity and unease. Without the assurance that there is a future, people mistrust the information that's given them. There's a kind of a 'Yeah, we hear that, but . . .' attitude."

Yet for all the anger, for all the distress, almost no one had retreated into a purely adversarial or self-protective position. This had not yet turned into a war of each against all. Underlying everything was a strong love—I use the word advisedly—for the old community, and a continued desire to contribute to the success of the company. Here, for example, is a woman who was briefly laid off and then brought back: "I blame my managers, not [the company]. I'm still a good worker for [the company] and I always will be."

Such comments reflect loyalty in the old sense: these were people dedicated to the corporation as an entity, as a community, people whose identity was bound up with the group. They were willing to do anything to contribute. In many cases their fathers and other relatives had also worked for this company; in all cases they had great difficulty imagining life on the outside. They talked with intense emotion about the bonds uniting them with the company, and with sorrow about the destruction of that community.

> "There used to be a real esprit de corps here and complete loyalty, a good relation to employees' families. Now it's much more impersonal, the spirit has gone. For the welfare of the corporation we need to rekindle the spirit."

> "My father worked here and when my mother was sick, they were very considerate. They did everything they could to help. People seemed to care more about you then."

These managers claimed, furthermore, that the company's performance was being profoundly damaged by the changes. This was not because people were sabotaging or resisting the change: they claimed—I am presenting their perspective here—to be willing to do whatever they were told. The problem now was that they lacked a *context for cooperation*. The old centralized, secure, caring community encouraged people to work together; the new state of confusion destroyed the bonds without creating anything in their place:

> "There's a lot more politics and influence managing now, because there's less formal reporting and less centralization. It's made people less trustful of each other. Power in this organization now is all based on information and withholding of information. Decentralization has increased the manipulation of information. The rumor mill is very strong."

> "There's too little integration now between groups. Every group is going its own way. I don't see the cohesive working environment that we used to have. It used to be when there was a new product everyone pulled together. Now the right hand doesn't know what the left is doing."

What is unexpected about these comments is that they are the reverse of what was intended by the leaders of change: the focus on products and delegation of authority was supposed to create better integration and faster decision making. Yet the structural change was producing, at least in the perception of the middle, perversely upside-down results.

Most lamented this state of affairs, claiming they would eagerly contribute to the whole if only they could understand what it was. A few had, in effect, given up the effort to make sense of things. One old-line manager said, "I'll tell you how I deal with it now. I manage my team and it's us against the world, and I don't give a damn about what happens in the rest of the place. It could blow up as far as I'm concerned." To which another replied, sadly, "But this used to be one big team."

These loyal managers, the bulk of the company, did have an enemy—not the company or its top managers, but the group of new managers whom they identified as "professionals." This term, *professionalism,* was used almost as an insult: it connoted people who were independent of the company, who stood outside the old enveloping community. And it carried with it a set of attitudes and perspectives that the loyal managers found abhorrent:

> [This company] used to be very supportive of the employees. Employees felt entitled to growth and development and benefits if they worked hard. Now it's changed to a new professionalism of give and get, give and get; the sense of entitlement is gone.

The professionals themselves, of whom there were a few at the middle levels, also saw themselves as a distinct group with different values. But they rejected the idea that they were less dedicated to the company's success than the loyalists. The loyalists objected to the professionals' limits on commitment; the professionals saw their commitment not as limited, but as structured differently:

> I'm more accustomed to change than many people. Change per se doesn't disturb me. I have a long, long track record in a lot of companies. It turns me on a lot. I like variety. . . . The people who have worked only at [this company] are much more concerned than I am. The old idea of progressive and predictable movement is no longer there.

These professionals were critical of the loyalists for their inability to go beyond the traditional, personal network of relationships to get things done:

> The dominant attitude here is I'll go along to get along. I tend to make waves and I'm seen as a bad guy. Most people are not trained well enough to deal with using persuasion and influence where they don't have direct authority for getting things done.

The professionals, incidentally, were no more *satisfied* than the loyalists in any simple sense. They were highly critical of top management's handling of change, and they did not particularly enjoy their work in the current environment. But they were able to make sense of the situation in a way the loyalists were not—neither lamenting the confusion nor giving up and retreating to personal protectiveness. They had conceptions of how the organization should move, tactical ideas about how to handle themselves, and a sense of alternatives if this job did not work out.

There were, in short, two unusually distinct orientations in this company. The loyalist majority had a set of expectations that involved what one called a "sense of entitlement": entitlement to security and caring in exchange for competent work. Within that framework they put few limits on what the company could ask: fourteen-hour days, changes in career lines, "giving myself"—all were part of the bargain. They expected treatment from the company and from their fellow employees that reflected a feeling of "family" caring.

The professionals did not expect the same things: they did not expect security or personal caring, nor were they willing to "give themselves" to the corporation. They expected rewards for contribution to the company. They were willing to work extremely hard on tasks, but to "give" only their professional competence. They were seen by their loyalist colleagues as measuring out their commitment in a spirit of "give and get, give and get," and therefore as violating the conditions for trust within the organization. But from their perspective they were the ones who should be trusted, because they based their relationships and their claims purely on matters of performance rather than on entitlement. They put great emphasis on clear understanding of business objectives, and strategy was crucial; these framed the standards of performance. When these were clear they knew, in effect, whom to trust.

It was quite clear that the top management of the division (though not of the company) viewed themselves as "professionals"; certainly they were viewed that way by their loyalist middle.[3] They offered a vision of a cooperative enterprise with a clear ethic of performance that would maximize flexibility and commitment. But this ethic had not been communicated effectively to those below. In the meantime the top had taken many actions, from layoffs to reorganization, that made sense within the "professional" paradigm but which had disrupted the expectations and relationships previously governing the organization.

By disrupting the prior basis of relationships without substituting a new one, they had made it impossible for people to cooperate. Thus the loyalists were left with only two alternatives: individual retreat or formal, rule-bound interaction—that is, "politics" or "bureaucracy." Both were profoundly upsetting to people who wanted to be part of, and to contribute to, a productive community.

The professionals in the middle ranks also felt left out, since the top appeared to have done a poor job of communicating the plans and business conditions framing the standards of performance. Thus they, too, found it difficult to cooperate and were therefore frustrated. But the depth of the distress was less because they had a wider range of options—they could conceive of an identity outside the company.

Patterns of Cultures in Shock

Now let me put this case in a wider context.

The responses at Nadir were in many ways similar to those of other companies caught during or close to the start of the downsizing process.[4] They do not fit any simple description; they are full of contradictions and confusions. At that initial moment people had not organized their responses into coherent and sustainable patterns. They often veered in single conversations from lashing out at their bosses, to hoping that those same bosses would save them, to diffuse self-pity, to teeth-gritting determination to last it out and make the company work again.

Occasionally people claimed that morale was so low that everyone had stopped working hard—that they were leaving on the dot of 5:00, no longer coming in on weekends, and so forth. But this was clearly the exception rather than the rule. Most believed, on the contrary, that not only they themselves but also most of their fellow employees were working harder than ever. They complained frequently of the stress and the extra hours that had followed the reductions.[5]

It is perhaps obvious that work would increase with fewer people. None of the troubled companies had made dramatic changes in the organization of work, so people had to work harder to get it done. Many managers spoke of having to "fill in the gaps" left by those departing.

But why should they put out so much? And how effectively were they working?

MOTIVATION: WHY WORK?

The Paralyzing Effects of Fear

When people all around are being shot, one is presumably stimulated to greater effort. Yet that is not in fact the picture that emerged. Those who spoke most strongly about fear—and there were a fair number of them in all these organizations—were not the ones who claimed to be working hard. Their reaction was rather to narrow their sights, to just get the job done and go home: "The reaction to fear is to scatter, and everybody's protecting their individual flanks."

What had happened for these managers is that the world had dissolved into chaos. The familiar laws of cause and effect had been violated. In the old world you did a good job, you had security. What produced security now? These managers could not say.

Their leaders had an answer: good performance. The human relations directors and line managers at Nadir and all the other companies were virtually unanimous on this point. Nadir, like most of the others, had tried to use performance appraisals—flawed though they were in a system that had never taken them seriously—as a basis even for its very first layoffs, and it had been actively proclaiming a new era of true performance-based rewards.

But this message, at least during the period of initial shock, had not gotten through. The layoffs were such a violation of prior standards that some managers—especially the most fearful ones—no longer believed in standards at all. They frequently mocked the claim that performance had played a role in the layoffs: they had plenty of stories about poor performers who stayed while better ones had been dumped: "There was a sense that the people who were laid off were not necessarily the poor performers. So people are feeling even if I do a good job, if I'm in the wrong place at the wrong time I can get hurt." What's more, even the notion of what a "good job" is had become freighted with uncertainty. Certainly the fearful had abandoned any notion of creativity: "People pull back and they don't support you. In communications meetings, no one asks questions, they are afraid they'll lose their job. If you write memos about why aren't we getting results, you're told to be quiet and not cause trouble." In the worst cases, the world now made so little sense that even doing the basic job was hardly worth it; there was—in their view— simply no way to know what would be rewarded, or even what was wanted. So you came in, did what was in front of you, and kept your head down. When the laws of cause and effect have been repealed, there's not much point in trying harder.

Counterbalance: The Desire to Contribute

This extreme fear reaction was, however, not dominant in any case, even that of Nadir. It was mixed to varying degrees with a countervailing emotion: wanting to do the best for the organization.

Wherever people could define to any degree what was needed, the crisis mode drew from them increased effort. The word used by many of them was *contribution,* as in: "What motivates me is the feeling that I'm contributing to a growing, healthy company." Everything depended on this sense that the company was moving forward, and that the current trauma was necessary to its success. Where this view existed—and most people managed to define the situation at least partially in this way—the comments about hard work followed; where it didn't, there was only despair.

The Search for Direction

I have described Nadir as a company that had failed to communicate a vision of the business. It was not alone: indeed, this was the dominant theme in every one of the troubled organizations, and was really the focus of the frequent criticism of top management. There is not much point in piling on examples: the comments from Nadir are nearly identical to those from the rest.

Now, the problem was not that the top was *unaware* of these criticisms. On the contrary, almost every manager I spoke to, at whatever level, had made very extensive efforts to inform and involve subordinates in the changes going on. In facility after facility I found meetings in which top managers presented business strategy information; these were typically supplemented by an array of measures that encouraged discussion, from 900 numbers to "face-to-face" meetings. Most had developed "vision" statements and "strategic priorities" that had been shared through every communications medium possible throughout the corporation. These efforts were in most cases radically new, and in every case greater in scope than they had been in the past. Yet they seemed to make no real difference.

To illustrate the problem, let me contrast comments from Lyco: the first from a high manager, the second from a very enthusiastic and active middle manager:

At the top:

> My ideal concept would be that we have to have the management so involved in the business that the supervisors and department heads know exactly how their efforts fit into the business plan. They can intelligently discuss this with their people at their group and department meetings. That's the ideal situation. I don't think we're there yet, and we're a long way from it. But that's where we gotta get to. . . . And to foster that type of thinking, the division has a four-level meeting once a year.

In the middle:

> I guess that to really summarize in terms of this communications problem this building has a big problem with morale, it's terrible. It's just terrible. I don't know how better to describe it. People don't trust anyone, the financials don't mean anything because they show financials one month and change them the next week. And since they don't have a strategy and they don't know who their customers are, and they don't have a plan, then nobody believes any of the numbers.

The middle is criticizing the top for not doing exactly what the top says it is trying to do. One interpretation of the discrepancy is implied by the first manager: the change takes time, and understanding can't be achieved all at once. We will examine this implementation problem later; the solutions vary, but the point here is that the *problem* is intense and universal.

How, then, did middle managers maintain any sense of what to do?

One important mechanism was an attachment to a particular leader. At Nadir the widespread definition of the situation went this way: the new divisional head, who had been brought in from outside, was causing all this trouble; but the CEO—a lifetime "insider"—really cared about people and would not do anything to hurt them. They could trust him: either he didn't know the pain they were suffering, in which case he would soon put it to rights; or else the pain was really necessary, because he certainly wouldn't knowingly allow it otherwise. A slight variation was found at Glover, without the "insider/outsider" element. Here the "problem" was that the CEO was a shortsighted financial type; but the heir-apparent was someone with deep roots in operations, who really understood the feelings of management; he was the one who could be trusted.

Another and related mechanism of hope was to stay attached to the old order. This was based on the belief that the crisis was a temporary one and things would soon return to normal; indeed, the faith in an old-time leader was in a sense a specific form of this overarching belief. It was not purely conservative in form: everyone[6] agreed that business would have to become fundamentally leaner and more efficient. I asked regularly whether middle management might disappear, and the vast majority answered that it had to be significantly reduced. They did not, therefore, expect a simple return to the old days. What they did expect was a return to the old sense of security. *Once the fat had been pared away,* this argument went, those left could settle down to something like the old relationship in a more successful company.

Indeed, most were quite positive about such a prospect. They had no problem admitting that there were too many middle managers, that systems had become bloated and that some deadbeats had hung around too long. A trimmed-down, focused organization with increased market success would be nothing but an improvement. The managers commonly looked beyond their own prospects to judge what was good for the company as a whole, and they generally felt some downsizing was laudable:

> "Even though I was laid off, I can see that a lot of the cuts were justified. There were a lot of people who weren't working. We had to eliminate underperformers."

> "The good things are that they are putting a lot of money into new products and there's a better focus on profits, and some cost cutting. Those are good. You can't live in your little cocoon all your life."

The usual assumption behind this hope, however—voiced only when people were asked directly—was that this slimming and cutting was a one-time affair, getting the company back to the kind of shape it should have been in all along. Hopes that included a basic change in the employment relationship were, in this group of companies, much rarer.

The continuing desire to contribute to the improvement of the company was, in short, an effective motivator, keeping most people going even through the darkest hours. It also helped to prevent any sign of organized opposition or resistance. But it also had its dark side: a conservative pull toward the past, rather than the embracing of fundamental change articulated by most of the leadership.

INTERNAL RELATIONS: DIVISION AND WITHDRAWAL

One reaction I expected to the trauma of downsizing was for people to turn against each other. This "scapegoating" phenomenon has been widely observed in many situations of social disintegration; I expected to find a lot of blaming and finger-pointing.[7]

Fingers were in fact frequently pointed at two groups: top management and "outsiders" (those hired in from other companies). But these did not harden into pitched conflict, because everyone continued to feel interdependent. While they blamed their leaders for the problems, they also looked to them for rescue; and while they were suspicious of newcomers, they also wanted to make them part of the family.

On the whole, discord was a minor note in these companies. Rather than turning on each other, most people drifted apart, becoming more isolated and looking to be left alone. This was an early form of what would later become a full-scale "retreat to autonomy."

Middle versus Top

Without question the most important fissure was one I have already alluded to: that between the middle managers and the top. Muted though it was by the hope that some top leader would save them from disaster, the feeling of distance and misunderstanding was consistent and unmistakable in all the troubled organizations.

Discussions of the relationship covered a variety of tones. In some cases they suggested something like a battle of enemy camps: "They don't know what they're doing and we do; they're trying to manipulate us." This was common in the two or three most angry organizations, of which Nadir is a good example: "The top is making big mistakes, they're not being held accountable, while the people in the middle are being held accountable for all the mistakes that are happening. Don't think for a minute that the people working in this company have forgotten how to think and observe and see things. They see things, and they say, what's going on in this company?"

Such open hostility was relatively uncommon. The far more typical response, even in the "angry" companies, was of frustration and confusion, of not knowing what was going on, a mixture of hope that the leadership might really understand what they were doing, and fear that they didn't. As one put it succinctly, "I'm sure there are good reasons, but sometimes they're hard to believe." Here the tone was not of hostile camps but of different planets.

All these responses started from a failure of meaning. This void marked a sharp division in the organization between those who had some responsibility and decision-making authority in the restructuring process and those who were merely affected by it. The former group saw events as fitting together in a pattern; the latter saw them as disconnected.

The contrast was apparent in all but three or four companies. An example from Emon will do for all. From the point of view of one of the top people involved in change, the process looked coherent and sensible:

> We built value statements, starting by asking for opinions at the bottom. Then we had a problem-solving skills training program which went all the way down to the worker level, with statistical quality control, process control, and so on. Then the next year the business units developed strategies and mission statements, a planning process with clear criteria for judging the business.

From the middle management point of view, it looked fragmented and senseless:

> It depends which program is popular at the time. Conway is the current fad. We used to go a year or two between big changes. Now it seems they happen every month.

In general those who had made sense of the change could not understand why others had not. This was the source of a universal paradox in these less-successful organizations: the top spoke constantly about how much they were communicating, while the rest spoke constantly of how little communication there was. Both were true. There was in objective terms a huge amount of communication in almost every case: newsletter articles, focus groups, videotapes, speeches. And in every case it made little impact, because it did not help people make sense of their environment. We will return to this theme in chapter 5, in exploring the failure of mechanisms of voice.

Insiders versus Outsiders

The second substantial split within these organizations was that between "insiders" and "outsiders." I have emphasized the strength of this at Nadir, and it appeared regularly in other companies as well. There was widespread agreement, and much objective evidence, that outsiders had a difficult time in establishing credibility and trust within the system.

A mistake that we've often made in the past is we want to change a culture. Let's say we've got a problem organization, where you look around for some guy who's very good, and you hire him, and you say to him or her, you know, go fix the organization. It doesn't work here.

There are two ways that you can [bring in new people to] change an organization. One is to change enough of the people that you get a critical mass so that the individual is not totally absorbed by the organization. Or alternatively the individual goes in, like a Carl Icahn or a Frank Lorenzo, goes in there with an axe, "This is the way I want it," bang! And everybody toes the line, or the organization blows up. Now you don't find those sort of people here, generally. What we tend to do is we tend to take an individual and put him in an organization, the organization eats them up. (Lyco)

Another:

I'm just telling you the kind of psychology that goes on here. Instead of saying "Look, we've got somebody from outside who can probably help," people think: "Maybe he's only going to be here for two years. Maybe he's going to jump jobs again." (Lyco)

It was frequently true that outsiders did jump jobs, and it appeared that a major reason for these jumps was frustration at an inability to change the culture.

Yet it is striking how little exaggeration there was in these comments: psychological projection, or scapegoating, was very much the exception. In general managers spoke with balance of the need for cultural unity on the one hand and the value of outsiders on the other. There was more demonization at Nadir than anywhere else, perhaps because of the freshness of the shock. The second Lyco manager just quoted, for example, went on to say about a new outside hire, "I have no idea if he's actually the kind of person to jump ship again. But at least when he's here he's done a lot more, he knows a lot more about the market than anybody in this building. And we should pay attention to what he has to say."

Divisions Among Peers

Hostility against peers other than "outsiders" was not common. I was especially surprised at how little racial and gender tensions emerged during downsizing. In almost all these companies there had been one or another version of affirmative action to encourage the advancement of minorities and women. In the society at large it is apparent that these policies lead to extremely complicated and intense reactions. In these workplaces there was certainly some continuing bitterness on the part of traditionally excluded groups, but I heard almost no complaints on their part that they had been treated unfairly in the restructuring process, and almost no claims by white males that equity had been sacrificed to such issues.[8]

There were many claims that the implementations of the downsizings were unfair. It is surprising, in this light, that so few claimed unfairness based on race or gender. One might be tempted to guess at self-censorship on this highly charged topic, but that does not account for all the facts. First of all, the minority and women managers themselves never spoke of experiencing this kind of resent-ment. They were frequently eloquent about the problems they faced in other respects—about the subtle pressures and isolation of their daily lives in the corpo-rate world—but not one claimed that this had worsened during the downsizing pressure, or that they were being made scapegoats for the difficulties of others.

Furthermore, if one follows this line of thought, there are many other splits that might have come to the fore but didn't: resentments between young and old, for example, or between functional units. I didn't hear comments like that. If it was a matter of people censoring themselves in the interviews, one would have expected the opposite: it would have been far easier to blame peers than to criticize higher management, yet the latter was far more common.

Drawing Apart

A major puzzle is why there was so *little* internal conflict. Here is a situation in which people have suddenly been put into intense and vaguely structured compe-tition, each one concerned that another may take his or her job. One would expect this to transform rapidly into some form of defensive hostility. In their analyses of similar situations, historians, sociologists, and social psychologists have converged, finding typical patterns of scapegoating and projection of anger onto outsiders to the group. Indeed, such hostility frequently gets very nasty even with little provocation. If you separate any collection of people into competitive groups, even on a random basis, they will quickly and reliably develop negative images of the others. Often they will find rationales for applying different rules to the outsiders than to themselves.[9] Most often they will exempt authority figures from this hostility, turning their anger on peers and seeking approval from above. These patterns seem deeply embedded in human groups.

Yet in the situation of corporate downsizing we have, if anything, the oppo-site: anger, when present, was turned against the authorities—top manage-ment—and almost never against peers. One could well imagine complaints, say, that the marketing department was escaping the cuts and getting fat, while we, the operations people who really make the business run, are taking it in the neck. Yet in fact I never heard this. Marketing did indeed often do "better" than other functions: the buzzword in several companies, especially Lyco, was "moving to a marketing-driven organization," and this group was rapidly growing rather than downsizing. Yet operations managers never expressed bitterness or a sense of inequity about this shift.

The difference between this situation and those that have historically pro-duced racism and ethnocentrism appears to be that the corporation started as a single strong community, and individuals were strongly attached to it as an entity. Although conflict among functions is endemic to any company, it has been a secondary theme within a recognition of interdependence and shared destiny. This emotional unity acted as a counterweight to natural tendencies to fragment and point fingers, producing strange results. The earliest phases of the shock were marked by a kind of schizophrenia, clearly visible in Nadir, in which people alternately and almost in the same breath would express anger at management, hope that the leadership would rescue them, frustration at change, and willingness to suspend judgment.

Very quickly, however, such inconsistency seemed to become intolerable, and most people adopted a different defensive mechanism: they withdrew from intense attachments into a cautious individualism. This response did not involve rejection of the company or its leaders. It coexisted with continued hope. People merely gave up trying to make immediate sense of the situation or to save the company, and focused instead on doing their own jobs well.

> "We used to be friends here. I don't see that so much anymore. People are a bit standoffish, because they don't know what's going to happen."

> "There are plenty of people to talk to, but they all have tunnel vision, because they have so much on their plate that they can't help others. I have a job to do and I'm the only one who can do it."

Nadir was one of the most intensely emotional companies in part because it was one of those I caught in the early throes of the transformation. Yet even there one could already see a tension between the high level of distress and a desire to pull back and smooth over. In the next chapter we will explore further how this dynamic worked itself out over time.

Cushioning the Blow: The Failure of the "Human Relations Approach"

Most of the companies in my sample followed what I call the "Human Relations approach" to change. By this I mean that though the substance of the change was driven by immediate business needs and crisis, the process focused on making people feel as good as possible about it. Thus there were generally very substantial efforts to avoid outright layoffs, and to rely instead on early retire-ments and attrition. When layoffs did become necessary—as they did in the case of Nadir and Lyco—the Human Relations department ran elaborate programs to help with placement, to ease retraining and skill upgrading, and generally to show "responsibility" for those let go.

One thing I can say confidently after this research is that I would not want to be a Human Relations director in this situation. It seemed to be an absolute no-win position. If Human Relations was visible and highly involved, as at Nadir, it became a lightning rod for resentment. If it remained in the background, as it did at Lyco, it was less directly the brunt of anger but became an object of scorn.

The morale of Human Relations managers aside, the surprising point is that their efforts made little difference to the morale of others. Being "nice" didn't make anyone feel better.

The avoidance of formal layoffs, to begin with, did not lessen the feeling that promises had been broken. Early retirement programs, a frequent alternative to layoffs were widely seen as just as bad because they involved hidden pressure—in effect, people were told (or at least they heard the message), "Take voluntary retirement now or you may get an involuntary layoff later." As a Lyco manager put it in this early phase, "There have been layoffs, there just haven't been official layoffs. It's kind of, you get pressure to leave, and people go."

Early retirement incentives were sufficient to break the "contract," even without layoffs, because they immediately put into question the traditional sense of security. What they symbolized was that for the first time managers were being looked at as a cost to the business, a factor to be manipulated in the competitive game. At Lyco, which was the only company I visited both before and after "official" layoffs, it was clear that as soon as downsizing began by attrition, rumors began flying and fear rose dramatically: one manager said, "I'm sure we'll reduce by attrition—but that could change tomorrow." From there to a layoff was another step, but not the largest.

I rarely heard anyone say good things about policies for cushioning the blow. Much more frequent was the opposite: a sense that it would be better to do things quickly and cleanly, to be hard-nosed about it. Interestingly enough, the figure of Jack Welch—chairman of General Electric, famous (or notorious) for his ruthless approach to change—was referred to with approval by several people independently. In the midst of one of the angriest conversations at Nadir, for instance, among a group that included people who had already been targeted for layoffs, one volunteered: "I know how much went into trying to make the layoffs work well and how screwed up it got anyway, because plans were changed all the time. If you are in Jack Welch's company, you know that if you are not a [top performer], you're gone. And you can deal with that psychologically." At Lyco a manager expressed both sides of the ambivalence at the seemingly humane practice of giving three months' notice:

Can you imagine laying off a group of ten people and having them stand around for three months? Do you know the damage that they could have done? I mean in most companies if somebody is going to be laid off, they do it quickly. Now, by the way, part of the reason they did it that way was to be sensitive to people, to give them a chance to find a job elsewhere. So in some respects I think that was very positive. But in other respects it just made the whole process more painful.

There are, it seems, two different dynamics at work in these surprising comments, and in the general tenor of the discussions. The first is a simple and common defensive reaction: if you're going to hurt me, get it over with fast. The kinds of comments just cited are generally embedded with others that show longing for the old world of security and hope for a return to it. In the background is the hope that things have not really changed—that the crisis is a temporary aberration and can soon be forgotten: the managers are saying, in effect, "Let's get the worst over and get back to normal."

This first response is profoundly conservative, but not, I should emphasize, generally selfish. This is not a simple matter of trying to get the unfortunate ones out of sight. These people were themselves potentially victims of the downsizing, and they were advocating policies that might soon affect them. In at least one instance, the speaker had actually been laid off and was in the process of searching for a new job. She nevertheless said, "I went through the outplacement program, but what I'm angry about is all the money they waste on that program. They just throw money away."

These loyalist managers had their eyes fixed to a remarkable degree on the company's welfare, not their own—or more exactly, the two were still so intertwined in their minds that they could not be separated. The pain of downsizing was psychologically tolerable if it could really be seen as contributing to the company's success. The implication in many comments was that if we have to suffer, then it had better really do some good; the worst thing is to suffer in vain. So if the company is wasting its resources or floundering around while conducting layoffs, it adds a deeper insult to the original injury.

There was another group, however, that took a very different attitude: these were the nonloyalists who were scornfully labeled "professionals." Rather than wanting to get it over with so that things could return to normal, this group wanted to make a real and clean break with the past. Here is another comment from Nadir using Jack Welch in a different way:

Jack Welch—you know, "Neutron Jack," right?—everyone asked him the same question: "Don't you think you were kind of ruthless in changing the organization?" and "Don't you think you acted too quickly?" And Jack Welch said, "Quite honestly, I should have gone faster, because I couldn't get through the culture."

The problem we have here is nobody wants to do anything, say, revolutionary, as opposed to evolutionary. Everybody wants everybody to be nice-nice to one another: We're not going to embarrass manager so-and-so by telling them, "Look, you've outlived your function, we're going to retire you early." None of that has happened. You know, I want to make the business go. You've got to have a revolution, I'm convinced of that.

This manager, unlike those in the first group, is embracing a fundamental change in the business. He and the other "professionals" seek a redefinition, not a restoration, of the relation of companies to their employees.

Though the reasons were different, both groups saw the attempt to cushion the blow of downsizing as wrongheaded. The two groups defined the immediate task in fundamentally divergent ways, but they agreed that what was needed was to get on with the task and to do it well. In this respect all retained a kind of loyalty, or at least an attachment to the good of the whole.

Conclusion: The Flight from Conflict

Perhaps the principal puzzle in companies undergoing the shock of change is that it produces so little outright conflict and disintegration. Many observers— not only journalists, but even some top managers I have spoken with—find this hard to understand, and continue to hold to a myth of imminent collapse. The middle managers, however, had little patience with this view.

The companies I observed in the first throes of this trauma certainly felt a great deal of pain, and some of this pain did translate into anger or withdrawal. But work was still getting done, and the tone was far more complex than either open hostility or an "every man for himself" scattering.

A powerful force intervened between individuals' trauma and their responses. This force was a *desire for meaning,* and more specifically a desire to draw meaning from contribution to a group effort. Those who could find no meaning in the downsizing were the most distressed and disoriented, their views marked by inconsistency and continual shifts of tone. A few managed to find a negative meaning, attributing to the top management some sort of destructive motive or major incompetence. Where the top leadership was new and outside the culture, as at Nadir, this was easier to do and produced a more polarized situation.

Most common, however, were those who even in the midst of the change were able to frame it as good for the company and therefore tolerable for themselves. This is why there was such a high level of overall support for the need to downsize and restructure. This mood was never entirely absent, even at Nadir, and in most cases it dominated, producing a kind of cautious tolerance for what was going on. The outcome for most was to hunker down, to wait for the problems to pass, and to believe that the pain of the moment was a necessary prelude to a brighter future.

4

The Retreat to Autonomy

Wᴇ ʜᴀᴠᴇ sᴇᴇɴ that the first shock produces anguish, bitterness, and deep distress. Yet there is no rebellion: the response is softened by more patience and loyalty than one might expect. But what happens over time?

The short answer is that patience and loyalty generally win out, producing an atmosphere of reasonable calm; but these very virtues quickly turn into liabilities, for they can be maintained only by denying the scope of change going on all around. Loyalists have to focus inward, screening out unpleasant trends in the environment; companies who want to maintain loyalty have to play into the dynamic by softening the blows and muffling the pressures. Neither individuals nor organizations do well.

This is not, of course, the intended purpose of restructuring. Most of these companies saw downsizing not only as a cost-cutting move but also as a way of creating a new culture. They hoped to develop more flexible, responsive organizations, to move away from rigid "bureaucracy." In every case there were programs of one form or another that sought to produce a common vision of the future and to encourage decentralized innovation within that vision. Many companies used the language of "entrepreneurship"—with elaborate training programs and communications blitzes—to symbolize this change; others put out images of upside-down pyramids and spoke of "empowerment"; all of them constantly stressed a focus on the customer.

Almost all communicated as well a new emphasis on individual responsibility and reward, and many instituted programs to tie compensation to performance. At the same time these companies were advocating "teamwork" and establishing large numbers of temporary task forces. These two thrusts caused considerable tension and conflict, which we will explore in more detail later.

Few, however, challenged the basic employment relationship: as far as middle managers heard, these companies were all doing their absolute best to preserve employment security and hoped that it could be stabilized soon. In most instances I spoke directly with top-level managers as well, and they told me the same thing. So the hope appeared to be that once the initial trauma was past, the organization would be leaner, less rule-bound, but still loyal and with a strong sense of teamwork. I found no instances of such a combination. Instead, where loyalty remained strong the organization seemed to retreat into an inward-looking immobility. In cases where I interviewed three to five years after the initial break—in Lyco, in Karet, and in Glover—managers consistently said that there was *more* bureaucracy than before, and their descriptions of how they did their jobs confirmed the view. These organizations did indeed downsize, and they did cut costs, but they failed to change their cultures. If anything, they froze them in place. The story of this failure can be exemplified by Glover.

Glover

PULLING TOGETHER IN A CRISIS

Like Nadir, this was an old company with a history of near-monopoly in its major markets, now faced with stiff foreign competition. In the previous decade its market share had shrunk so dramatically that it faced an unmistakable crisis—not a threat to its existence, but certainly a threat to the primacy it had come to expect.

When I first visited the company in 1988, the crisis was about four years old. Top management had responded with a number of major change initiatives. The first, beginning around 1984, was a 25 percent downsizing of the salaried ranks through attrition and early retirements. The second was a reorganization that pulled together many product-based organizations into larger divisions based on product families: Glover was one of these new divisions. The third was a series of revisions in the pay system to introduce more reward for performance. More recently there had been the start of an ambitious quality program that aimed to build task forces and interfunctional groupings for improved customer responsiveness.

Beneath these three major themes were the choruses heard at most other companies. "Entrepreneurship" had become a widely shared buzzword through constant emphasis in management training and communication. Information about the competition and the company's performance had enormously increased. The CEO and his top officers had gone on a retreat for a week to establish a new vision for the company, which had then been "rolled out" in meetings down through the hierarchy. The results had so far not been positive. It was difficult for anyone I spoke to, up to rather high levels, to be precise about the financial results because of the complexity of transfer cost allocations and marketing relationships between divisions. But sales continued to drop and the product's quality reputation continued to be poor.

Many of the same patterns we observed in Nadir were also visible here. There was a very strong sense of loss of community: the old product divisions had been powerful centers of identity that had been destroyed by the reorganization:

> "The restructuring was much more difficult than I expected. It is difficult to internalize. I underestimated the old allegiances. There are still feelings of division in this company. People still feel that damn [product division X], they took us over."

> "The idea of consolidating different activities was a good one, but the loss of identity has hurt. To say you work for Glover is almost an apology now."

Yet despite superficial similarities, the tone in this organization was very different from the bitterness and confusion of Nadir. There was still nostalgia for the past, but also more acceptance of the need for downsizing: people had generally come to terms with the new environment.

Almost everyone agreed, to begin with, that the changes, however painful, were necessary and were moving in the right direction—unlike at Nadir, where an abstract support for change was coupled with rejection of what was actually going on. The person, for example, who had complained, "to say you work here is almost an apology now" added immediately, "but we had to do it, there were too many pieces before. Now we have a unified focus which we never had before." Another old-line manager commented: "The goal is positive, and change was definitely needed. I'm not sure this was the right change. But generally speaking, the heading seems right."

Most of the people in the company were strong loyalists. They had spent their entire careers in the company, they felt personally obligated to it, they emphasized its nature as a "fair" and "caring" organization. Yet what is striking here, unlike at Nadir, is that the loyalists were making a positive effort to adapt to the new rules. Though they felt personally pained and often lonely, they understood the need for the breakup of the old communities and a new focus on the business. The result was often a complex ambivalence:

> "There is a move toward a more general business focus, the reduction of specialization and over-the-wall thinking. Reorganization tried to get people to do an entire job, not a simple task, especially for the older people. But it has gotten us to focus more on customer satisfaction, which was not our focus in the past."

"Ten years ago many parts of the organization were not in touch with the total product. They were technically good, but they were centered on small pieces. So the reorganization was positive in that sense, we made some real gains. The change is enormous, but it takes a lot of time. There is the problem of getting the network back together. The reorganization disrupted the network of relationships among people at all levels."

And they were clearly working hard on it and thinking creatively about the problem:

In terms of roles, there are going to have to be a lot of changes, because we have to push responsibility down. For example, if we can organize the supervisors into self-managed groups, then the general supervisors can begin to do scheduling and forecasting and planning and I could do more strategic or tactical planning.

The response to changes in the compensation system was a particularly interesting instance of this attitude of dutiful support. There had been considerable anger and resistance to the new performance-based system at lower levels of management, one to two levels above the supervisors. But the middle managers above that range were philosophical, which is another way of saying that their responses were extremely complex. Not a single one had a good word to say about the implementation: they felt top management had crammed a system down everyone's throats with no explanation or warning, and that many of the details of the system were unworkable. Most of them were also critical of the basic idea of increasing the emphasis on individual performance. They saw a conflict with the professed value of teamwork, and they argued that the most effective motivation did not come from money. Yet at the same time most also believed that the company should not retreat from the present plan too quickly. They often suggested that maybe there were some benefits from it, and in any case it was important to maintain a stable direction, even at the cost of short-term problems, rather than responding too quickly to initial reactions—even their own!

In terms of the effort to change the culture, then, it seemed that this company had moved beyond the turmoil visible at Nadir. On the surface there was far more positive feeling. Most managers were "on board" to a significant degree, willing to put in the effort to bring about a change even though they felt personally hurt by it. They consistently professed continued loyalty to the company and dedication to their jobs. In the face of reductions in the managerial force of over 20 percent, this might seem an excellent outcome.

But below the surface there was much trouble. One sign was in the relationship to top management. Although the middle was supportive of the company overall, they were consistently scornful of the corporate leadership, who were seen as financial types with no understanding of operational realities. (One said of the CEO, "If it were my choice I wouldn't follow him to the men's room.") The middle managers saw themselves as struggling to make the company work in spite of the interference of top management.

There was clear disagreement on a major policy decision, for example: the company had decided, for cost and efficiency reasons, to contract out some design and engineering work. The middle levels saw this as plain foolish—damaging to the integrity of the product, and more costly in the long run because of quality problems and the need for rework.

> "The upper levels dictate things which sound good in theory, but are inefficient in practice. For example, this idea of doing the engineering outside the company. You have a few options: you can do it and help it fail, or do the best you can but just knowing it's inefficient and a bad way to do things. That way of doing things also pulls the best engineers out of the organization and sends them to the subcontractors, and there are all kinds of losses when you are trying to work with people outside the company. It's a classic case of the failure of the top to understand the real world. The goal is OK—don't engineer what you don't make—but the implementation was poor. The ability to make correct decisions has been removed by people who feel they know what's best from a policy standpoint. If I can't make these decisions day-to-day, then it raises my frustration level."

> "There's enough momentum building in the middle ranks to ignore what's coming down. It's really a matter of learning what to ignore. We are also learning to work around the systems that have been set up. For example we set up some engineering outside of [the company], but under our control, so that gives us some sense of controlling our own destiny."

One can be confident that this was not mere self-interested resistance. The middle managers, as I have emphasized, were clearly trying to change, struggling with the new policies; they were not simply trying to justify the status quo. Their reasons for opposing the plan were well-thought-out in terms of the company's needs. The clincher, moreover, is that they turned out to be right: when I came back three years later the contracting-out policy had been reversed, and there was general agreement even at high levels that it had been a mistake.

This conflict appears to be a distinct example of a phenomenon I saw at several other sites: the top, assuming the middle would resist, tried to force change rather than engaging them in a discussion of how to implement the new directions. Thus they ended by creating the very resistance they feared.

The middle managers were making a claim, in effect, that they were the experts at operational implementation. They were willing—and many were explicit about this—to follow the top's strategic direction, but they objected when the direction got into the operational level. Then they felt invaded, mistrusted, and overcontrolled.

But did the middle managers in fact understand the changes that needed to be made? Though there were few common sets of concepts that they referred to, they agreed about one basic thing: the need for greater autonomy in their roles. They criticized upper management, as I have indicated, for interfering in their domains; but they also sought clear delineations of their responsibilities in relation to their peers. Their vision of the future was of an organization that had eliminated excess checkers and administrators, slimmed down, clarified roles and responsibilities, and delegated effective authority to each of those roles.

"I think we could combine bureaucracy and entrepreneurial culture if we took a consistent stand like this: as a unit, you have total autonomy except for x and y."

"We are trying to reduce middle management because its function is not value-added. It just adds to the chain-of-command and communication problem. What we are trying to get is where everybody has complete responsibility within his own role. I have complete responsibility for my piece, which is different from the way we have done it in the past. Usually in America we have a tendency to get input from a lot of groups that we can share the blame. Now we have complete accountability, which creates more tension, but also more responsibility."

These managers were showing signs at this point of pulling back to a narrow vision of bureaucratic responsibility, where each person is accountable for a particular job, and conscious cooperation falls to the background. They were asserting their knowledge of their own territory against their higher managers, and despairing of consensual working together. They continued to be loyal to the company, and to do their best; but the framework for cooperation was broken.

This attitude is in essence a retreat from the sense of shared community that, as I argued in chapter 2, is essential to lubricate the clumsy mechanisms of bureaucracy. So it should not be surprising that over the next few years the organization fell increasingly into fractionalization, confusion, and ineffectiveness.

THREE YEARS LATER: WITHDRAWAL AND DENIAL

I returned for further interviews three years later—that is, more than seven years after the initial downsizing. I spoke to seven of the people I had interviewed before, as well as seven more who were new to me.

In the interval the company had been pressing ahead with its cost-cutting moves: the managerial ranks were now down by 30 percent from 1984, and plans were in place for further cuts over the next two years—all through retirement incentives and attrition. The shift toward a team-based organization had also continued apace: the product-focused units had strengthened their authority over functional groups, and task forces had become ever more popular—especially around quality initiatives. *Quality* was the magic word: training, organization, incentives were all focused in relation to it.

A new CEO was enormously popular within the company. The division head was seen as decisive and positive, moving aggressively to improve the quality of the product. Managers felt, on the whole, quite good—they believed that enormous strides had been made and that they were positioned for success. There was far less sense of crisis than during my previous visit.

The only problem was that this confidence flew in the face of all available evidence. On the whole the performance of the company and of this division during the previous years (and in the year since) can only be described as appalling. Market share had continued to erode dramatically, and despite the severe cost-cutting moves the company was losing money in its core business at a great rate. Only a few divisions, relatively peripheral to the main business, were doing quite well; this was the main factor preventing the crisis from turning into disaster. Within Glover, however, the figures were horrendous no matter how you sliced them.

How can we explain this discrepancy between the numbers and the perceptions of the middle managers? Perhaps the latter knew something the market didn't—for example, that they were now fundamentally stronger than the competition and would soon turn things around. But if they knew this, they hid it well. "How does your quality compare to the competition's?" I asked, consistently. "Have they improved as much as you have?" Not one could give me a good answer; indeed, it seemed to be something that they hadn't thought of before. It became clear that these managers, almost without exception, were focused *inward.* Their pride and sense of accomplishment was based on having improved over their own previous performance; they had no reference point on the outside.

There was only one exception, which was so striking that it did help to clarify the rule. This was an operations manager with over twenty years of service at the company. By the time I spoke with her, I had heard repeated self-congratulations about quality improvement. She alone pointed out,

> Quality is a moving target, and we are where the competition was eight years ago. So we can't be lulled into saying we've got the quality problems licked. Quality is your union card, it's your ticket in. If you don't have quality you're not even going to be in business; but the quality alone is not going to get you market share.

This manager was also the only one I spoke to who had gone out to check her operation against that of other companies. "I knew I was perceived as world-class by the corporation," she said, "but I wanted to make sure that was true."

She explained (without prompting from me) an impression I had been forming: that the sense of urgency in the company was sorely lacking. It felt to me as if the organization was wrapped in cotton wool—signals from the outside arrived muffled and distorted. She said:

> Though there's a great deal of information shared with the organization, on a working day-to-day level there's a sense of disconnect, the sense of urgency is not there.
>
> Just for example, here's one teeny thing that's indicative of what I mean by mixed signals. Throughout the building there are large plants, and Glover pays a company to come in and water these plants. Now if we're hemorrhaging so much money, how can we afford to do that when it doesn't add value to our business? It makes us feel better, one might argue that it helps the quality of life of people working here; but if we don't have jobs in the future, that's what's not going to help the quality of life of the people working here. That's just one little signal that I think we're missing the boat on trying to create a sense of urgency so that people understand why we have to do the very serious things we have to do in terms of business and head count.

The second dominant theme, besides this misplaced sense of confidence, was the continued power of loyalty. If anything, people were more sure of this than they had been three years before. I asked, "Do you consider yourself a loyal employee?" The answer was almost invariably "Oh, yeah." It seemed that the passage of time had only consolidated their insistence on this value and clarified the emotional resonances I have discussed before—a desire to hang onto loyalty, distress that the society no longer seems to value it. One exchange went like this:

> When I hired into this company there was no question in my mind I hired in for the duration. Young kids today—I think they're taught, my kids come home and tell me what their professors say—go into a company to get all they can for a few years and get out. They parlay each move into a few more pennies in their income. I've only sensed this in the past ten years.
>
> *I hear you saying that the loss of loyalty is not anything the company has done, it's in the society.*
>
> Yeah, don't get me wrong, I'm not blaming this on the company. It's just that [the young people look for] an opportunity to make another hundred bucks a month or whatever it might be.

That comment comes from an interview with a group of four managers. Let me follow that conversation for a while, to explore how this breakdown of loyalty was linked to their overall interpretation of the situation.

The discussion of loyalty followed from an exchange about the old product divisions that had been eliminated eight years before. Recall that in my earlier visit, most (including three of these same managers) were mourning the loss of community resulting from the breakup of those divisions, but they nevertheless supported the direction as a necessary consolidation. Now, three years later, when I repeated the gist of their earlier comments, they went into reverse. To my astonishment, they not only expressed an undiminished attachment to the old organizations, they also were no longer sure that the breakup had been necessary. The loss of identity, mentioned so often before, had not become less painful with the passage of time:

> We are still out there searching for what we used to be. And we could be what we used to be, but it would defy everything we just got through doing. We've commonized everything.

They even went so far as to suggest that there had been no real need for change. One posited that

> [the former CEO] was in search of a problem. He didn't know how well he had it under the old organization. I think he felt, if I'm going to make my mark, damn, I've got to do something, so I'm going to shake up everybody. And we're still paying for it.

This attitude seems far more disconnected from reality than the earlier interviews: here, in a company already in serious trouble, you have managers saying that the problems were figments of their superiors' imaginations. This was not, furthermore, a matter of lack of knowledge. They knew that the problems went back for many years; they knew the basic figures on how much money had been lost by the division; they knew they had had a plan to be in the black two years before, and then another one to do it in the current year, and that the red ink had only flowed more swiftly.

There is so much distortion here that one has to look for nonrational mechanisms behind it. What was linked most consistently with this altered perception, as they talked through the problem, was the emotional pull toward the sense of identity, meaning, and safety that they remembered from the time before the current troubles.

Throughout the conversation a major theme was criticism of the matrix management system that had been central to the reorganization from its earliest days. What this meant was that people reported simultaneously to an organization focused on making the final product and to an organization based on function (such as finance, engineering, and so on). They had, in other words, two bosses—sometimes more. They complained at length about this ambiguity. They admitted, somewhat reluctantly, that it allowed a greater sharing of knowledge and talent; but then they described tugs of war among different units to control people, and mistrust flowing from the need constantly to negotiate and work things out. This moved into a yearning for stronger leadership:

I think it's human nature to want direction. Any of us—we want someone to tell us what is it we're trying to accomplish, and you want direction. And then you'll go do it—you don't need to get fifteen guys to buy in before you can go. We don't run our personal lives that way. My parents didn't give me that opportunity and I don't give my kids that opportunity, to poll all our input and a nine-member family makes a decision about what to do with little Johnny. That was the strength of the old units: a guy came in and said here's what we're going to do, and Christ, we did it.

They stressed also another theme that was widely echoed by others: a desire for more autonomy, to be left alone to do one's job. "When you have a clear responsibility," said one, "there's less political games, you can control your own destiny." This was clearly consistent with the idea of strong leadership. The ideal situation would be, as expressed in the comment just quoted, someone telling them what to do and then getting out of the way while they did it.

Yet there was an apparent inconsistency between this desire for autonomy and the lamentations for the old community. What was stressed about the old days was not how independent everyone was but how collaborative; not the clarity of distinctions among people but the ability of people to pitch in informally and help each other out.

> "Starting with the major changes in 1984 the working relationships were disrupted. There are new people, new faces. And trust is something that's built up over time. That's a major downside in reorganization: you do break those working relationships and bonds. You know, my boss used to say, 'Take care of this meeting, I don't have time to go to it.' And I knew this guy well enough that I was pretty doggone sure how he would lean. Those kinds of relationships have been disrupted."

> "A lot of close working relationships were built up years ago when we were youngsters in the organization. There isn't the camaraderie of the more mature workers on the job of stopping for a cocktail after work."
> *Does it feel lonelier?*
> "Oh, yeah. When you're an organization that has to keep tweaking itself because you're not doing things right, it breeds that kind of a thing—you know, 'We're all in the group, but we're sort of here independently.'"

WHAT THE TOP THOUGHT

After this second visit I met with the entire top team—the division manager and those who reported directly to him—to discuss my findings. This group had spent much of the previous year in an intense strategic planning review culminating in a reorganization that had recently been announced. Now, like men emerging from Plato's cave, they looked at the reality rather than its shadow in their plans, and they blinked in a puzzled way.

They focused on my comments that the managers I had spoken to did not understand the business well and were sanguine about the company's future. At first they wondered if this was really true. They emphasized how much time and effort had been put into communicating about the business. This is a nearly universal response: upper management always feels they have communicated as much as they can. When, in companies I have not studied, I talk to leaders about the general lack of business understanding in middle management, they are always quick to say they are different: they blame my findings on benighted policies in other companies, and they run through all the training programs they have initiated. But the companies that *were* in my sample felt exactly the same way, and had put just as many resources into communication.

After thinking about it the top team at Glover agreed that the problem was not, in any simple sense, a lack of communication concerning strategy. The middle managers I had spoken to described frequent briefings on strategy, in many different forms, and they could all describe the part of the overall strategy that applied to their own part of the organization. A great deal of information had been flowing down to the middle layers—information about profitability, about market share, about the competition—far more, indeed, than ever before in the company's history. The top was well aware of the importance of building this kind of knowledge. One said, "In terms of understanding strategy we've been very consistent with them, and there's been an awful lot of effort put in this division. If it really is the case that people don't understand it, then we really need to step back and examine how we're trying to communicate with people, how we're trying link individual performance with the business plan. Because that's amazing." It was not that the incentive system wasn't highlighting the problem: the human relations director pointed out that managers had had their pay cut by as much as 50 percent in the prior year or two through foregone bonuses.

Gradually, as they reviewed the evidence and their own experience, they decided the basic point was nevertheless probably true. "I don't disagree with anything you've said," one commented; "but I don't understand why." One suggested that the problem went far deeper than the "communications" issue:

> I'm not sure how much of it's a communications issue, versus denial. Let me go back to this conference we had last fall, of the top people in the company, when [the CEO] laid it on the group, 'By the way there's not going to be a bonus this year'; and we had people walking around that room with their mouths open. And these are all people who were looking at financials every month; I would say half of them were flabbergasted by those remarks. We talked about it in the smaller group afterwards and some of us found it incomprehensible because they had been exposed to that information. It's not a matter of they're not smart enough to understand. I think that there's a denial thing. People don't want to look at it, they just push it away. I don't know how else you can explain it.

As they struggled with this "incomprehensible" problem, they gradually closed in on two major issues. The first was that they had been too worried about discouraging their managers to really lay out the depth of the problems that they were experiencing. The division leader agreed that he had "not emphasized the negative." Another asked a revealing question:

> How can you be frank and straightforward with the organization and still keep morale on the positive side? How do you lay the facts out for them and still don't let them get discouraged?

As they thought about this problem, they suggested that perhaps it was more important to be honest than to protect people from bad news. Referring to the severe downsizing pressure, one commented, "We saw the importance of honesty in things we tried to do personnel-wise two or three years ago. We would soft-pedal things, and we had more trouble with it than if we'd just laid the facts out. In hindsight I think it proved out that if we laid the facts out we probably wouldn't have had any trouble at all."

The second realization was that although they were communicating persistently about strategy, they were not creating a context that gave people a sense of being able to *do* something about it. The strategy remained disconnected from the day-to-day implementation issues faced by middle management:

> The folks hear the strategies, they can't deal with them or keep them straight. And they're thinking, "Oh, here we're losing money, but what can I do? I'll just cover my own little area here." I'll bet you they don't know their product line is losing money. And they're hoping that this astute set of leaders can deal with it— if they work on a couple of strategies that they should and get the quality up, all will be well. . . . I've heard people say, "All I need to do is do Total Quality, and run my couple of strategies that are key to my platform, and all will be well."
>
> We have been successful in translating the customer's concern over quality into something which I have been asked to do and is expected of me and is expected of my product. But we have not made yet the same translation into, "The company is losing money, this is what it translates into for my product and to me." And therefore when things happen, like my salary is reduced, I cannot put it in the context of the total job to be done, and in the absence of that I say it must be enough, when it isn't.

This was a soul-searching discussion, with many long pauses and much questioning of what they had done. It ended on the point I already have stressed in relation to Nadir: that when the changes didn't make sense to people, they simply hunkered down and ignored them as much as possible, focusing on the piece that they did understand, as in "I'll just cover my little area here." This was a new thought, different from the emphasis on simply communicating information about the business.

The Revival of Bureaucracy

Looking beyond the single case of Glover, there is here a long-term, very stable pattern. It was very clear in the two organizations that I saw over an extended period (Glover and Lyco), and also visible in several others that I only visited once. Its major elements are:

- an inward focus, taken to the point of a denial of business reality;
- a strong sense of loyalty;
- a desire for autonomy, clarity, and strong leadership, along with its converse: a resistance to consensus-based management styles; and a longing for the past community.

Beneath this pattern, which one can see at a given moment, is a dynamic unfolding over time and effectively blocking change. At the start is an organization with a significant level of trust based on shared loyalty. As this is threatened, people pull back into a more isolated and narrow focus on their own particular roles. Decentralization, which is typically a major part of the shift, only increases this fragmentation; links across the decentralized units fail to establish themselves. And the end result is a more bureaucratic organization than before: "bureaucratic" in the sense of rule-bound, conservative, unable to mobilize people around a common task.

The managers I talked to didn't articulate the dynamic in this form. But they did keep telling me a surprising thing: that despite downsizing and team-based reorganizations, bureaucracy had *increased* in recent years. This was a question I asked consistently, and the answer was also consistent: the substantial majority—especially at Glover, Karet, Lyco, and JVC—said bureaucracy was on the rise. Sometimes it was qualified; some people said that they were left alone more than in the past, which felt like less bureaucracy, but they went on to say that when they did interact with others, there was more rigidity and negative politics. This response was so strong that it begs for an excavation of the underlying reasons.

WHAT WAS LOST: THE LEAVENING EFFECT OF TRUST

In the view of middle managers, the "old order" was not a bureaucratic one—or more exactly, it was not bureaucratic in the bad sense of the word. It had some elements of the Weberian model but not others. It combined a clear structure and defined responsibilities—the key ingredients of classic bureaucracy—with an atmosphere of cooperation and shared commitment that is generally seen as its opposite.

One can draw from stories about the past that contrast it to the present a picture of life before the "break." It is romanticized, as one can see from other comments and other studies. There is nevertheless enough truth in it to help in understanding what happened in the process of restructuring.

I have cited in chapter 2 a few examples from the many people gave me of informal working together to get the job done. Although the formal structure stresses up-and-down relations, both research and the impressions of the managers indicate that far more time is spent on lateral ties. This communication across lines is often referred to as a manager's "network," and the ability to build a good network is, or was, the key to being effective in the job.

There was always a certain tension between the formal hierarchy and the informal network. Formally, people were held responsible for accomplishing their own tasks and achieving their own objectives. In order to do that, however, they needed the help of others, which went outside the system of accountability. Therefore people constantly made deals. Sometimes these were fairly explicit: if you'll help me out here, I'll do something for you later. More often they were just part of the atmosphere: I'll be open with you about what I'm doing because I assume you'll be equally forthcoming with me.

There is a rich anthropology to this deal-making which has rarely been explored.[1] Clearly there was variation in how well it worked. Most often this collaboration was portrayed as a matter of filling in, or implementing, the higher-level commands—showing enough independence to get the job done, but continuous with the direction of the top. In a few organizations—most notably in Glover and Karet—it appeared to have been more disconnected from the bureaucratic apparatus. The stories centered on the middle levels getting together to do things *in spite of* the directives from above. In some instances (especially that of Marks) it had never worked well: as far back as people could recall there had been jealousy and backbiting rather than cooperation. This was called "politics," in the negative sense described in chapter 2.

But for most of the organizations in my study middle-management networking had functioned well at least some of the time. When it did, it was almost invisible; it was simply a critical part of daily managerial life. There was a climate of trust that facilitated getting things done. This is what defined the quality of the lamented product divisions that had been taken apart in the reorganization at Glover: people knew each other, they could work out informal agreements with confidence that they would be honored.

This networking meant that the organization was not fully bureaucratic in the key sense: people were not restricted to a narrow focus on their little pieces, ignoring the rationality of the whole. They could, as cited before, "pull in" people from different areas through informal mechanisms to accomplish a task, crossing formal organizational lines to focus on the main objective.

In this structure managers had never simply played a bureaucratic role: they had never been mere transmitters of information upward and orders downward, never just technical or expert performers of a defined job. Their sense of their role had, quite consistently, two major components. First, they were generally managers of a small team, providing support, career counseling, and developmental opportunities as well as coordinating their work. They inevitably spoke about this role in terms of leadership rather than of bureaucracy. The modern language of "coaching" came naturally to them. For instance, an Emon manager said,

> The bottom of the organization does better with people-centered management than the top. The lower levels give good coaching and training, and all of us look at the long term.

In general, direct supervisory relationships seem to have been good. For example, I regularly asked what happened when there were real disagreements with directives; the vast majority said not only that their subordinates felt free to come to them but also that they themselves felt free to go to their own bosses. This easy relationship rarely went further. Immediately above the direct supervisor the organization began to look formal and impenetrable. But within the "team," most reflected, both upward and downward, a very non-"bureaucratic" definition of their roles.[2]

Second, they were coordinators of tasks, reaching through the organization to gather the resources and people needed to implement the top's strategy. To take one example: in many different companies people spoke of the practice of "borrowing" personnel from other parts of the organization. This appears to have been a common way of dealing with temporary task pressures in the classic organizational setting: rather than formally reassigning employees, with all the paperwork and procedural clumsiness that would involve, people simply lent expertise and manpower from their groups to each other for limited time periods—with the understanding that the favor would be returned someday.

This sense of teamwork in the traditional organization explains at least in part the lack of fundamental resistance to de-bureaucratization. If one were to judge from popular management consultants and texts, the idea of teamwork—one of the chief buzzwords of the past decade—is a radical innovation. They convey an implicit assumption that managers are typically stuck within the rules of their narrow job titles and never act cooperatively. It is true that there were many barriers impeding certain types of cooperation, but it is not true that teamwork was absent. The current move to "de-bureaucratize" organizations, reducing rules and emphasizing working together, is just a formalization of the best aspects of traditional roles.

All of this cooperative activity at the middle levels depended, however, on underlying expectations of stability and loyalty. Stability was critical because one could count on people to be around to return your favors; loyalty, because one could trust that they were oriented to something other than their own self-interest. Those who tried to play games, putting themselves ahead of the group, were quickly identified and excluded from the networks of peer cooperation. And because of the long-term continuity, they could not easily get away from damaged relationships. These two aspects of the traditional system created the objective conditions for trust; they turned potentially negative and fragmenting deal-making in a constructive direction.

Now, I cannot let that image stand for long without pointing to its limitations. It was clear that the old sense of community described by so many of the managers was a partial and limited one. The negative side of it was that there were in-groups, among whom the informal trust worked as a basis for common action, and "out-groups." The distinction might be made on legitimate grounds, such as excluding the overly self-interested, but it was often made on illegitimate grounds as well. Race and gender, for example, could be such grounds. It was a woman who was the only dissenter from the overwhelmingly idealized picture of the old product divisions at Glover, noting their narrowness: "What a hidebound old-boy network that was!" For the most part the minorities and women I spoke with were less romantic about the past, and saw more opportunity in the present, than the white males. That is not difficult to understand, given past evidence of the ways in which they were kept on the outside of the old peer networks.[3]

Even the mainstream managers, however, would frequently remark on dysfunctional aspects of the old system—the "politics" that interfered with proper cooperation. The most obvious problem was that subunits, rather than the company as a whole, would often become foci for loyalty and community; at that point communication across those units became strained. The old product divisions at Glover did not work well together. That was why they had been broken up, and why the majority of managers reluctantly agreed that the breakup was necessary. Functional units likewise often fought each other, and there was some evidence—less than I would have thought—of personal empires, in which people developed primary loyalty to a particular leader. These dimensions defined local areas of cooperation and often interfered with the unity of the whole.

Finally, the hierarchy was a major barrier to cooperation. Apart from direct supervisors, *no one* felt a sense of "teamwork" with higher levels.[4] The informal cooperation I am describing was almost purely a horizontal matter.

The "old order" was, in short, a traditional community: stable, homogeneous, strongly hierarchical, and based on personal ties and relationships. When cooperation was called for across these boundaries on the basis of a common task, or needed expertise, or competence, without the shared informal network, it quickly degenerated into in- versus out-group dynamics. But within these bounds there was a level of trust and cooperation that kept the system functioning and responding smoothly.

THE RETREAT TO AUTONOMY AND THE "FREEZING" OF THE ORGANIZATION

A major effect of the changes in the troubled organizations was to undermine informal teamwork. Existing political networks had been torn apart, and the underlying sense of traditional community had been largely abandoned. I have noted this in the two cases I have described:

> "The reorganization disrupted the network of relationships among people at all levels." (Glover)

> "There's too little integration now between groups. Every group is going its own way. I don't see the cohesive working environment that we used to have." (Nadir)

And it also appears in most of the other cases:

> "We lost the sages, the people who helped you along and gave you advice, the people who figured out how to work out problems and disagreements." (Fixx)

> "Basically you operate as an individual here." (Marks)

> "We're all alone out there. It's been very stressful." (Crown)

At Nadir this "pulling back" seemed to be a reaction to the confusion and fear caused by the initial shock of downsizing, where no one knew what to expect from the system any more. But in other organizations, including Glover, it had settled into an apparently *stable* way of dealing with change.

The undermining of political networks had become at Glover and other companies a quasi-permanent state, for the change had fundamentally weakened the expectations on which they were based. The traditional community could not be maintained where there was constant restructuring and movement of personnel, and where loyalty was not reliable. Many people spoke of "trying to get the network back together," but all agreed that it did not work as well as it had before the reorganization.

This in turn produced two results for the organization as a whole: a formalization of relations and an increase in dysfunctional "politics." The dynamic is this: the old organization at its best combined formal systems of accountability with an informal system of cooperation. The latter "lubricated" the former, as it were, and made the formal system adaptable enough to deal with the constant demands of a market-based organization. This informal system, as I have stressed, was "outside" the official management process. People consistently portrayed it as a kind of benign and necessary evasion of the formal demands of the hierarchy. But it was nevertheless channeled in a positive direction by the stability of the system and the shared loyalty to the whole.

When these latter conditions broke down, there were two possible responses. Those who continued to feel deeply loyal to the corporation, now unable to mobilize a cooperative network, would have to put their heads down and do the best they could on their own. In their relations with others they would need to rely more heavily on the formal procedures and rules—the bureaucratic framework—because trust was less widespread. Meanwhile, those whose loyalty was less secure—and there is of course a wide range of shadings in this—might seek to shore up their personal positions at the expense of the company. Hence the negative form of "politics"—empire-building and making deals for personal advantage—though it had always been present, would tend to increase.

> I think at the lower supervisory levels there's incredible competition for jobs. And I think that's really created an environment where people compete in a very unhealthy way with each other. Instead of sharing information, they close information. Quite frankly, I do it, too. I don't like this part about myself, but I'll share information, I'll offer things, I'll be open, and I'll give and I'll give and I'll give—but if I don't sense anything reciprocal, I'm gonna stop. (Lyco)[5]

Part of the general trend in almost all of these companies, as I have said, was to push responsibility down in the organization. One would think this would be well received, since it would allow people more autonomy and reduce "micromanagement" from the top. But that is not the way middle managers, for the most part, saw it: they viewed decentralization as further breaking the sense of unity that supported cooperation. One manager at Nadir remarked,

> When we were more centralized, we were more like a family. We socialized more. I personally have gained from decentralization, but it has reduced the family feeling. The teamwork spirit has deteriorated, because of decentralization.

The final element driving the retreat to autonomy was the growing distance between supervisors and their subordinates. The reduction in numbers and the "delayering" of organizations had clearly increased the span of control; perhaps more important, the emphasis on customer satisfaction and quality management meant managers were out of the office and moving around more than they had traditionally.[6] In any case, there was a consistent sense that bosses were less available than in the past. Since the supervisor had been almost the only point of penetration to higher levels of the organization, this meant that there was an intensification of the vertical separation.

I used to do business face-to-face with [my boss]. We would have lunch every week. Now his replacement has a much broader responsibility. There are fewer informal relations—you can't talk to him informally the old way, you can't work things out by saying "Bullshit!" to him. Now working things out is a formal process of negotiation.

All these forces in effect pushed people to withdraw from communal life:

> This company has probably gotten more bureaucratic. Top management wants a lot of details and information from the lower levels. The vice presidents are not being allowed to manage their divisions. We've had decentralization but more procedures and control.
>
> Before there was more focus on how do we do this together; now we'll work to make our divisions profitable if we can, in some cases at the expense of other divisions. Now there is less of what is the best thing for JVC. Now things are required to be solved at a higher level. Before they were solved at lower levels.

Conclusion

If the initial shock of change produced confusing and contradictory responses, as we saw in the last chapter, the passage of time brings more coherence. But the movement is not progressive; it goes backwards. Initially people pay at least some attention to the challenges posed by the environment, but eventually they settle back into an increasingly inward focus, building walls between them and the outside world. Whereas at first the desire to maintain a community is in conflict with contrary emotions of fear and self-protection, what dominates over time is the desire for autonomy; the sense of community becomes increasingly abstract, a memory of happier times.

Then, in the kind of irony often characteristic of social transformation, the changes made in the name of teamwork and de-bureaucratization end by increasing both bureaucracy and internal infighting. Decentralization is linked to *more* procedures and control—just what the top managers at Glover and elsewhere do not want. Yet how could it be otherwise? If you decentralize, and also break the informal pattern of expectations that keep people pulling together, how can you avoid formalizing procedures to keep the decentralized units in line? If people lose the sense of what holds them together, how can they cooperate? It seems inevitable, in retrospect, that attention should narrow and turn inward.

The downsizing among these companies certainly reduced costs, and it may have eliminated much duplication and waste. It did so, furthermore, without destroying the essential loyalty of managers, their desire to do a good job for the company. That is the good side.

The negative results are deeper, both harder to see and more profound. Along with cost and waste, the transformation also eliminated, or at least damaged, the links among people. It did not make them selfish or bitter, but it did make them more isolated, more cautious, less able to enter into informal and spontaneous agreements. The organization therefore became more rigid and "bureaucratic" than before.

Such, at any rate, was the pattern at Glover. Let us turn now in more detail to efforts to overcome the problems through systematic transformation of the culture.

5

The Walls of the Box: The Failure of Participatory Management

I HAVE DESCRIBED a kind of trap, in which attempts to cut and streamline middle management produce more rigid, isolated organizations than before, with managers who seem strangely disconnected from reality. "But," one might reply, "these companies have simply not gone about it right: what they *really* need to do is . . . "—and here one fills in a favorite theory of change.

A common theory is that the transformation should be *participatory,* involving employees—middle managers, for our purposes—deeply in the planning process, and working to build shared understanding. One of the most sophisticated theorists in this area, Albert Hirschman, has suggested that participation, or voice, is particularly important to declining organizations, for if the most active people cannot express their views, they will tend to leave—thus depriving the system of the very people who are most needed to pull it out of its decline.

Hirschman further adds loyalty to the mix. Loyalty tends to hold people in an organization even when their rational self-interest would prompt them to abandon it. In staying, they have a greater incentive to try to change the system for the better.[1]

The danger in the current situation (it would follow) is that if participation is blocked, managers will face an intolerable conflict. Their loyalty holds them to the organization, yet at the same time they are (or feel) excluded from shaping its future. They must either withdraw—make a physical or emotional "exit" from the company—or force upper management to listen through some sort of rebellion.

Many of the managers I talked with concentrated on this theme of voice: by and large they believed that their views were not adequately listened to. Their frequent railing against top management, which I have already emphasized, had this motif: they don't understand our position, they don't respect our knowledge, and they don't listen. The middle managers usually felt they could speak freely to their own bosses, to be sure; but they were convinced that the channels of communication were shut off somewhere near the top.

They also believed and argued that their input would be valuable. In this they tended to make fine distinctions. They did not claim that the company should listen to their views on corporate strategy and finance; this they accepted as outside their domain. But they did argue that they had a deep operational understanding of the company, and that they could therefore contribute useful ideas. In at least a few cases I managed to track, they were right. For example (as I mentioned earlier), at Glover upper management decided to contract some engineering functions to outside suppliers. During my first visit many of the middle managers described this as a stupid decision, because the short-term cost savings were achieved at the expense of coordination in the complex design process. When I came back two years later, upper management had acknowledged that they had made a mistake and had reversed the policy.

These managers did not only believe that their input was valuable; they further believed that their loyalty to the company created an obligation to contribute their views, even if it might hurt them personally:

> I think we have an obligation—particularly those of us who are in middle management—I think we have an obligation to make things better. . . . We have an obligation, even if it does give somebody some heartburn.

Thus we have basic evidence for Hirschman's view: that loyalty is the basis for a climate in which people want to help, and that they in fact can help. The interviews are also full the tension and conflict caused by the prohibition of voice. Some were bitter:

> When you have complaints you keep them to yourself. You do things yourself around here. You solve your own problems. You don't try to go through the hierarchy and you definitely don't voice your opinion to [higher levels].

And many were merely confused and torn, simultaneously trying to express their views and despairing of the possibility; simultaneously loyal but thinking about exit:

> I think we have an obligation, regardless as we keep options open or whatever, and I think we would all do that—to try to make things better where we are [even if we're looking for something else]. I see that in terms of in some cases working both ends of the fence. . . .

All this seems to lead to a logical solution: to break the walls of bureaucracy while building on loyalty by involving people more deeply in decision making. There is, of course, a great deal of rhetorical support for this concept in the speeches of business leaders and the books of consultants. Participation has been a major theme of the age at least since the (re)discovery of Japanese "quality circles" in the 1970s. A number of companies in my sample had moved beyond rhetoric by developing extensive programs to increase participation by managers.

These efforts were, to put it simply, failures. Participative management is not, in itself, capable of breaking through the walls of the bureaucratic box. The story of why it fails involves a complicated exploration of the cultural stability of these traditional companies.

Increasing Participation and Voice

One set of companies went to great lengths to give managers a voice in the change process. Karet, for instance, had established two years before an "assembly" in the managerial and professional ranks: each year representatives from various levels and functions met for several days to express their concerns to the top, to hear about the company's strategies, to explore ways to improve things, and to develop action plans for organization change. Isony, which was a much smaller organization, had a system of ongoing committees to discuss employee concerns, extending through the managerial ranks and including also shop-floor workers. And one division of Lyco, which I will describe shortly in more detail, had tried a radically participative management style in a newly renovated site.

These were only the most substantial of the efforts to involve managers. Leadership in almost every organization, with the partial exceptions of Clark and JVC, expressed the same ideology of participation. At a minimum, managers at all levels were told to treat their subordinates with respect and to listen carefully to their concerns, to act as "coaches" rather than as supervisors. Almost all went beyond that: they had "open door" policies that enabled lower-level workers to bypass their supervisors when they felt they could not be heard; they held "focus groups" in which higher managers had breakfast with small groups of subordinates; and so on. The uniformity of the overall direction, and the sincerity and variety of its implementation, were impressive.

The pervasiveness of the participative approach should be gratifying to the large number of management writers who have been advocating such an approach for at least the past decade: it shows that their work is taken seriously.[2] The case has a basic plausibility, of course. The managers in my interviews were quite convinced that if they were listened to they would be more loyal and better performers. They didn't ask for much, on the whole—they didn't expect that they would actually change decisions, certainly not that consensus should be a requirement; it would help, they said, if only they knew that the higher levels really understood their concerns. Their tone was typically humble, moderate, hesitant:

Obviously we all want some voice, and in every decision maybe that's not necessarily possible, but if somebody can convince you that they have given some
consideration of what maybe you would have said or some element of that . . .

But signs of a problem are already there in these plaintive comments, for the
laments were just as consistent as the programs that were meant to alleviate
them. There is a contradiction here: somehow the open doors, the focus
groups, the stress on coaching did not solve the problem. What is more surprising is that neither did the more ambitious efforts: the assemblies, the teams,
the committees that tried to institutionalize participation in a more systematic
way. In those organizations, the complaints about not being heard were just as
loud as anywhere else; and the programs were seen as marginal and irrelevant.
This makes the walls of the box seem more impenetrable.

Let us take a closer look at one of these cases to judge better why there are
so many failures.

THE LYCO ENGINEERING DESIGN BUILDING

High Ambitions

Lyco made one of the most concerted efforts to transform the culture—an
effort I followed closely over some time. The background story is the same as
almost all the others: an old-line, highly stable, paternalist, bureaucratic company, faced with a rather dramatic development of new competitive pressures in
the early 1980s; these led to a major reorganization and then, more reluctantly,
to layoffs.

Part of this overall change involved a strong affirmation of the importance of
human values, including participation and security, and of cooperation in the
improvement of the business. As in most of these cases, a statement came from
the highest levels expressing this commitment, and the heavy machinery of
training programs was brought to bear. During the period of the story I am
about to tell, all managers learned to refer to themselves as "coaches," and all
employees learned to discuss their jobs in terms of "serving customers,"
whether "internal customers" or "external" ones.

The particular site I studied tried to take these approaches as a foundation
for a new style. It was an engineering design building that had recently been
renovated to accommodate the latest in equipment; thus it had an unusual
opportunity to try new styles. It was a large operation, returning over a few
years from 100 engineers toward its original capacity of nearly 1,000. When I
first saw it the scaffolding was still up around the building, but the future managers were hard at work planning to make it as advanced as a social system as it
was technically.

Groups who normally had been walled off from each other by functional divisions had agreed to work together. They had formed a committee of five middle managers—who soon came to be known as "the Governors"—to cooperatively plan the organization of the site. They brought together, in particular, two groups who traditionally were on poor terms: the technical staff and the support staff. The former were engineers and draftsmen responsible for product design; the latter provided everything from building maintenance to information systems to labor negotiation. As in almost every organization I have ever observed, the former felt themselves to be the real core of the business, and the latter felt that they were treated with little respect.

The five Governors had been encouraged by their superiors to be innovative and daring. Their immediate boss remembered:

> We had a meeting to just think about the possibilities. I said to them, "We've got a clean sheet of paper. We've got this fantastic opportunity to do something different, and there are no holds barred. We can do anything we want, starting with a clean sheet of paper." They didn't want to use that terminology. They said, "What do you mean, a clean sheet of paper? We don't have a clean sheet of paper, we've got all these constraints." I said, "No, you don't. You can do anything you want." And they kept saying, "I don't like this . . . "
>
> These guys, I mean, they thought I was wild. Now sometime between that meeting and today, they stopped saluting and started doing it themselves. I mean, I don't have to push them anymore.

And indeed within a few months, the Governors developed a rapport and a shared vision of an ideal site. They planned for an informal atmosphere, a high level of involvement, and close working relations among all the groups in the building. The Governors early on modified the physical design so as to encourage casual interaction; they worked hard with their own subordinates to develop a participative style of management. Most important, from our point of view, they established a "Congress" of people from all levels and functions of the building to help in its management.

The Congress was viewed by the building leadership as a way to shake up the old bureaucracy. All had a sense, as expressed by the manager just quoted, that the traditional order was a powerful constraint on change. Most employees (including, initially, The Governors) had developed extremely strong habits of mind: expecting to be blocked, looking for the rules that limited them, fearing to be bold. The problem, then, was to find a concrete way to assure them that they had a "clean sheet of paper" and could be active participants in filling it in.

The Congress was a group of about twenty people covering as much diversity as possible: middle and lower-level managers; technicians, marketers, and support staff; both sexes and several races. The Governors met with them at their kickoff, but then backed off in order to give them as much freedom and room to create as possible. The Governors' message at the first meeting was very much like the one they had received from their superior: go forth, be bold, we will support you actively in any effort to make this location more effective, involving, and satisfying.

After a few meetings in which they sorted themselves out, the Congress focused on an issue that might seem peculiar to an outsider but which was freighted with significance for them: they requested that a space be set aside for an employee lounge. This was justified in terms of creating a cooperative and supportive atmosphere, and so on. But the real significance was that the top management of the organization had already ruled that some other facilities could *not* have employee lounges—that this was a waste of money in a time of retrenchment.

Thus this first major issue set up a direct confrontation between top management policy and the commitment to participation. There were, of course, many layers of meaning and expectation below the surface. The members of the Congress took, in public and in private, an ambivalently challenging tone. A minority were reluctant to push the issue, but the majority tied the culture of bureaucracy in a neat knot: they argued that in voicing their needs they were *simply doing what they had been told to do* by their superiors. It followed that it was not their problem or responsibility if they were rejected.

The higher levels of management—the Governors and their own superiors—recognized that they were in an uncomfortable bind. As they saw it, if the employee lounge proposal was turned down, they would simply be proving that the old order was still dominant. Breaking the mold required responding to the request. They therefore put their personal influence very heavily on the line by pushing all the way to the division head for an exception on this issue. One of the Governors expressed his deep discomfort with the situation:

> It was frustrating when they started testing. It was almost like, "This whole concept isn't going to work unless we get permission for an employee lounge." The employee lounge became a cause célèbre—it really became a cause célèbre. And I got very frustrated trying to understand where they were coming from and the reaction that I was getting from my supervision. Their reaction was, "Make it go away, Jim. We don't want to discuss this. You know how sensitive this is. Nobody else has one. We don't want to talk about it." So, you know, I had to find a way to package this such that they would find it acceptable. Because it was that important to these guys.

To their relief (and considerable surprise), the answer from on high came back positive. The Governors were jubilant: they felt that the deadlock had been broken, that a definite sign had been given that business would not continue as usual, and that a new, more responsive, more cooperative order was starting.

The Congress's response to this momentous event, however, was much more muted. Though there was a certain amount of satisfaction, there was far less sense that something fundamental had happened. Rather than showing a surge of enthusiasm and energy, they floundered about for a number of meetings trying to figure out what to do next. In retrospect, the mood indicated severe trouble ahead.

Stopping Short

The next phase centered around an effort to shift the focus of the Congress from quality-of-life issues to business concerns. In this they were encouraged, both directly and behind the scenes, by the Governors and other managers with relations to the site. Their view had always been that the real importance of the Congress would be in pulling together the various functions—service, design, marketing, production—into a collaborative unit. The initial discussions of things like the employee lounge were seen as a phase necessary for trust building, but not the real point.

The chairperson of the Congress, a young technician, was strongly in favor of pursuing questions in this expanded domain—projects such as gathering information on changing customer demands, exploring new product ideas, increasing the flexibility of personnel assignments, and so on. But he found the majority of the committee strongly resistant. Despite the overt support of their bosses for the enlarged agenda, they continually argued that these areas were not their concern—that they would be trampling on the domains of other groups, and that they lacked the needed expertise. Success in one area, in short, had failed to unleash self-confidence in others.

Their reluctance to forge on did not mean that the issues were minor or irrelevant. The problem was not that the majority didn't *care* about the state of the business, or that they felt they could safely leave it to others: on the contrary, they overwhelmingly believed that the company was in serious trouble, and that top management really didn't know what it was doing. In this respect the tone was very much like that of Glover during my first visit.[3] Over the first few months after the reopening of the building, the pressure increased as layoffs began in nearby facilities. I heard no direct criticism of these layoffs, which were unprecedented, but I heard an increasing drumbeat of criticism of top management's incompetence and lack of communication.

In this environment the Congress found itself—about nine months after its inception—in an enervating stalemate. Its meetings were on the surface devoted to increasingly trivial issues, such as orientation programs for new employees and social hours, but underneath the situation was highly charged. Their chairperson and their immediate superiors were urging them, almost pleading with them, to voice their real concerns, to tackle issues of how to make operations more effective and thereby improve the chances of security. But the more the pressure grew, the more the majority shied away from facing it.

This same dynamic was repeating itself at a higher level—among the Governors. At the urging of one of their superiors, as well as a consultant's they met to discuss the strategic future of the building. They were encouraged to develop their own view of the priorities and concerns to be addressed. There followed one of the most curious meetings I have ever been part of, for this higher-level group reproduced the very pattern that they were trying to change in the Congress. They spent the first half of the meeting complaining vociferously about the lack of leadership from above:

> We don't know who to believe. . . . People don't know who's running the business. . . . They continue to pour money into technical development when what is really needed is a better focus on the marketplace. . . . We're not reaching the right customers: we're getting too dependent on single large customers. . . .

Then they spent the second half of the meeting *refusing to do anything about it.* When I say "refusing," I mean that the level of resistance to all options was so high as to amount nearly to panic. Their superior suggested formulating their views to be passed to higher levels; they thought that would be worse than useless. The consultant suggested developing at least their own definition of strategy for the building for the issues they could control; they only returned to further criticism of the top:

> Meetings with top management won't help. They're flailing, too, and we'll just get the same answers we always have.

Meanwhile, back in the Congress, the private complaining continued to increase in intensity. A particular focus was the recent renovation of the divisional headquarters offices, which they saw as ostentatious and increasing the distance from the "troops"; there were plenty of complaints as well about missed business opportunities, the closing down of promising projects and so on.

An Opportunity Lost

One day at lunch Allan, a senior technician, was reciting the litany of criticisms and also putting unusual emphasis on his own willingness to stand up and be counted, to tell it like it was, no matter what the cost. The consultant suggested that the Congress arrange a meeting with the division head to convey their views. This set in motion a chain of events that further illustrated the difficulty of participative change.

- The chair of the Congress took up the idea with enthusiasm, but few followed her. Allan, who had prompted my suggestion, quickly withdrew into grumbling silence.
- The Congress nevertheless appointed a focus group, including the chair and Allan, to meet with Randolph, the division manager. Randolph, for his part, expressed great openness, even delight at the prospect of the meeting, and encouraged them to be frank and open.
- The focus group, when it met to prepare for the meeting, spent its time arguing about who had called it and whether they should have an agenda for it. Allan and others insisted that this meeting was not *their* idea—they were merely respond-ing to Randolph's request: "He called the meeting, why do we have to set an agenda?" They frequently erupted in complaints about top management ("We're bobbing around in the ocean and no one's steering the ship"), but they flatly refused to bring up those complaints unless they were asked directly.
- The meeting with Randolph was wary, tensely calm. He began by saying he wanted to communicate more. A few members of the focus group voiced the gen-eral feeling of drift and powerlessness; but everything was said so guardedly that it lost all urgency. One young staff employee asked about the issue of layoffs. Randolph explained that the business was very uncertain, but that he did not expect layoffs in the building in the foreseeable future. He said he didn't quite understand why people felt so lost; he had explained the state of the business many times in public forums, but somehow people didn't seem to get it: "Either they don't *agree* with the direction we're going, or maybe it's that if you don't feel ownership, then you just hear it—you don't remember it." He promised to spend an hour a week getting out to talk to people in the building, and they discussed an expansion of open meetings where people could question him about business issues. Randolph suggested maybe they should celebrate successes more and concentrate less on the problems. And he commended the Congress for opening up communication.
- Nothing changed. Over the next months complaints continued in the same form and with the same intensity as before. Randolph and other top leaders felt the mood was improving, but the middle managers, in private comments to me, saw no change.

Long-Term Inertia

Now let us fast-forward three years. The business environment did not change a great deal in the period. The prognosis was, as it had been during the above events, guardedly optimistic with lots of turbulence ahead. Though the company continued to downsize, in most business units it avoided forced man-agerial layoffs.

The Engineering Design Building itself had had no "official" layoffs, but there had been several waves of early retirements with pressure applied. Layers had been eliminated: indeed, the whole management level that had formerly composed "the Governors" was gone. The day-to-day operations of the building were now managed by a cross-functional team of people one level lower, reporting to a "coach" based at a distant site.

So what had happened to "participation," "morale," and "loyalty"?

As far as *participation* went: the Congress continued to meet, but it had never moved beyond the peripheral issues on which it was stuck in those early months. A nonmember said: "I don't know what the Congress is doing. I don't really know who is on it. I don't remember seeing anything significant from them. I guess they did some stuff with the fitness room and new furniture. I was very pleased with the initial response on the Congress. . . . But now a lot of that focus has been lost."

Morale had a lot of the quality of Glover: most people were trying to keep on doing their jobs and hoped for the best. Some groups, however, were more disoriented than that—in particular the cross-functional leadership team. These managers felt isolated and out of control: they did their jobs, but had no sense of whether they were helping the company or not. They said that they worked together moderately well, but they were furious with upper management and especially with their "coach." They did not feel "empowered" by the elimination of close supervision; they felt abandoned:

> The negative side of coaching is that we don't get any recognition or feedback. I feel we've been abandoned. We don't hear from anybody.

There had been an incident in which the team had gone to the manager two levels up and suggested they needed a superior on site, rather than hundreds of miles away; the "coach" retaliated by giving them a low performance appraisal, which was later changed after much agitation.

The overall sense of floundering was, if anything, stronger than it had been three years before. The dominant theme of my conversations was that they had no faith that the business was going in the right direction, and no sense of connection to it.

> What's wrong with the business unit? First of all, I don't understand how we're running our business from a marketing point of view—who our competitors are, our strategy for entering markets, and so on. Second, we are terrible in manufacturing. We've focused on meeting the customers' needs, all right, but not on the bigger picture of the whole system and the market and the capacity and how we get things out to the market.

And *loyalty?* Like a building after an earthquake, it showed severe cracks but still stood. The attitude of most people, though they seemingly had not thought it through in any coherent way, was that they would still call themselves loyal—but they were not sure to what. I asked a few people the question, "What would you say about loyalty?" and got these ambivalent replies:

"My loyalty to my people is higher. Loyalty to immediate management is low because I haven't seen any sharing and trust. My loyalty to Lyco, I don't even know if I can define it. I'm not going to violate the code of ethics, but that's about all I can think of."

"There should be a greater sense of belonging, that's a need. I don't feel a sense of belonging except to my team. Lyco is too far removed."

Despite these expressions of confusion and pain, I should emphasize, the general sense of loyalty remained very high: all of those I spoke to (with the exception of one or two very new employees) continued to expect a permanent relation to Lyco, and most expressed a strong emotional connection as well. The dominant reaction was not an abandonment of the company or the adoption of any calculating individualist orientation, but a cry of pain at the company's indifference. They still hoped to reestablish the bond. If they had withdrawn, it was to focus their emotions on a part of the corporation—but not to reattach them to anything else, whether it be their own personal careers or a wider professional responsibility.

Why Problems Can't Be Discussed

The key point to be drawn from this story is that it is difficult to change the rules of communication in the traditional community. No matter how much higher managers talk about new ways of doing business, they are not likely to be heard; no matter how much they listen, they are not likely to be told the real problems.

What strikes me, as an outsider, in Lyco and most of the other troubled organizations, is the degree of self-censorship. Managers may boast about their fearlessness and willingness to speak up to their bosses, but when the opportunity comes they hold themselves back. Their superiors may emphasize their own openness, they may even beg and plead for people to bring out the real issues, but it doesn't happen. The result is that meaningful interchanges become all but impossible, even when they are clearly needed.

The explanation sometimes given for this reticence is fear—fear that people who speak out will be punished. This is undoubtedly partly true, but I have come to see it for many reasons as insufficient. Simple fear of retaliation is not predominant in most of these companies. Though there were a few cases where upper management was seen as punitive—JVC and Marks in particular—they stood out as exceptional. At Nadir, undergoing the first shock of layoffs, there was a strong generalized fear of the future, but not particularly a fear of punishment for speaking out. In most cases people believed, as one put it, that "the company is fair in the long run." If this were not so, it would be hard to understand the level of continued loyalty and positive effort that I observed.

As I probed for views about participation, moreover, it became apparent that the self-censorship is not uniform across all issues: some things can be argued about, some cannot be. I could distinguish three types of issues that elicited very different responses.

IMPLEMENTATION ISSUES

There is one category, and only one, that is truly open for debate: issues involving the technical implementation of policies within the middle managers' domain. Here they feel themselves on absolutely firm ground and are willing to speak out. Quite a few had stories about how top management had tried to "micro-manage" problems in ways that showed their failure to understand implementation issues. The middle then did one of two things: either they banded together to go around the dictates of top management (I have recounted tales of this in chapter 2) or they aggressively pursued their objections through the hierarchical layers. There were many examples of these proactive responses in *this* category of issues.

The willingness to take on fights in this arena is one proof that fear is not all that is shutting down discussion. In the area of implementation managers are willing to confront fear, because they feel they have a legitimate position. In other areas they back off:

> On product issues you can have an impact. Otherwise not: you channel every-thing through the boss.

"PERSONAL" ISSUES

As soon as one moves to issues that have to do with managers' own concerns about their jobs or working conditions, the possibility of dialogue is shut down. In the current period of downsizing, increased work, and high overall stress there are naturally many intense concerns in this area. But to raise matters like compensation, recognition, or promotion policies in public is out of bounds.

Of course there is no formal or explicit prohibition on these issues. On the contrary, all companies say that they have open doors and open ears and encourage managers to voice their concerns. Few of those I interviewed ever admitted that their subordinates might be reluctant to speak to them.

But just as universally, middle managers recognize a clear boundary beyond which one gets "labeled"; if one wanders into this domain it is "career-threatening":

> "If you bitch about parking spaces you will be labeled. We are still being cautious about the new plant manager and how much can be said."

> "As far as voice on these kinds of issues, it doesn't do you any good to be a malcontent. I have so little faith in our compensation system, but I feel, 'Why bother?'"

It is clear that the self-censorship evident at Lyco exists in the other companies as well. Indeed, I have often tried in group sessions to get managers to talk about their own needs: if their superiors are in the room, they will talk only about the needs of the company or of their subordinates, not about any needs of their own. Issues of discrimination, of family concerns, or many other areas of personal commitments were also part of this restricted area. It is as if there is a taboo on voicing personal, "quality-of-life" concerns.

It was for this reason that the proposal for an employee lounge became such an emotionally laden issue at Lyco: this was an attempt to break the invisible barrier. The lounge was quite simply a quality-of-life issue for many managers. Members of the Congress were extremely tense at the thought of even raising the subject. When they got a positive response, it was seen as revolutionary. Yet so deeply rooted is the taboo that even this critical event had no long-term effect.

How does one account for this barrier to communication, so well-marked even though leaders deny its existence? It is both hard to talk about and hard to cross because it defines one of the boundaries of loyalty. The ethic of loyalty defines good employees as those who subordinate their needs to those of the organization. Those who raise *personal* needs (in a public way) are marked as not truly loyal, people who think about themselves rather than the organization.

Many people used similar language: they told me that to raise such issues is "career-threatening." The career, of course, is the major validation of loyalty; the expectation is that if you stay loyal you will advance. This language indicates that to raise personal issues breaks the bond.

Loyalty is (to use Lewis Coser's term) "greedy," seeking to subjugate all other commitments.[4] There are degrees of greed—corporations are not sects or utopian communities, and they allow their employees (nowadays, though it has not always been thus!) to live in the outside world. Yet their policies have always indicated that commitment to the corporation should come first. Until very recently, for instance, it was a totally accepted part of corporate careers that managers would move frequently. The possibility of competing claims from spouses and families was not taken seriously. Outside activities were expected to support the corporation: involvement in the Rotary Club or the Boy Scouts was a way to build the company's reputation, while involvement in independent professional activities or (worse) controversial political activism were "career-threatening."[5]

Most middle managers seem to accept this definition of what is legitimate to talk about. They censor themselves, they boast of their willingness to do whatever is required of them, and they avoid like the plague being "labeled" as self-interested. So the strain of change remains largely hidden.

BUSINESS STRATEGY AND ORGANIZATION

The third domain is equally restricted: it involves issues that go outside the speaker's own job responsibilities. The rule of bureaucracy, accepted by most of the managers I spoke with, is that any given problem should be solved by the person responsible for it. That leaves people who see a problem with two choices: either they must accept responsibility, or they must give it over to someone else. In either case there is no way to talk about the problem. If they accept responsibility, an attempt to have a dialogue may seem like weakness or avoidance; if they give it over, talking about the problem may be seen as interference and questioning the ability of others. Thus, the only outlet is private complaining, which is rife in almost all companies.

This rule shuts off public criticism or questioning of other functions. Even more important, it shuts off discussion of the *strategic* domain of high-level business strategy and organization.

Here is where much intensely contradictory, seemingly irrational behavior takes place. Middle managers are frequently loud and vocal, to me and among themselves, about the stupidity of their leaders in failing to take the right technological or market initiatives, or in pursuing useless organizational "fads." But they don't express this kind of feeling upwards *at all*—and indeed reject any opportunity to do so.

If the tension around the "personal" need for an exercise room marked the first stage of the Lyco Congress, frustration at the strategic level marked the second. The meeting with Randolph was doomed by his middle managers' refusal to raise in public the strategic and organizational complaints they were so vocal about in private.

The disconnect here is huge and extremely important. Top management *typically* insists that its top priority is to enable people to understand the business. They have engaged over the past decade in increasingly intense efforts to build this understanding. The level of information sharing at almost all of these companies has grown enormously: middle managers regularly receive information about productivity and costs that used to be guarded with intense secrecy by corporate staff. At Lyco, as Randolph noted above, upper management has engaged in meetings every month or so to go through the entire state of competition and business conditions. Videotapes, newsletters, and computer e-mail amplify the drumbeat.

Despite all this effort, middle management *typically* does not understand business strategy. What they understand is product performance: they are extremely concerned with how well the object or service they turn out every day does its job. But a strategy cannot be built merely on good products: it has to be considered in relation to the investments required, the market for capital, the changing desires and composition of customers, the directions of the competition. Top managers build sophisticated pictures of how these factors come together in a coherent plan. But few of the middle managers could speak intelligently at this level.[6] So one finds expressions of frustration on all sides—in the case of Lyco, the Governors trying to push the Congress to take up business issues, without success; Randolph expressing his bafflement that despite all his explanations, people just don't seem to get the business reality; the middle managers feeling they don't understand what's going on, and angry at the top for making, to their view, nonsensical moves.

The situation is no better, by the way, in the companies that create formal and systematic middle-management forums than in those that rely on informal communications. Isony and Karet, as mentioned earlier, had established versions of Lyco's Congress—indeed, theirs were probably even more far-reaching. Yet they too made no dent at all on the essential failure of communication around business strategy.

There are many reasons for this extreme disconnect. Certainly the simple question of skill is important: it is hard to teach large numbers of managers who have spent their careers thinking in terms of product performance to understand competitive niches and the cost of capital. But there is more to it than that. There is in addition a fundamental resistance to really making the connection on the part of the middle managers themselves. Their refusal—the word is not too strong—to engage in real discussions about strategy indicates a *motivation not to understand the business.*

The reasons behind this peculiar attitude reveal much concerning the vision of middle managers. They see the organization in terms of legitimate domains and roles, and as surely as technical implementation is their domain, business policy is not. They do not believe that they have the knowledge to make valid judgments, but even more to the point, they don't believe they *should* be involved in this type of judgment. That is the job of the top leadership.

The consistent underlying logic across all the troubled organizations (but not, as we shall see, in the four more successful ones) is that top management should watch out for strategy and middle management should implement. This is fundamentally the same distinction made by Alfred Sloan during the creation of modern corporate bureaucracy. This simple principle organizes the world and keeps things in their places, so that the whole operates smoothly. When it breaks down, the result is anxiety and fear as well as anger. We have seen these reactions when the top pushes into the implementation arena, but the distress of the middle ranks is equally high when they are asked to push into the domain of top-level planning. That can only mean that *they* (the leaders) *don't know what they're doing*—a thought that was consistently seen as "scary":

> I say, tell us the plan for change and let us get prepared for it. But what's most scary is sometimes I think there isn't a plan.

Note that they say, "Tell us the plan"; they don't say, "Involve us in planning." Indeed, they reject the latter idea both in theory and in practice.

Higher management reinforces this self-limitation on the part of middle managers. They reinforce it unconsciously even when they are eagerly seeking in every conscious way to break down the barriers to shared understanding of business directions. They reinforce it because, in trying to preserve the sense of "family" loyalty, they feel compelled to shelter and protect their people from the harsh truth, to maintain a climate of caring.

Randolph, the division manager at the center of the events above, was a perfect example of this prevailing contradiction. On the one hand, he spoke insistently of the need to build business understanding, and he was proud of his efforts to achieve it. On the other hand, he admitted to me that he tended to pull his punches in telling people of the enormous changes that he saw in the not-too-distant future. He felt, he explained, that middle managers and workers were not ready to hear the extent of the problem—that they would be overwhelmed and unable to cope. This fear of speaking the truth to subordinates—for their own good!—was typical throughout these companies.[7] It is therefore not surprising that all the effort, all the meetings and communication, yields so little real understanding.

Like most responses to stress, this pattern is complex. There is no psychological restriction on complaining in private: middle managers are quite willing, in water-cooler conversations among themselves, to accuse their leaders of all sorts of stupidity in the most vehement tones. Yet something different happens when they are being serious and reflective: they typically speak of "giving [our leaders] the benefit of the doubt," and they assume that the top must know what it's doing, even if it isn't apparent from their vantage point. And the big divide comes when they are asked to go public, to openly voice their concerns or debate their leaders about policy issues. Then their reaction is near-panic. It is as if the idea that the top needs to hear from them undermines the norms that hold their world together.

This pattern reveals the bureaucratic ethic in crisis. From both above and below there are pressures to maintain traditional distinctions that defined the roles in a bureaucratic order. These barriers result in a systematic lack of honest discussion, no matter how earnestly everyone may speak of the importance of such discussion.

Today this lack of open discussion turns into a crisis because the structural foundations of the whole system are being assaulted. The informal, personal networks that allowed managers to implement effectively; the security that supported a sense of long-term trust; the strategic constancy that allowed business plans to work their way down through the organization in a methodical way—all these pillars of the old order are being dismantled. Yet there is no way to talk about the change.

In a sense, loyalty itself demands that certain types of issues not be discussed. For loyalty is attached to the company as it has existed, including the comforting clarity of roles divided between strategic planning and implementation. To question that distinction, to *really* attack the ability of the top to set directions, would bring down the whole structure—which is what makes it so "scary" and leads to such intensely contradictory behaviors. The only way out, psychologically, is to withdraw to a focus on what an individual can do, and for that individual to hope fervently (despite the evidence!) that the top does have its act together,

> They're telling us that we are going to be competitive with the industry. I have complete faith that eventually we will.

Conclusion

Speaking of the tensions around some of the Congress's initiatives, a Lyco manager summarized the situation nicely:

> There have to be boundaries on this kind of participation. . . . Even though I take risks, I know where the line is.

The "line" operates at two levels. It rules out public discussion of personal needs, whether of individuals or of groups—of any needs that conflict with the corporation; loyalty demands subordination to the organization. It also rules out real discussion of strategic matters, which are supposed to be the province of top management.

These two restrictions are ways of protecting the two sides of the loyalty bargain. Employees are supposed to do their jobs as well as possible, and companies, in return, are supposed to take care of them throughout their careers. To give weight to personal commitments means that one is not focused on doing the job. And to question strategic directions puts in doubt the ability of the company to provide security. Without an alternative, both sides are reluctant to threaten the bargain by loose talk.

The overall situation is, in a phrase, one of rapid change without the ability to discuss it. So of course it doesn't make sense. The experience of Lyco and similar companies indicates, moreover, that the barriers to making sense are so severe that they cannot be dismantled by even the most earnest and sustained efforts at better communication across the traditional levels.

The result should be (to return to Hirschman) a contradiction: here is loyalty without voice. That is, middle managers complain a great deal about the policies and actions of their superiors; they feel unable to express their complaints in any effective way; yet they continue to be loyal to the organization. What keeps this contradiction from breaking out is withdrawal: in their hopes that things will return to the comfort of the past, middle managers are willing to play down the problems they feel in the present.

But the contradiction, even if covered over, is nevertheless a problem: the maintenance of loyalty is achieved only at great cost. The most important issues are effectively ruled out of bounds for learning and discussion, thus frustrating efforts to "unfreeze" the organization.

6

The Loyalty Trap

Introduction

The ten troubled companies in my sample were part of a single pattern: though I have focused on Nadir, Glover, and Lyco, the other seven are quite similar. In the first shock of change, many mangers were bitter and angry—Nadir represents this period. But soon these intense emotions subsided, to be replaced by resignation and withdrawal. Thus in the majority of companies morale seemed, if not outstanding, at least tolerable. There was no sign of rebellion, and people continued to work hard.

I was surprised at the level of continuing loyalty on the part of the middle managers, despite the shattering of the promise of job security that was thought to be a key condition of that loyalty. Not only is there no rebellion, but there seems to be little conscious resistance of any kind, individual or collective, to the changes sweeping through the corporation. This is not to say that there isn't a great deal of grumbling, not to mention fear; these are very much present. But despite their complaints managers are working harder than ever before, and with generally good will, to help their companies succeed:

> I'm still loyal because that's what I knew starting out. I've always given 100 percent, and it's hard to stop. It started with my family and my whole way of working for GM.

The problem, however, is that this good will has not led to coordinated and effective organizations. Rather, it leads managers—after an initial phase of shock and rage—to dig into their own trenches, trying to do their narrow jobs as well as possible, but losing touch with the whole. Their reaction has all the earmarks of defensiveness: denial of reality, avoidance of difficult questions; they consistently underestimate their company's competitive problems and sidestep questions about future careers. Thus they remain inwardly focused and reactive, unable to grasp the full import of the changes they are facing and therefore unable to respond creatively to them.

Is the glass half-full or half-empty? My initial reaction, as I conducted my interviews, was on the positive side: that managers were far less angry and negative than I had expected, given the enormous change for the worse in their condition. For a time, then, I saw loyalty as a remarkably effective protection against the negative effects of downsizing.

It was only gradually that I became aware of the ways in which this attitude was tied into a complex that, while not consciously *resisting* change, effectively smothered it. Both the leadership of organizations and their middle-management foot soldiers sought to preserve the community of loyalty, but to do that they needed to shade and distort reality, softening the magnitude of the change they faced. The results:

- Confusion was generally high: people were quite aware that what they were hearing did not square with what they were experiencing.
- The gap between the top and the middle grew: the top leadership, being more in touch with the long-range transformation they were undergoing, were using a different logic to make decisions, while the middle frequently felt their leaders were using no logic at all!
- Middle managers, faced with a context that made no sense, increasingly narrowed their focus to the immediate and clear task, leaving aside the long-term as well as the overall good.

There is an unconscious but powerful conspiracy between individuals and organizations to preserve traditional relationships. For individuals, the community of loyalty provides a core sense of identity—one *is* an IBM or a GM or a Pitney-Bowes employee, in many cases as one's father was before; this defines who one relates to, how one lives, what one's expectations are for the future. If that is removed, identity is lost. For the company, the community of loyalty provides dedicated, flexible, cooperative employees willing to go the extra mile when necessary. Neither wants to abandon the bargain.

The majority of the organizations in my survey, in short, appeared to be trapped by loyalty. The very community that had been the basis of trust and flexibility within a bureaucratic structure now blocked the ability to grasp the magnitude of their current challenges.

The Fundamental Failings of Corporate Loyalty

The ten troubled organizations were trying many things, but none were working well. Not all had blatant performance problems, but all of them were failing to confront the fundamental challenges of the current economy.

The two basic forces now undermining the traditional corporate organization are continuous change and diversity. Historically, these forces have always been enemies of community, making it more difficult to work together. Traditional corporations, like traditional societies, are built on the permanence of an order or system. People cooperate in part because they know where they fit, in part because they know that their relationships are lasting, and that violations of the order will come back to haunt them.

The "fit" is not only an objective fact but also has a moral dimension. A stable community determines that certain behaviors are appropriate for each "place" in the system. Corporations, as we saw in chapter 5, have strict codes—for instance, that lower-level people are not supposed to challenge those in the higher levels on strategic issues, or that functional expertise cannot be questioned by those who perform other functions. Attempts to change these codes cause unease bordering on panic, especially among those in the lower levels.

Corporations have held out against change and diversity through sheer size and organizational power, building artificially stable and homogeneous communities of loyalty. That option has now vanished. When rapid change breaks into the cloistered ranks of management, the codes of order break down. Knowledge cannot be sorted rapidly enough to the right place in the system: often lower-level people know more than their bosses about technology or customers, and often functions must work together on the fly to solve complex problems. Stable relations and obligations that held things together in the past no longer function:

> When loyalty starts to go, when the young people start leaving and older people are moved all the time, it makes it hard to get things done. How many times I've cut a deal and they say, "Yeah, but you might not be here when the time comes to pay it back."

Many of the loyalists expressed a fear that if everything was opened up for discussion, the result would be chaos. In this view, the ability to get things done depends on the fact that large areas are *not* open to discussion: if lower-level managers can openly debate strategy with their superiors, where will it end? How will decisions get made? This fear, as we saw, led managers at Lyco to refuse to voice openly doubts that they held privately.

The problem becomes even more acute when a company tries to adopt a strategy of "continuous improvement." At this point the difficulty is not limited to environmental crises; even in stable markets there is pressure for constant change. There would seem to be little motive for cooperation and trust when you don't know who you will be working with tomorrow.

Now add in diversity, defined as a mix of people who are not only different— so different that it is hard to know how far to trust them—but who also insist on *expressing* their differences publicly rather than assimilating quietly; that is, women, minorities, gays, the disabled, and others who increasingly demand that their commitments to their social groups be openly recognized and accepted. So a good loyalist will never be able to tell whether such people will answer the call of corporate need when it competes with their private concerns.

It is no wonder, given these forces undermining the traditional bases for trust, that people retreat into a desire for autonomy, wanting to be left alone or to be told clearly what to do, avoiding the need for spontaneous working together.

There were many signs in the troubled companies of a fundamental inability to cope. Even when they were holding their own in the short run, in many ways they were drawing down their social temporary reserves, which cannot be sustained forever.

One immediate problem is that troubled companies are keeping their heads above water simply through harder work: there is a speedup going on within management. With few exceptions, respondents in the troubled organizations (though not, for the most part, in the dynamic ones) said that they were working harder than they used to:

> "They cut 25 percent of the organization without analyzing the value added; they just cut across the board. So we end up with a same workload with a fewer number of people."

> "There's a phenomenally high level of stress in this place, and management doesn't understand that. The general manager and his staff don't see it. People are hurting, yet they're so dedicated to this place that they'd never admit it."

Further, the emphasis on autonomy often results in a sense of isolation and loneliness, even among those who support the direction of change.

> I'm self-driven on the job. That's my motivation. I just want to get the project done well, but it's lonely and frustrating. I'm the only one who really cares about my programs. . . . It's a terrific challenge, but it's also scary and there's a lot of pressure.

There is no question that stress levels are high in the troubled organizations. As I have indicated, most feel that, at least in part, this stress is positive, either because it is necessary to the firm's success or because it is part of the new autonomy. Still, it is a real question how long such stress can be sustained without more grouping and mutual support. If there is no public community, then private communities of personal relationships are likely to undercut the cleanness of the bureaucratic structure.

As a further indication of the inability to grasp the need for change, there is evidence that those forces that had produced a "fattening" of the bureaucracy in the first place were continuing to operate, even during the period of slimming.

For example, I found frequent instances where the formal reduction of layers was, on closer investigation, more illusory than real: old positions were popping up again with new titles. In at least two instances, managers told me explicitly that they needed to recreate the old layers to give subordinates something to aim for, to reduce the growing opportunity gap as the hierarchy was cut back. In other words, without wider changes in career systems, there is enormous pressure to snap back to the old patterns.

Finally, there is a more profound problem: it is doubtful, even if career systems could somehow be brought into line, that the rationalist mode of autonomy could support an effective organization. If earlier analysis of the function of managerial politics is correct, the focus on autonomy will produce a more rigid organization that will not be able to adapt smoothly to environmental change. When an organization is first restructured (assuming it is done well) it will run for a time because the new structure is good for the situation. But as that situation changes, the structure must change to meet it. If the middle managers are thinking of themselves as individuals fulfilling tasks, they will not restructure their own relations—they will wait for someone to tell them how to adjust, to replan. And the result will be a jerky series of frequent restructurings instead of a more continuous process of spontaneous adjustment mediated by middle management relations.

That is indeed what appears to be happening in many of the organizations in which the old communities have been disrupted without adequate replacement: this dynamic is the primary source of the tension between middle and top that has been noted at the start. Nadir, as described earlier, went from centralization to decentralization and back again; Lyco, similar in mood, had a series of rapid-fire major reorganizations; and there were similar issues in JVC, Hardin, Glover, Fixx, and Emon. In all these cases the middle managers felt that change was proceeding in "jerks" as it were, through edicts from on high that did not make sense in their terms:

> The bias for action is too much. That's what Peters and Waterman say we should be doing, but the top is just doing action for the sake of action. These new people are moving too fast, they just want to change everything. The bias for action philosophy creates yes men.

The existing organization was, in short, incapable of keeping up with the pace of outside pressures.

The Dynamics of Organizational Loyalty

These twin developments—continuous change or improvement, and increasing diversity—seem to be inescapable; they are also incompatible with an ethic of loyalty. Loyalty fosters stability and subordination, when what is needed now is change and creativity.

The question is how this dynamic works, how the attempt to hold on to loyalty results in an inability to adapt to change. It is not a matter of rationality: resistance is not conscious, and most managers believe they are acting every day in the best interests of their company.

First, let me reemphasize that managers do not act as purely rational, obedient "agents": their attitude is not "Tell me what needs to be done and I will do it, because it is in my interests to do so." On the contrary, they constantly go outside the bounds of what they are asked in an effort to do right by the organization. Often this is for the better, as they apply their intelligence to the good of the company; indeed, that is what loyalty is all about, and why companies seek to foster it. Sometimes it is for the worse, as they fail to understand what is really needed. In short, they are constantly structuring their actions based on what they think the good is. They seek to help the company because they are attached to it, and their definition of what it is they are attached to—what is good about the company—shapes what they do.[1]

The core of this notion of loyalty (recalling themes from chapter 2) is attachment *to an organization*. It is distinguished from personal loyalty on one hand and commitment to a purpose on the other. The connection is to an organization as an entity—not what it does, but what it is. This emotion leads to many distortions in responding to change. Let us try to trace, in a kind of ideal description, the boundaries set by the loyalist ethic.

THE PROTECTIVE "FAMILY"

In all of the cases marked by traditional loyalty the organization is widely defined in terms of a "family." This term came up most frequently, in many different organizations, in contrast to the new or emergent system. The contrast was rarely favorable to the new.

> I am an extreme loyalist, but because of the pain that I have been put through for twelve years now, I am heading toward free agency. You begin to realize this isn't a family, this is a business.

"Business" in this context means heartless, unfeeling, and also untrustworthy: the stories people told had to do with promises broken, values destroyed.

The key aspect of the family is caring—both being cared for and caring for others. On the receiving end:

> I am very loyal because I feel as though the company has provided everything I needed.

On the giving end:

"It's a family type of thing, where you look at the people that look up to you for the leadership and the guidance, and that's probably all part of what turns us on as managers."

"Managers are fighting tooth and nail to protect their people, and this encourages real loyalty."

It is, in short, a traditional "paternalistic" family, where the stronger protect and care for the weaker.

An important aspect of middle managers' roles in such a system is to be parents to those below. They speak frequently not only of "fighting for their people," but also developing them, nurturing them, mentoring them. They look to their own superiors for the same. This nurturing relation is almost always narrowly defined by the hierarchy: if your boss doesn't care for you, no one will.

The contrast between the family ethic and the business ethic was frequent. For loyalists, *business* is almost a dirty word: it refers to the unfeeling abandonment of those who have given their lives to the company. This is a key reason why loyalty produces resistance to the business focus so widely sought by top management.

HIERARCHY

This picture of a protective family provides an emotional support for hierarchy. Because the company is strong and powerful, because it dominates the individual, it can be counted on to provide safety and a stable identity; loyalists need to believe in the power of their superiors. Dependence and protection, in other words, make the hierarchy worth defending.

One common theme, for example, is individuals' gratitude for the benefits they have received from the company. Typically managers will say that they are nothing special, but they were extremely fortunate to be taken in by their organization and made part of the "family."

I traced in the last chapter the way in which the need to believe in the power and wisdom of higher levels shuts off communication across levels. Lyco is a model of consistent distortion in which people turn into "children" in the presence of superiors. When the boss is absent they may complain bitterly about all kinds of issues, from corporate strategy to personal treatment; when she is present they are abashed and submissive.

The dependence is not a personalistic, feudal one. In large part, people are emotionally connected to the company itself rather than to any individual. That is why, if they believe that their superiors have told them to do something stupid, they feel it is right to go around them. They have a job to do within the total system, and within that domain they feel comfortable and justified in speaking their minds. They do whatever their job demands, not whatever they are told. But the job is thought of as a piece in a bureaucratic hierarchy, and the barriers marking it off are difficult to penetrate. One does not try challenge superiors on their responsibilities for strategy and direction, any more than they (legitimately) challenge subordinates on the details of implementation. You have to believe that those up the line know what they are doing on strategic issues, or the whole structure of dependence and protection is threatened.

INWARDNESS

The intense "family" orientation also leads, psychologically, to the inward focus that we have noted, which seems so hard to eradicate, and which creates a resistance to outside criticism and ideas.

How severe this is varies. Today, with all the emphasis on "customer-driven" management, it is rare for anyone explicitly to reject anything that customers say about them: they are eager to please. Yet managers remain deeply defensive about outside suggestions for change. They typically believe, for example, that they *are* responding to customers, even when evidence to the contrary is overwhelming. GM managers I spoke to uniformly cite the success of their quality efforts; IBM managers I spoke to informally in the late 1980s consistently praised the strength of the company's customer orientation—this while, in both companies, customers were deserting in droves.

The defensiveness shows itself in a curious pattern that any consultant will recognize: there seems to be no room at all between "We can't do that" and "We're already doing that." Any suggestion from an outsider will be tossed into one or the other of these rubbish heaps. Though they are opposites on the surface, these two responses come to exactly the same thing in the end: both imply that the outsider doesn't really understand (and therefore has no standing to speak); and both negate the need to change.

EXCLUSIVENESS

Exclusiveness is closely connected to inwardness, but it is worth stressing. These companies had great difficulty dealing with outsiders. In Nadir managers were particularly eloquent on this point: they had built up an entire collective image, restated independently by several people, of the invading "professionals" who were destroying the old harmony and loyalty. JVC was another company where the theme of "blame the outsiders" was particularly strong—although the trauma lay somewhat further in the past, and the dominant reaction was therefore more one of withdrawal and resignation than of anger.

These two are notable because the presence of outsiders was actually an issue. In the other companies, aside from some specialty areas like marketing that were very well insulated from the main body of the operations, there were almost no people who had come to the company at other than an entry level. But even in these cases there were often emblematic stories of a few exceptional cases that expressed the resistance. In GM they centered on Elmer Johnson, a lawyer who had been brought in by Roger Smith and who became a lightning rod for all the complaints about top management; he left the company under pressure. The same happened at AT&T, some years earlier, to a leader brought into the top levels from IBM to transform the company; his aggressive innovations were rejected like a transplanted organ.

Outsiders, according to these stories, did not understand and did not value the strengths of the company. This is, of course, by definition true: both knowledge and values in a community of loyalty are located within the company. The fact that outsiders may bring a different perspective with value of its own is unacceptable when the loyalty is to the company as an entity, and not to something independent of it.

The exclusiveness has another dimension: while it keeps outsiders out, it also keeps insiders in. The managers I interviewed had extraordinarily few strong attachments to communities beyond the corporation. They spoke about their families, of course—and that was generally it.

This was, in fact, one of my original points of interest in entering this research project: I asked people what kinds of groups they belonged to outside their work lives, what causes they were committed to, what communities they valued. After a while I dropped this line of questioning because I got so little back. There were those, to be sure, who worked for their churches or for the United Way; but the level of passion around these causes was far less than that around the company. There were not very many, for that matter, who were active even at that level: the high mobility that many companies require of their managers made it impossible to develop deep ties to outside groups. Most important, there was almost never a sense that outside activities might legitimately compete with the demands of the corporation.

Very few, even among engineers, had significant professional ties to outside work organizations or associations. The role that one might imagine such groupings could play in helping people deal with downsizing was not a reality. Not a single loyalist, during discussions on how to deal with restructuring, brought up professional associations spontaneously; and only two or three responded when I probed specifically.[2] For most, the gulf between the supportive world inside the corporation and the cold world outside was untempered by intermediate attachments.

MORAL RIGHTEOUSNESS

A tone of moral righteousness often accompanies exchange with the outside.
A vignette: recently I heard a rather high-level manager from Lyco's parent, a
man with extremely progressive and participative conceptions of his role,
become enraged when a union leader accused his company of racism. "I sort of
feel," he said, "that if you accuse the company it's like you were attacking my
family." His reaction effectively shut off discussion.

The emotional charge of this response is related to the exclusiveness of the
community. Because there are few outside anchors, the company *must* be seen
as good—otherwise individuals would see themselves as having their entire
emotional attachment to something bad. Who could admit that, even to themselves? The company must be valued as an entity.

This does not mean that *no* criticism is tolerated—these are not cults. But
criticism must essentially be framed in terms of improvement within an overall
framework of good. Thus at GM, to take one example, managers regularly
accept that they need to become more focused on quality—but they admit that
only in the context of stressing that they are already moving rapidly in the right
direction. They believe in quality and believe the company believes in it. When I
challenged them on the point, suggesting that perhaps their competitors were
more committed than they, they either denied it heatedly (despite their lack of
evidence on the point) or returned to their inward focus, insisting that they
were doing a great deal better than they used to.

Given the long-term nature of the employment relationship, loyalists are also
willing to take the long view—to admit that the company is in trouble at the
moment, may even be doing bad things—but with the clear proviso that it will
work out later.

What is not acceptable is challenging the basic fairness and value of the company. To return to my vignette: calling the company racist implied to that manager that the company was violating his deep beliefs. This would be intolerable,
because the exclusiveness of loyalty requires that the company embody high
values. Therefore the subject was undiscussible.[3]

Warding Off Change

Managerial layoffs and reorganizations undermine this pattern of corporate loyalty characterized by a "family" image, hierarchy, inwardness, exclusiveness,
and moral righteousness. Loyalty under stress turns into defensiveness: it leads
a range of behaviors designed to keep change at bay, even at the price of ignor-

ing reality. Common counterproductive responses include regression to a narrow focus on the immediate task; denial of competetitive pressures; and enthusiasm for a limited version of change that involves no fundamental reordering.

The word *defensiveness* is a dangerous one, because what the observer calls defensiveness the protagonist is likely to call truth. It needs further explanation.

One can recognize defensiveness reasonably clearly when it causes people to miss major aspects of what is going on around them. When a company is in big trouble (as were Glover, Karet, Lyco, and Nadir), yet managers persist in saying that everything is all right, that is a sign of defensiveness. When people say they can and will voice problems with their superiors, but then flee the opportunity (as happened at Lyco) that is defensiveness. When people try to deal with big problems by tinkering around the edges, or by doing what they are already doing harder, that is defensiveness.

Several patterns were visible frequently enough that they can be called typical.

REGRESSION

Many of the people I spoke to had clearly put their heads down. Their loyalty to the company, while continuing strong, had become abstracted—not a genuine enthusiasm about what the company was now, but a conviction based on past experience that someday it would work out. In the meantime some held themselves together by pulling back. The pulling back I most often heard about, which I have stressed in describing Glover, was a focus on one's own job. In doing this employees came closer to the image of the "true bureaucrat": just doing the job, often enthusiastic about it and dedicated to it, but losing the connection to the overall goals of the organization.

A different form of pulling back, which I heard about in a smaller but still significant number of cases, was to focus at least temporarily on a narrower loyalty to the immediate group. I never heard about this in relation to a superior: *none* of these managers said their primary attachment was to a boss or mentor.[4] Instead, what I did hear at times was a dominant connection to a small peer group or to subordinates. This was sometimes explicitly a reaction to the disconnection from upper management: "Within our group of six, . . . we're dependent on each other. Survival has required successfully working together. We all know we're not going to get any help from the outside, so we don't let each other down, we help each other out on vacations, pick up each other's due dates."

The reason this reaction of "small-group inwardness" was not more common, I suspect, is that the personal networks had in almost all cases been greatly torn up by the restructuring process: immediate bosses had been moved out, peer groups had become very unstable. Thus there was relatively little to hang on to between the individual job boundaries and the organization as a whole.

Both forms of pulling back—focusing on the job and attaching to a small group—had the same basic effect: they severed the connection between the individual's efforts and the welfare of the organization as a whole. Not that there isn't such a tension in all organizations—there are "empires" within every company, and conflict between representatives of different functions is almost a given. But in "healthy" cases they are arguing about whose ideas are better for the company's success, while in these distressed cases they had given up even trying to understand what was going on at the company level. To pick an illustration from a company that I *have not* focused on so far.

There is a feeling of what are they going to do next because every year they are changing the policy. (Karet)

In almost every organization these were complaints that "politics," though always a problem, had grown much worse. The regression to narrower versions of loyalty almost by definition creates fragmented "politics," because there is less united focus.

DENIAL

There was a persistent tendency to downplay the magnitude of changes and problems, and to assume that things would "settle down" after a period of trauma. In some instances, such as at Glover, the business problems were so severe that one could say without question that this attitude reflected defensiveness and not reality. It seemed, there and in Lyco most clearly, that the managers were separated from the world by cotton wool that softened the external blows. I can add that, in general, managers at GM, which was suffering at that time from horrendous business results, were startlingly sanguine about it all and convinced that they were on the road to a turnaround.[5]

In at least one major area the denial came through unmistakeably in internal inconsistency. I always asked about careers—whether people expected to stay with the company for the rest of their careers, whether career patterns were changing. What I found in the majority of cases, especially in those over 40, was a bland expectation that they would continue with the company; I found very little thought about the long-term consequences of the current restructuring. This was an instance where active interviewing helped, because when I probed further many people agreed that there was probably a serious issue present that they hadn't thought much about: opportunities were closing down, security was declining. They explained their lack of attention by saying that they would be able to hold on, since they had passed through the fire so far.

The denial was not total. Many had their resumes out with headhunters;

most agreed that they were thinking more now than in the past about the possibility of leaving the company. Yet almost all insisted they expected to finish their careers at their current firm, and they expected things to return to normal in the long run.

The fact that a fundamental shift had taken place in the implicit contract between employer and employees seems both inescapable and of paramount importance to the lives of these managers. It could be escaped only by not thinking about it—and for the most part these managers didn't.

INCREMENTAL IMPROVEMENT—"CLEANING UP THE BUREAUCRACY"

These first two responses—regression and denial—are ways of avoiding dealing with change. The third is a way of embracing it while keeping it limited. The most pervasive positive reaction to change was to focus on incremental improvement—tightening up the systems, clarifying the rules. I class this as another defensive move because it aims to preserve the past rather than to accept fundamental change.[6]

What most people seemed to be looking for in the ten troubled organizations I studied was a sharpening of the basic principles of bureaucracy: a clarification of job descriptions and procedures, stronger leadership from the center. I have already discussed at some length in chapter 4 the twin desires for autonomy and centralization.

> What we are trying to get is where everybody has complete responsibility within his own role. I have complete responsibility for my piece.

The desire for autonomy is a prime characteristic of bureaucracy: the core of the bureaucratic ethic is "Let me do my job (well)." It is generally linked to a desire to get the systems clear:

> We are getting back to the basics. People don't know the costs now, where the money is spent. We used to be excellent at that, that was our reputation. We knew exactly where every dollar went. Then we lost it. The organization just got too big and too sloppy, but we are starting to do it again. The competitors have forced us to evaluate costs, to do good analysis and paperwork.

So strong was this diagnosis that it led most people to agree that it was a good thing to cut back on middle managers. They frequently agreed that there was a certain amount of fat in their ranks which needed to be trimmed. I always asked, "Do you think middle management will disappear?" The most common answer by far was along the lines of this response from a Nadir manager:

I see a smaller, leaner company in the future. I could see us operating with one-third less people in five years and much more efficiently.

Or another from JVC:

Could middle management disappear? It might get to a span of seven to eight people instead of five to six, but you couldn't replace middle management. You couldn't replace their functions.

The prevailing view was that, to a greater or lesser degree, a certain amount of trimming *would* be valuable. Many went on at length about the unnecessary levels that had grown up, and the time they themselves wasted in paperwork and needless control. They were not looking to protect themselves, or to preserve the company *as it is*. They want to make it better, but "better" in this case means the stronger, clearer implementation of the fundamental values of the past.

From the point of view of dealing with change, this reasoning exemplifies profound ambiguity. On one hand, they believe enough in their company to support measures that might hurt them personally. That's the strength of loyalty. On the other hand, the measures they support involve a return to first principles—preserving the basic "functions" of the existing system. At a time when evidence is piling up every day of a need for more profound transformation, that demonstrates the shortcomings of loyalty.

Limits to Change

All of this adds up to limitations on the range of acceptable change. It is notable that highly loyalist companies are very flexible *within certain boundaries,* then seem to crack beyond them. GM, for example, was a model of responsiveness for decades, coming up with new car models with great dispatch, learning to customize, innovative in its relations to its unions. But the shift to smaller, high-quality cars seemed to be completely unmanageable. Similarly, at IBM the first CEO not from the founding Watson family made very public his frustration at his inability to get the system to make fundamental changes.

What defines those limits?

LOYALTY AND ORGANIZATIONAL IDENTITY

Each of the troubled organizations seemed to have a strong core identity, thought of as eternal and rooted in company history. They had, in other words, what is normally referred to as "strong cultures." Many writers advocate such strong cultures because they provide a framework for trust and working together; what they do not note is that culture can also become a conservative force.

There are several ways of building strong group identity. Perhaps the simplest is to focus on a person—a revered founder. IBM, by most accounts, has been such a company: the figures of Thomas Watson and his descendants still loom large, and stories about what they would do shape managerial behavior to this day.[7] It is probably fair to speculate, at second hand, that these ghosts have presented a powerful obstacle to the last two CEOs of the company, the first nonmembers of the Watson family; both have had great difficulty changing the culture.

Among the companies I studied, the memories were more complex. AT&T, for instance, has a rich folklore based on its history as a regulated company. The identity that motivates many employees is left over from that time, now more than a decade gone: an identity as a provider of universal service. This image frequently conflicts with attempts to create a more "businesslike" culture.

GM is typical of another large group in which the traditional products are the source of identity; this means that efforts to change the products in any fundamental way are very threatening. Many managers grew up not loving GM vehicles, but loving Chevys or Oldsmobiles, and have a strong image of the kind of vehicles these are. The attachment can be highly emotional:

> We think we can build specifications for a vehicle and then build that vehicle. That's wrong. A vehicle has a character; it has genes. There has to be a core of people that retain the genes of the vehicle. I want a sense that it's my car like a wife—it's your family, it's part of you. You can't have two wives, you can't have two cars.
>
> We have lost a lot of loyalty because people lost their identity—that is, their identity with the car, Chevy or Pontiac or whatever.

Now, if your identity is tied up with a car, you are not going to take kindly to attempts to treat that car as a "business" matter. The tie to the product defines who you are. Even further, it defines whom you can trust; to put it into question is a sign of disloyalty and arouses deep resentment from loyalists.

> The society has changed. We've got people on our staff who've probably been here five years and buy a competitor product. And that just drives the living shit out of me—I mean, that just makes me mad. Needless to say, I always think of those things come promotional times: I might question your judgment.

These fierce attachments make product modifications difficult. One could see it clearly at Glover, and also at GM when upper management restructured the old car divisions to achieve market efficiencies; the internal complaining was intense. This type of loyalty is an obstacle to market adaptability, and seems to have been an important factor in the failure of many of the troubled companies to keep up with market shifts after the mid-1970s.

RESISTANCE TO TEAM-BASED ORGANIZATION

Loyalty facilitates one kind of teamwork: the informal relations of people trading favors. The maintenance of informal networks is aided by stability and the sense of shared commitment to the organization. But loyalty also, by promoting dependence on the hierarchical "family," makes it harder to work together formally in flexible teams without a clear leader.

Thus loyalist managers were highly skeptical of the "team" systems that have become widely popular in the past decade. The use of task forces, cross-functional groups, "SWAT teams," "skunk works"—all forms of linkage that cut across levels and organizational structures—has grown at the same time as the downsizing of middle management. These are in part seen as ways to use resources most effectively, and in part as ways to achieve more flexible response to demands and problems.

Virtually all companies I studied used the rhetoric of team-based transformation and "empowerment."[8] To the middle managers in the troubled organizations, this language seemed like a prescription for chaos. The overwhelming sense, with few qualifications, was that these innovations undermine effectiveness by making it harder to reach decisions. By bringing together people who do not have a clear hierarchical relation to each other, they raise the problem of consensus, here voiced by a Glover employee:

> In my previous job . . . there was nobody else that I had to get consensus with to get a decision. In my current job I am confused about which decisions are mine. Does the marketing division have the right to define product specifications? No one is ultimately accountable. I would like more autonomy, not more consensus.

For the bulk of the middle management in these companies, "empowerment" is fine as long as it means allowing each person a clear domain of responsibility; they are quite happy to have their superiors stop "micro-managing" them, and they generally believe they should allow their subordinates the same autonomy. Where they grow deeply uncomfortable is when empowerment means the blurring of individual responsibilities and roles, or the loss of clarity in the decision-making process. They want to know what they will be held accountable for, and where to go to resolve a dispute.

Flexible teamwork presents another large problem for the loyalist world view: it is no longer clear who will take care of you. The traditional system works because your hierarchical bosses represent the corporation's supportive side. They are the ones who listen to personal problems who may (if they are "good" bosses) help their subordinates manage the demands of the corporation, who advise about careers, and who protect "their people." Effective leaders build warm "teams" out of those who report to them, and loyalist managers view their immediate superior as the key to advancement and success. But when people are part of *many* teams, then they have no consistent relationship with higher levels. Having many bosses means having no protector: every relation is focused on a particular task, and no one takes care of the person.

These reasons for resisting flexible teams are not necessarily valid: as we shall see, there were a few organizations where consensus decision making was embraced with enthusiasm, and apparently worked pretty well. But these were organizations *not* marked by loyalty and the deference to hierarchy that is linked to it.

A Brief Case Study of Managerial Loyalty

Now I would like to let one person speak for himself, with little editing. Until now I have been mixing many people together to build a composite picture; here is an example of how it fits together in one individual, and how it came out in my interviews.[9]

Sam Lax is a third-level manager—that is, two levels above the supervisor— at Lyco. I have picked him because he articulates many of the themes I have sketched:

- Continued strong loyalty, now under siege and focused on a smaller scale— together with a pained longing for the wider community of the past;
- An implicit contract trading a secure career in the company for hard work.
- A continued sense of dependence on the company.
- A mixed desire for *clear direction* from the top, laying out a detailed path of change, combined with a desire that things not change too much;
- Great emotional difficulty in dealing with open-ended or continuous change;
- Bewilderment about what he is supposed to do, and what his leaders are aiming for;
- Support for traditional bureaucracy, cleaned up to get rid of unnecessary "politics" and empire-building;
- Skepticism and difficulties in dealing with team-based management systems;
- Insistence on the parental role of middle managers toward their subordinates: coaching, nurturing, protecting, settling squabbles, and in general "championing your people";
- A focus on his own particular position, with little effort to engage broader strategic issues such as market demands;
- Resistance to a "business focus" as breaking the mutual caring and support of the old culture.

Lyco, recall, was actively experimenting with participative systems and autonomous teams, eliminating levels of supervision. Lax was particularly concerned about one group of six managers, one level below him, who had been operating for over a year with essentially no direct supervision. This is what he is talking about when he refers to "the group of six."

We started with a discussion of recent moves to take out layers of management. His comments show a lack of understanding of top management's intentions in the restructuring moves; he continues to do the same things as before with fewer resources:

> When you abruptly take out a level of management, you arbitrarily impose what is going to amount to a strain—a major strain.
> *How does that strain manifest itself?*
> I feel that one of the major problems with doing something too abruptly is that I don't know what I'm *not* supposed to do anymore. Therefore, I continue to try to do everything. And that snowballs into a sense of not doing anything as well as I'd like to or as I think I'm capable of doing. Also that gets expanded into a personal image, if you will: people ask me to do things and look towards me to meet commitments, and then those commitments don't get met, and it snowballs into a general bad feeling.

Then he moves spontaneously into a discussion of why team-based systems make him uncomfortable. First, they break the hierarchical logic of who is supposed to do what:

> That leads us into a discussion about the group of six here. I've worked for Lyco for eighteen years and that's been my career; I've not worked in other organizations. And so I have grown up through the standard, normal organizational structure. And this self-managing concept is something that's very new to me as a manager. How it manifests itself for me personally as a manager is that that abrupt dislocation, if you will, [resulting from the elimination of a layer,] doesn't provide organizations or managers at either side of that interface time to decide what they are not going to do.

Second, team-based organization undermines the ability of managers to "champion their people": to coach, nurture, protect, and resolve fights:

> The concerns I have with the self-managing group as a model, is that, if you don't grow up in a self-managing mode, there's historic baggage. There are what I believe to be natural points of conflict. Natural points of conflict occur, in my view, anytime you have an organization [within which] you have two different functions or groups. There's always the dilemma of who has more value. And as a manager of those groups, you need to champion your people; and to champion your people, you have to figure out ways that they are as valuable as

the competing group. And that causes conflict—particularly when there's threats of downsizing.

So, when those conflicts that I believe are natural in an organization arise, if it's 100 percent self-managing, there is no person to step in and arbitrate it, listen to both sides, say, "Okay fine, I've heard both sides, this is what I think you should do." The counseling that (excuse the gender) "You're big boys; you can handle it yourself" is absurd. If they were big boys and could handle it themselves, the problem wouldn't exist.

Note in that last paragraph the paternalistic imagery behind the leader's role.

[The pyramid] is what I happen to be most comfortable with because that's the way I grew up. Professionally, I grew up in that environment.

Just as you need the coach/manager to champion someone in their movement, in their mobility, you also need someone to act as an observer who says, "Sam, you need to take a course in finance, a course in business case studies." And that's where I think just saying we're going to have a self-managing group here of six people isn't enough. Yes, the basic functions will get done, and will probably get done from the customer's standpoint very well. Will it get done as efficiently as possible?—I don't know.

I then raised the issue of shifting toward a business or market focus. He resisted: first by saying that that was not his domain; then, on being pressed, by questioning the value of a business focus. Though he seemed to accept it as an inevitable fact of modern life, he didn't like it because it undercut the old community.

Let me just bring in another theme. I think what was in people's minds is that this should become a more marketing-driven organization rather than a technology-driven one.

I can't comment on that. As much as I can share with you my thoughts about the self-managing team, my role has been more one of administration with the type of organization. In all candor, in the two and one-half years that I've been here, if I've been downstairs [outside my immediate group] once a month, it's a lot.

My role is to make the technical manager's life easier. And we make it easier by taking all the classic corporate instructions and guidelines that come in 4-H binders and reducing them to a paragraph. We keep the need for them to know all the intricate details of a bureaucracy away from their day-to-day lives so they can do the technical work. I do not, in my current capacity, get involved with the projects in a product realization way [such as] the marketing people would.

One way of thinking about the change that's going on, that I think is certainly widespread in the business culture, is the shift from technical focus to a business focus, which would mean presumably that these people would have to change.

I think that it's recognized by most people.... When you say, "We have to get more business focused," one of the concerns I have with this company and the United States in general is that we tend to equate business with our quarterly reports. And we have to be conscious of our responsibilities to shareholders for increasing shareowner wealth, which is the classical reason we have for businesses and our people realize that. But that doesn't take away our responsibility for sharing the wealth, the longevity of the corporation and so on. We have to plan for the future.

I think in the past five years people have been much more sensitive to the importance of the business in terms of how it affects them as individuals. I think what we all struggle with is how much we can influence the business—because we know the business can influence *us*. It can either keep us employed or downsize and get rid of us. But other than taking whatever direction we're getting from our immediate supervision and trying to do that as best we can, we still question how much we can influence the business.

Now we took up the leadership role of higher management. He expressed again his concern about too much participation, and added his wish that if there had to be change, that it could be laid out clearly and dealt with quickly.

Let's just do a little science fiction for a moment. How would you imagine better influencing the business if you could talk to the CEO and say we need . . .

If I could talk to the CEO, I would say, "I don't believe in 100 percent participative management. You're not going to have votes on certain things. There's going to be one [basic] policy for the corporation. Now each of you may tweak that policy any way you want locally but there's, you know, some limits. So you are 'empowered' to manage an operation locally, but you are going to get some direction from above." And in everything I see happening now with the redefinition of the organization, I don't know that I see that occurring.

As far as how much I can influence the business, I guess where I struggle with that is that—it may be a personal struggle with adapting to change, and this may contradict what I said earlier—but it's easier if someone says, "We're going to change, and it's going to be an abrupt change, and here's going to be the new state. We're going to go from state A to state B, and this is what state B is." I can operate in that mode. If you say, "We're going to go from state A to some future state, we'll figure out what the future state is when we get there"—I have a real difficult time operating in that mode.

Somewhat contradictorily, he then added the classic concern that the top level is being too directive, pushing into the domain of middle managers in the effort to change:

One of the dilemmas that I see at work is that we have people who are involved in business strategy and that, if you pardon the expression, there are the poor schleps around that have to worry about how we implement that strategy. And there seems to be a disconnect at times. The strategist says, "I'll only be able to do this, this, and this." And the person who's got to implement it says, "Well, wait a minute. I've been doing this function for twenty years, and I'm not going to tell you you can't do that, but did you consider these points?" "No, no, I've looked at the problem and I've strategized, and I have a vision of where we should be and that's it."

At some point in time managers, including myself or my boss, should be able to say, "Look, I need this done." We don't have the time to participate in a consensus type of environment to figure out is it the right thing to do or not. We create inefficiencies for ourselves by not, as individuals, accepting the fact that in an organization somebody is going to come down and say, "I need it." Now I could spend three weeks telling you exactly why I need it, laying out all the details and talking about it with you. Or you can accept that at my level, I need it, and I need it by this point in time. If you don't give it to me by Friday and we spend three weeks talking about it, we missed an opportunity.

I probed for his view of bureaucracy. He expressed his support for good, centralized bureaucratic systems, and a concern for what decentralization will do to the sense of unity and caring:

You used an interesting phrase earlier about bureaucracy driven by political turf-building, as opposed to—what? I mean, is there a good form of bureaucracy?

Oh, yes. Many times, myself included, people will talk about the horrible bureaucracy. But I view bureaucracy as part of an infrastructure that helps an organization move ahead. When you have a bureaucracy as big as Lyco, and something is wrong within it, you try to fix that dimension of the bureaucracy. I equate it to the body, if there's something wrong with me because my arm is broken, I fix my arm. I don't yank out the whole skeleton. If I yank out the whole skeleton, I'm left with a blob. I can't move a blob forward to achieve any goals that the corporation may have. So that a level of bureaucracy is important.

When I say a bureaucracy motivated by political turf building, it's when people say, "My bureaucracy is better than your bureaucracy."

Right. And would you say—I'm just trying to see if there's a connection among some of the themes we've talking about—that there's been an increase in that kind of political use of bureaucracy?

In my opinion it's gone from one to fourteen. It's gone from one Lyco to fourteen business units. Everybody is driven for their business results and they want to have control.

You brought up downsizing earlier. [When this organization downsized] I was amazed by the amount of effort that was put out by other organizations to help us place as many of those people as we possibly could. As we move forward in the business structure, I guess I get concerned that we're going to start only worrying about ourselves—that even though I may have talents here, they're *my* talents and those people are going to work for *my* organization, and if somebody else has to go through a downsizing, that's their problem.

Finally, in a discussion of loyalty, he showed his continued attachment to the company; his effort to preserve the attachment in the face of all the changes by putting his head down and narrowing his focus; his sense of dependence, and a gratitude that an average guy like him can be part of a powerful company like Lyco; the implicit contract of career security in exchange for hard work; and a fear that if this deal is broken everything will fall apart.

> *Let me just shift back to the philosophical level. This company is going through tremendous cultural and systemic changes. What would you say about loyalty?*
> I'm hesitating because it is a tough question. I have been described by two of my more recent principals as being very loyal because I feel as though the company as it was has provided everything I needed—in terms of my career development, my self-actualization as a professional.
> One of the things that has concerned me over the past year or two is that part of that loyalty comes from what you give the employee in terms of a career. A brief definition for me of a career is [this:] allow me to use my skills, recognize those skills, help me develop those skills. Don't constrain me by bureaucracy that's motivated for political reasons. What I believe has happened is that the company has taken the *careers* away from a lot of us and given us *jobs*. The difference between a career and a job is that I can get a job anywhere. I may not get paid as much, but I can get a job anywhere. And not everybody, once you pass a certain point of income, not everybody works for the income. We do ourselves and our employees an injustice when we don't recognize that coming to work should be fun.
> One of the things that excited me, in terms of working at Lyco, was the opportunity to work in an organization as well known as Lyco. I came from a small school, and did some graduate work at University of Tennessee and then came to work here. I viewed myself as an average type person with maybe an above-average drive. And I looked upon Lyco as providing the opportunity to be exposed to every dimension of business because of its supportive development. It was a big enough organization that it required people to deal with the financial aspects of business, the facilities, the personnel, every business dimension that you can name.
> My basic mindset was, there's an implicit contract. I expect that the company will provide me a career, development opportunities, and reasonable pay and benefits; and they, in turn, should expect from me that I'm willing to work very hard for them. When either one of us is unhappy with that situation, the contract is broken. And up until the past two years, . . . I had faith that that [contract would hold]. On a very microscopic level, I still have faith that that contract holds with myself and my immediate boss. But I don't know that it goes

beyond that, and that's why I said earlier that I believe that the corporation is headed down the path of taking careers away from people and giving them jobs.

And they are doing the individuals and themselves an injustice. If they think that they can continue to get away with it because the recession is here and there aren't job opportunities, that's just postponing what could turn out to be the inevitable, and that is a mass exodus of people.

Conclusion

Sam Lax, like most of the middle managers I talked to, is loyal to an image of a traditional organization. He doesn't like the idea of it changing too much. He holds on firmly to the notion that the company should care for him and all employees, and that in return everyone should work together. A "business focus" represents a short-term, bottom-line mentality that destroys the bonds holding people together.

Like most loyalists, Lax is quite willing to accept that there may need to be pain and turmoil in order to get the organization back to its former healthy state. What he cannot deal with is the idea that there may never be a return to a steady state—only continuous change. His view is, if there has to be a change, tell me what I have to do and let's get it over with. But, to repeat his phrasing, "If you say, 'We're going to go from state A to some future state, we'll figure out what the future state is when we get there'—I have a real difficult time operating in that mode."

The problem is that today's business environment, if not the world in general, is characterized precisely by the condition that Lax rejects: we *don't* know where we're going; at best we'll figure it out when we get there. No large company that I know of, and certainly none in my sample, had confidence in even a rough picture of what markets and economic conditions would be like in five years. They are searching for a way to be continuously adaptable.

Therefore, to put it bluntly, managers in most of the companies I studied were spending their energy avoiding reality—by denying it, by focusing on their own jobs, by seeking a cleaner and purer form of the old organization. Their superiors, right up to the top levels, often played into that defensiveness by playing down harsh realities, letting people go on believing that they would be taken care of and things would soon go back to normal.

This state of affairs is not a benefit to anyone. It certainly is not good for these companies, which have to deal with continued denial of the outside world. Nor is it good for individuals, who are unable to make sense of what is going on or to prepare intelligently for the future.

Managers in these companies continue to want to do their best for the organization. Most of them are even reasonably content. But it is a contentment born of denial, of a refusal to look outward and to recognize the magnitude of the challenges their companies are facing. The paternalistic culture leads to a childlike attitude: make it go away.

Most of all, it leads to an attitude of "hanging on," trying to wait out the problems rather than confronting the future, as typified by this person from Karet:

> I have no doubt that it's going to get worse, but I have no doubt that we will recognize it and turn it around. The only thing we can do is just wait. We have a good organization here, when we get directed to do it, we do it, but it is so damn difficult to get a voice into the organization. I can't help but think that the pendulum will swing back. We will just have to wait it out, because there is really nobody to talk to.

PART III

The New Relationships

7

Breaking Through:
Creating the Community of
Purpose

ATTEMPTS TO HOLD on to the protective "family" of the traditional organization produce a deep freeze. But there is an alternative—not a Darwinian
free-for-all, but a way of pulling people together without subordinating them
to a dominant organization. Several organizations in my study showed what I
call a "community of purpose": a shared commitment to the accomplishment
of a mission, without a permanent and dependent relation of employee to
employer. Before we try to analyze it too deeply, let me tell the stories of
these organizations.

I found four cases in which middle managers were largely positive about the
future and enthusiastic about their own jobs. If we see upheaval and change as
the source of the distress in the other companies, we might expect that these
happier cases would be the organizations that had changed the least—where
the traditional security and perquisites of the managers' role had not been challenged. The truth, however, was the opposite: these were the organizations that
had changed the most.

A key transformation was that expectations of lifetime security and unques-
tioning loyalty had largely been abandoned—far more so than in any of the
organizations we have looked at so far. Two of the organizations had experienced significant managerial downsizing in the recent past, and all knew that it
was likely in the future. Unlike the bulk of my sample, no one seemed to think
that things would eventually return to "normal."

The top managers did not expect loyalty from their employees; that is, they
did not expect people to be there permanently, and they did not expect them
automatically to subordinate other identities and attachments—families, communities, ethnic identities—to corporate needs. And the expectations were reci-
procated: middle managers generally did not see the corporation as a perma-

nent and all-encompassing home. Yet relations had not moved to an attitude of me-first competitiveness or free agency. The managers in these organizations appeared to work together far better than usual, and the level of trust was high both among peers and across levels.

There were not many of these successful organizations—four at the most, out of the fourteen in my sample. Since two of them I had sought out particularly because of their progressive reputations, this is probably a higher percentage of success than in the corporate world at large. Even these four, moreover, fell far short of their own ideals. Yet they provide suggestions, at least, of a different conception of the relation between managers and their employers, and indeed of the basis for human cooperation.

The four organizations I will take up now are Apex, Barclay, Crown, and Dest. I will call them, for short, the *dynamic* organizations, in contrast to the ten *troubled* organizations we have reviewed so far. They shared a number of features:

- These organizations had all been through intense change processes aimed at dismantling bureaucratic procedures and building a sense of flexible teamwork. Though the rhetoric was not dissimilar to that of many other companies, these four had pushed it deeper into their practice.
- There was a marked acceptance of open-ended change—not a desire to return to the clean and tight image of the past, but a willingness to explore an uncertain and messy future.
- Middle managers had an unusually deep understanding of the complexity of business strategy, incorporating not just the creation of products or services but also the competitive and market context that shaped production.
- They did not have high levels of loyalty, in the traditional sense. That is, people did not necessarily expect to stay with the company throughout their careers, and they did not identify strongly with the organization as an entity. It appeared that there was relatively high movement in and out—or at the least, the managers were far more accepting of this movement, and of outside influences, than was the loyalist group. At the same time, the managers did not see themselves as "free agents" seeking the best offer. They were strongly committed to their companies and expected to stay *as long as they could contribute effectively to a company's mission.*
- They did not seek strong, centralized leadership. The top leaders in these cases were unusually low-key, mild-seeming people who rarely issued decrees or intervened personally to settle disputes. Unlike the more bureaucratic companies, this did not unsettle their middle managers.

How did they do this? The evidence from the companies we have looked at so far has been that traditional organizations—bureaucracies—create for themselves a closed circle or a trap: efforts to change only push people deeper into a defense of the core elements of the past. These four companies, however, seem to have at least partially escaped from this trap, and what we need to know is how they did it.

We have seen that traditional corporate loyalty creates a motive for coopera-tion, and that it is therefore essential to the functioning of bureaucratic organi-zation. Trust, in these systems, is intertwined with loyalty: people trust others who, they believe, are oriented to the basic good of the company and who will be around long enough to bear the consequences of their actions. It turns the inevitable "politics" of organizational life in a direction that supports the whole, rather than fragmenting it into warring factions.

So there is a problem here: to explain cooperation without "organizational identification"—at least of the familiar sort. If the four "best" organizations were succeeding—and three of them pretty unquestionably were, at least in the short run—then they must have found another way to create a motivation for working together. What I will argue from these cases is that they manifested a form of community different from that of loyalty, one built around a common *purpose* rather than a common history. And if this is true, it has implications not only for the management of organizational change but also for the problems of commu-nity fostered by the rapid changes in the larger society.

The Four Dynamic Organizations

These four companies were very different from each other. None is perfect, but they are imperfect in different ways, so they help reinforce each other as exam-ples of what is possible.

Apex, a division of a large company, was created about ten years ago and has pursued a deliberately experimental course. This is not uncommon: the Cana-dian divisions of General Electric and IBM, the Commercial Aviation division of Honeywell, and the NUMMI plant at GM are all examples of a strategy of test-ing out new ideas in a single part of the company.

While the parent company of Apex has been downsizing significantly, Apex itself has not (though there have been severe cost and hiring constraints). This may affect the mood for the better, though everyone is aware that the division is subject to the universal problems of closing opportunity and uncertainty for the future.

The company has been highly successful in bringing products to market and in trying innovation at all levels.

Barclay is a production plant. It has had significant managerial layoffs—not merely reductions by attrition—in the recent past, which make it a particularly good test of responses to downsizing. Since it is a single plant employing over 2,000 people, however, its lessons may not be directly applicable to larger-scale organizations.

Four years before my visit it was an organization in serious trouble; by the time I arrived it had turned its results around dramatically.

Crown is a division that went through a sharp change process in the mid-1980s and achieved great success. In the year before my visit, however, it had endured a series of traumas, in particular a merger with a considerably larger company that had absorbed much of the parent company's resources and attention. Under these recent pressures, Crown employees had gone through a partial "retreat to autonomy," of the kind described at Glover—people were frustrated, felt out of touch with the overall company policies, and were focused on getting their own jobs done. Nevertheless, the established foundation of shared understanding and commitment continued to contribute to relatively good cooperation and performance. As in the Apex case, the parent company here had been laying people off, but Crown itself had not cut back managers in the previous few years.

Dest is a company that has seen very bad times as markets have shifted; it was not performing well as a whole when I interviewed there, and it has done very badly since. Layoffs have been harsh and frequent. Yet managers were largely enthusiastic and optimistic as they redefined their corporate purposes and goals. As far as I could tell, they were performing well, though they had not overcome the effects of bad investment and design decisions in the past.

This case suggests that the positive mood in these companies doesn't automatically breed success. On the other hand, it also indicates that good morale doesn't depend on success: it shows the possibility of continued commitment and enthusiasm even in a crisis—yet without denial of the reality of the crisis.

To fill in this picture I will focus primarily on Barclay, with some parallels from the other cases. Barclay has several advantages as an example: it has been through serious downsizing, and it is an old site transformed rather than a brand-new site with all the advantages of starting fresh. Furthermore, I happen to have a very good comparison site in my sample: Hardin is another plant in the same company, making nearly identical products, pursuing the same formal strategy, yet with far worse results.

Both Barclay and Hardin, then, were when I visited them in the midst of a move that is very common these days in manufacturing plants: they were tightening up their processes, adopting just-in-time inventory approaches, reducing quality inspections by putting more quality responsibility in the hands of line workers. They had divided their large plant organizations into smaller "focus factories" with a great deal of responsibility. The mandate for these changes came from corporate management, and both had begun the process about three years before. There were, however, differences in approach.

Hardin, the less successful of the two, had started with a very tough, controlling manager who had enforced cuts and instituted tight new performance measurement systems. She held daily meetings of her managers to give them their marching orders, and those who failed to perform were terrorized. She had been succeeded by a milder, more "humanistic" old-line manager who was trying to rebuild trust by listening and allowing more autonomy. The plant was performing very poorly, though there was modest improvement under the new leader.

Barclay, by contrast, had focused quickly on the business task, informing everyone of the grave competitive situation and the danger of massive layoffs, and establishing performance goals around business outcomes rather than individual achievements. The two leaders of the effort—the plant manager and his operations head—had pushed the restructuring to focus factories and the decentralization of responsibility very fast. Performance had improved dramatically: product defects declined by 75 percent in two years, indirect labor performance improved by over 100 percent, and asset utilization by over 50 percent. As a result of these achievements the layoffs, originally projected to be around 1,500, in the end were closer to 200. These did, however, include several dozen managers, for the first time ever.

The difference in tone was dramatic. At Hardin, the higher-level managers were superficially content because their lives were so much easier under the new plant manager. They complained vigorously, however, about the petty, controlling corporate policies that kept them from effectively doing their jobs. And there was no spontaneous discussion whatsoever of the competitive situation of the plant. In these and other respects, they fit almost perfectly the pattern of *defensive satisfaction* described earlier at Glover and other troubled companies.

Going down a level at Hardin, to the shift supervisors and equivalents, there was simple rage: this group was closer to the mood at Nadir. Their focus was on the loss of perks: they saw the new policies as depriving them of the privileges that they had fought their way through the hierarchy to get. They railed against the loss of special parking places. They complained that to express their dissatisfaction would be suicidal—no one would listen, and their careers would be cut short. They also turned their anger, as at Nadir, against the newcomers, whom they saw as "me-firsters" with no real commitment to the company. They felt they were working harder than ever, making the new just-in-time system work, and getting no recognition for it. And, by the way, they continued to express their loyalty to and affection for the company!

At Barclay, by contrast, I noticed none of this finger-pointing or displacement of anger. The corporate policies that were such a target for anger at Hardin existed also at Barclay, but they aroused little passion. Some, like the reduction of perks, were actually welcomed; others, like individualized measurement systems, were seen as nuisances that interfered with the goal of teamwork but which could be dealt with in getting on with the work.

The middle-management level that had been most distressed at Hardin was of an entirely different frame of mind at Barclay. In the latter they enjoyed the increased responsibility and collaboration. They did not feel overworked; they believed that the new systems had on the whole reduced their job pressures by sharing responsibility more widely, and had left them time to follow more interesting and creative avenues. They stressed their own growth on the job in the previous two years.

How much of this was reality, and how much rhetoric? There were two particularly telling bits of evidence that there were real changes in the role of middle managers. First, their numbers had in fact been significantly reduced—while at Hardin, by contrast, efforts to reduce this level of management had caused such production problems that their numbers were in the process of being increased again. Second, these midlevel managers at Barclay told how they had come up with the idea of seeking bids for their products—which were normally used by other internal divisions—from external European companies, and had worked through the negotiations to a successful conclusion themselves, saving many jobs.

In short, the middle managers here had largely transformed their own self-definition. Those at Hardin saw themselves as controllers and problem-solvers, fixing difficulties that came up from the workers on the line. When their numbers were reduced, they simply had to deal with more problems apiece. Those at Barclay, by contrast, saw themselves as a team of people trying to build the business, and they demonstrably had the time and the power to take new initiatives. There were relatively fewer of them, yet they were less pressured than those in the traditional mold.

They knew that their jobs were not secure: a significant group had been involuntarily laid off already, and they knew enough of the business to recognize that the turmoil was far from over. Indeed, they were far calmer and more realistic about this prospect than managers at Hardin or many of the other companies, who veered inconsistently between confidence that they were safe and deep fear that they were not.

Lack of job security did not diminish for managers at Barclay and the other three companies a sense of real pleasure—one might almost say joy—in their work. For them, unlike those we have looked at earlier in this work, the change process made sense. One remarked, "The last one and one half years has been a revolutionary change with this just-in-time system. People feel very proud of what they have accomplished."

The sense of personal growth is one theme that appeared again and again in all four of the best companies, and it sharply divided them from the rest: "Apex is a remarkable place. It's a growth experience especially in terms of decision making and working with other functions. The sixteen months I have been here have added four years of experience."

Enough testimonials. What were the dynamics enabling people to achieve this remarkable state of mind in the face of disruption, dislocation, and rapid change?

It is not always easy to tell what made the difference. Much of the rhetoric of change was similar across all fourteen companies: the words *empowerment, teamwork,* and *flexibility* were heard everywhere. A number of "hard" changes were also very common in both the troubled and the dynamic groups, including restructuring around customer needs, changes in measurements, new relationships to suppliers, and the development of vision statements. But there were a few factors that seemed to make a real difference.

UNDERSTANDING THE MISSION AND BUSINESS

I have described the efforts at Lyco and Glover to spread information about the business and to clarify their vision. These basic points were common to nearly every company I studied: vision statements hung on walls everywhere and presentations on the business were legion.[1] But only in the dynamic group had the knowledge been internalized by middle management.

One of my major tests of understanding was whether managers could talk about the competition in informed ways. Amazingly, in most companies, they could not. At Glover, to take one example, there was great satisfaction about their quality improvements, but they were befuddled when I asked them whether their competitors were improving as well. Indeed, as I have pointed out, in the loyalist companies *business focus* was a negative term. It represented short-sightedness, selfishness, and dishonesty, as opposed to the warmth and caring of the old community.

The dynamic companies contrasted sharply with this: they spoke in positive terms about focusing on the business, and their level of understanding was extraordinary—a quantum leap beyond anything in the ten troubled organizations. At Barclay middle managers and supervisors knew what outside firms as well as other plants within their company were doing, and what they would be likely to do in the longer run. Middle levels spoke constantly of their efforts to create a planning mentality throughout the organization. First-level supervisors said. "We are involved in forecast, budgets, business team meetings. We have much more responsibility and challenge. The days of just doing the job are gone."

The result of this approach to change was a highly unusual degree of communication and understanding across levels of the organization: the top management (within the plant) had direct knowledge of the implementation issues, and the lower levels had direct knowledge of the strategic goals. This communication produced a unified picture of the world, in which the means of implementation (focus factories, just-in-time, and so on) were linked to the strategic objectives.

This unity of view was what made possible initiatives like the one mentioned earlier, in which middle managers sought out and conducted negotiations with fundamentally new types of customers. It also produced stories like this (from Crown):

Just yesterday there was an important customer who called me up and told me they needed a shipment right away if not sooner. There is one person who can sign tags to get a product out the door. He left for the day, so I ran over there to see if someone could shake the tree. Finally I found a quality supervisor who got the guy to come back.

Later on I ran into [the division manager] in the hall; I told him, "This shit can't happen. Our real business is supplying hardware. Our real business isn't security."

So today I've been thinking about how we can develop a new procedure for this kind of shipment. Because we shouldn't have to hold up a shipment because of guards' schedules. But we have to find a way to get the security needs met and still focus on the the business.

This little tale brings together a number of elements common in this group of companies: the willingness to push back against established procedure, the ability to talk freely with superiors (up two levels to the division manager, in this case), the focus on "our real business." In countless examples I have witnessed and heard about in "typical" companies, managers react to this kind of obstacle by complaining and wringing their hands, complaining about the bureau-cracy—in effect, complaining about everyone else in the company. The mindset that tries to do something about it is rarer: it appears in a few individuals in most companies, but in most people only in a few companies.

Still rarer is the reaction of finding a high-level manager and discussing the problem in a constructive way. And rarest of all is this man's interest in drawing lessons from the event—spending time trying to sort out the competing issues so that it wouldn't happen again. In most companies, even if an individual case was worked out, it produced a grumbling sense of "we'll always have these problems"; here it produced learning and a plan of action.

How did these organizations develop this level of business knowledge and commitment? In the larger number of organizations that failed at it, it wasn't for lack of trying. Top managers in almost every case "knew" the importance of developing business knowledge and, like Randolph at Lyco, boasted of the great increase in information sharing and education over the previous decade. But like the efforts at Lyco (which I described in chapter 5), these programs generally failed to "penetrate."

As I explored this question at length in my interviews, two things stood out. First, the four had generally done a more thorough job of business education than the others. Glover and Lyco's unsuccessful efforts had used newsletters, leader-ship speeches, and large-group presentations; several of the dynamic companies, by contrast, had multiday small-group interactions. At Barclay, for instance,

We took a group of about thirty people made up of 80 percent hourly and 20 percent salary and worked with them for a week on our business plan. The focus was, how do we get that business plan to come alive for the rest of the work force? In conjunction with that we get a lot of involvement in people doing their own layouts and getting buy-in from their peers.

This session led to a wide range of initiatives involving management at all levels in constant review of the business information. Apex, similarly, had several days of orientation to the business for new employees.

But the real reason for the penetration of business understanding, I think, lay at a deeper level: in the dynamic companies most managers *needed* this understanding, whereas in the others they did not. In the troubled companies managers could be successful in their jobs by focusing on their particular pieces—on the quality and cost of their own product, for example—without understanding that piece's strategic relation to the rest of the organization. In the dynamic companies they had to have a wider focus. The core reason for this was that among the latter, managers were constantly involved in decision-making teams with other parts of the organization, and therefore needed to see their relation to the bigger picture in daily practice. In short, it was the deep-rooted change processes focused on organized teamwork, which all the better organizations had experienced, that made the business information meaningful and valuable to middle managers.

FORMAL AND FLEXIBLE TEAMWORK

The change process in the dynamic organizations had in every case greatly increased the importance of temporary, formal, cross-functional teams. Teams were a common goal in most of the companies I studied, but not many had succeeded in doing much. In fact, only the four organizations I am calling "dynamic" gave evidence that teamwork had become more than a slogan, and had seriously cut across traditional lines of function and hierarchical level.

Let me stress the significance of *temporary, formal, cross-functional* teams. The word *teamwork* as used in traditional organizations has a different meaning. In that context it refers to improving existing relations in the hierarchy— usually getting a supervisor to relate better to subordinates. In the dynamic organizations, by contrast, "teamwork" continually reconfigured the hierarchy by putting people together across lines and requiring that they work together.

Apex and Crown had taken extraordinary measures to create such team-based structures. Crown had had a long process of divisionwide strategic planning a few years before, involving representatives from many levels and functions. Out of that enormous effort had come not only a general strategy but an elaborate set of cross-cutting groups with varying business and personnel functions. Apex had started with a participatory, multifunction design process, and it operated more thoroughly through teams—many of them including shop-floor workers—than any other company I have ever seen. It was routine there for shop-floor workers and managers from several levels, representing engineering and different divisions of manufacturing, to meet together for problem solving or objective setting.

Or consider once again the contrast between Barclay's success and Hardin's problems. At Barclay the factory had been thoroughly restructured into small units that had independent responsibility for results; this, by all accounts, had melded those within the units into tightly focused groups working well together whatever their formal rank or function. At the same time there was effective cooperation between the units, and among higher-level managers. Managers two or three levels below the top regularly met together across units on their own initiative, and at times took major strategic actions like the international marketing effort mentioned earlier. They frequently stressed the spontaneous working together among their peers. By contrast, at Hardin, though the rhetoric and the corporate mandate were similar, the factory manager continued to be the center of all attention; there was no effective teamwork because everything went through him. Focus factories had never been instituted. Managers never met among themselves except for specific tasks defined by the top.

A measure of the reality of these team-based organizations was the attitude of the middle managers. In the last chapter I reviewed the situation in the troubled organizations. There most managers viewed cross-functional teamwork skeptically: they were widely resistant to the use of task forces, freewheeling involvement, and skip-level communication. All of this was seen as tending toward chaos, violating the principles of order that gave them faith in the future. Teamwork was fine as long as it remained bound by the hierarchy—a relation between a superior and a subordinate; but it became dangerous when it began to cut across the lines and to create new decision-making structures. This attitude was so widespread in the troubled companies that I hardly need add the usual qualifiers ("generally," "for the most part") to my characterization.

In "the old days," as these managers recalled it, it was common for people to come together informally to deal with problems. That ability had been largely lost in the restructuring of the troubled companies, because personal networks had been torn apart and because people had withdrawn to a focus on their own areas. As a result, in the troubled group all the examples of cross-functional teams that I could trace carefully—about ten in all—were criticized by managers as confused, ineffective, and subject to irrational politics.

In the dynamic organizations teamwork was widely seen as exciting and fruitful:

> "I've never been involved in a corporation where I've experienced stronger group dynamics, camaraderie, making sure the people understand, and throwing up flags when you see team members heading for trouble."

> "We work as entrepreneurs and cooperate together, both. A lot of the systems that drive the performance here are linked together so that if something does fail, it's no longer people trying to cover up something. It's discovered very quickly, then the attitude is you get to the root cause of it and get it fixed. And that creates a team environment to deal with problems."

It was only in the dynamic organizations that managers enthusiastically took advantage of *formal project-centered* teams as a way of coordinating their efforts. A manager from Dest describes the difficult but exciting building of that process:

> The first couple of meetings, when you brought together people from all kinds of different functions, were like mating dances. There were three or four meetings where all of us were wringing our hands saying, "Ain't it awful, but it's not my problem." Then someone said, "We don't have anyone representing the management of customer engineers." So we got someone in from there. We started out in a state of semiconflict and expanded to bring in others who could contribute and were team players. Then it mushroomed more to cover all the bases.
>
> This process was very educational because we all saw that though we could agree on 80 percent of the problem, we all saw it from different facets. And then we saw that other people have problems. The next step in maturity was seeing that the problem was not on any one of us, the problem was that we didn't understand the entire transaction cycle in enough detail to understand each other's issues.
>
> Now a friendship has developed and the barriers have fallen. Then we became excited with this process. We're not just covering our asses, but we have a chance to really make some progress if we all pull together. The whole thing took about six months, and we've made enormous progress.

OPEN INTERACTION

The better organizations, in contrast to the rest, had created wide areas of open and cooperative dialogue across organizational lines. The avoidance of conflict and discussion—the pattern we observed at Lyco in chapter 5—is common to all the ten troubled organizations in my sample. But the four best organizations produced story after story of the opposite: the ability just to talk about issues, to fight about them openly on occasion, without creating back-room political games.

I have given one example already in the story of the manager at Crown trying to get the shipment out. When he ran into his boss (two levels up), typical behavior would have been to say nothing, for fear of looking like he had failed in his responsibility, or else to complain and dump it in the boss's lap. Instead (as he told it) he described the problem to the boss, put it in terms of its general significance for the business, and then went off to work on it further himself. There was, in short, a back-and-forth process, a dialogue.

At Apex shop-floor workers told me, "We've changed the operator description sheets five or six times. We consensed [*sic*] and then we went to our resource, that is the engineers, and they were very good about it."

In almost any other organization, the idea of engineers being "very good about it" when workers brought changes to them is hard to imagine. Yet it should be emphasized that this was not just an abdication or shift of responsibility: the engineers could and did disagree, and occasionally there were pitched conflicts. In all cases in memory, I was told, they were worked out through further analysis of the issues:

> What happens if there's a serious disagreement? Well, if you don't buy in, you have to present an alternative, or else we do a root-cause analysis and try to define the problem further.

I observed also at Apex a meeting in which a half-dozen people from a wide range of levels and functions—from the shop floor to a level below the division manager—met to develop an assessment of the organization's progress. The tone was exploratory, experimental. The hierarchical superior was not the leader of the meeting. Leadership shifted several times with the topic, and several different people stepped up to make facilitating comments when necessary. All of this contrasted sharply to meetings I observed at Lyco and Fixx, and to what I was told at other companies: the hierarchical superior always controlled the meeting and took ultimate decisions.

At Barclay, our main focus here, I did not directly observe interactions, but the stories were of the same type. The plant manager said, "The next thing now is semi-automated assembly. That will be a big change. You have to put together the story of why, doing it bit by bit with volunteers. We have been doing studies, all this jointly with the union." A couple of levels down, managers described the same kind of engineering-production relations as at Apex: "We're heavy into designs of experiments as well which are coordinated with the engineering group. It's a team of hourly people who work on issues which come up. It's a process where an experiment is designed to take into account various factors which may contribute to a problem on the floor. They design the experiment and carry it out themselves."

At Dest I found similar patterns, including one middle manager who volunteered to subordinate himself to another who was his formal equal, because he thought that would advance the business strategy.

Let me not leave a utopian impression: in no case was there equality or democracy. Hierarchical positions remained a key mechanism of decision making, and therefore affected communication. At Barclay the first-level supervisors had not been brought into the culture of dialogue: though they were pleased at the improvement in the plant, they avoided skipping the chain of command. Similar comments in every other case showed that "chain of command" thinking—the killer of dialogue—continued to exist everywhere.

Yet a clear distinction remained: in these dynamic organizations, unlike the ten troubled ones, there was widespread enthusiasm about the violations of the chain of command—about the ability to speak freely and cooperatively without threatening others' positions. Managers rejoiced in this openness; in the less successful companies, they feared it. At Lyco, as described earlier, middle managers fled from the chance to meet with their division leader as from a sinister trap; at Barclay and the others, they welcomed such opportunities.

LEADERSHIP: INTERMITTENT FACILITATION

It struck me that in all four of these cases leaders were very low-key—not dominating "turnaround" managers. Much of the time people seemed to forget they were around.

The most visible, "hands-on" leaders were found in the less successful cases. At Nadir, the division manager was an enthusiastic exponent of innovation, very visible, always wandering around, cheerleading, sponsoring experimental groups. JVC had another variant of top-level activism: the leader was a strong numbers-oriented, directive, hard-nosed type. At Marks there was a powerful visionary who was attempting to drag the company into a high-technology age by a combination of inspiration and detailed prodding. For all their differences, these men were similar in that they were the center of the action. And they were notably unsuccessful in the terms of this study—in mobilizing their middle managers as an effective and committed team.

In the four best cases one heard much less about the top managers from those in the middle. A second-level Apex manager asked half-seriously, "Is [the division manager] still with us? I haven't heard from him for a long time." But this did not mean the top's role was unimportant. They moved in a quieter way, but moved nevertheless.

At Barclay there was a paradoxical reversal of roles. On the one hand, the two top leaders (the plant manager and operations manager, who clearly worked well together) played down their role in the development of long-range strategy: "We used to have to plan for a five-year horizon, and we just bullshitted. Now we focus on eighteen months." Instead, they stressed their connection to the day-to-day problems. They were proud of the fact that when the just-in-time system was implemented, they went through the entire two-week training program themselves—not just the two-day introduction designed for leadership. As a result, they said,

> For the first time in a long time the top managers actually knew more than the middle about the production process. Most of the higher management know nothing about making the product. Business is business. But in the just-in-time switch we had a hands-on feel for what had to be done.

On the other side of the paradox, the middle levels felt much more involved in long-range planning than most: according to them, they regularly worked on projects with two-year time horizons, including major strategic initiatives like the broadening of international customers mentioned earlier.

This might sound like a prescription for chaos—as if the top and the middle had switched places. One might expect the former to be meddling far too much in details, or the latter to be dreaming when they should be guiding. But that was not what was going on. Both sides gave a similar picture: instead of the bureaucratic model—the top planning and the middle implementing—here *the middle planned and the top wandered around.* Various people described the top pair's role as one of keeping things moving, "looking for trends," "looking to improve," "throwing visions around":

> They come down to us with a lot of ideas and suggestions, egging us on to continue to improve. They need to keep us from getting bogged down in the day-to-day.

Others in the middle levels expressed uncertainty about what the two top leaders did do; when I reported this back, the plant manager was amused and not at all defensive.

My interpretation of the pattern was that because the concerns of the two levels had in a sense crossed, they were able to communicate far better than usual. Typically the higher levels feel they have a monopoly on big thoughts and wide understanding, and the middle in turn feel they have a monopoly on understanding the day-to-day demands of the business. This "cognitive turf," as it might be called, creates a divide that is hard to cross. Plans that look elegant and complete to the top leadership are regularly derided by the middle as impractical and faddish—we have seen many examples of this in earlier chapters—and of course the middle seem to their superiors to miss the big picture.

At Barclay there was respect from both sides: from the top for the important planning abilities demonstrated by the middle managers; from the middle for the "hands-on feel" that their bosses had. This shared respect made it possible for the top to play a more intermittent role. Instead of feeling constant responsibility to make sure the strategy was being implemented, these leaders could trust their subordinates to do a lot of that—so that they could focus on providing *as-needed* support in the form of occasional teaching, pointing out new opportunities, and so on.

This quality of intermittence is quite descriptive of the CEO at Apex as well.[2] I followed for over a year, for example, a dispute between two high-level managers about their respective responsibilities. These disputes did come up here as elsewhere, despite the generally high level of teamwork. What was unusual was, first, the openness of the issue—it was fought in public rather than through back-room maneuvers—and second, the role of the CEO. In most companies he would have been the arbitrator in such a case. Instead, he stepped in at several points to reinforce the basic norms of the organization: to get the disputants to formulate clear proposals, to develop facts, to check with other stakeholders, and so on. Other than that, he let them work it out—which they did, with considerable ingenuity and success.

Intermittence, I should stress, does not mean passivity: these managers could be intermittently very powerful. Certainly at Barclay the operations manager was widely seen as having forcefully driven the structural move to a just-in-time system and focus factories: he appears to have been extremely visible for a time. This made it all the more striking that when I visited, less than a year after this period, he was widely seen as a helpful but somewhat distant figure, certainly not a daily force to be feared. A year and a half after that he was gone, with no apparent effect on the momentum of the plant.

PUBLIC DECISION PROCESSES

Decision making varied considerably. Two of the cases (Apex and Crown) were very elaborate examples of what organizational consultants like to call "process-based" organizations: that is, they had highly formalized consensus decision-making mechanisms, starting with widespread training in group dynamics and team building, and including heavy use of teams with stakeholder representatives and strong facilitators. The other two did not use such approaches.

What linked them all, however, was that decision making was unusually public. Whether or not there were formal processes of involvement, there was a great deal of dialogue about the logic of the changes as they developed. At Barclay, since it was a relatively small and localized organization—a single plant, albeit a large one—this seems to have been accomplished largely through the wandering around of the top leaders. At Apex and Crown, which were larger and more scattered divisional organizations, it seemed that more formal processes were necessary.

The contrast with the failed approach at Glover could not be more sharp. There the top management team of the division literally withdrew for much of a year to a windowless room in the basement; in "the vault," as they called it, they held an intensive series of meetings to work out their strategic plan. When they emerged they announced a series of reforms—and then seemed surprised that their ideas didn't make a lot of sense to everyone else.[3]

At Barclay, although the basic just-in-time transformation had been decreed from higher levels and was not optional, its recent implementation was clearly very interactive. This had not always been true, according to those who had been there: the first time through it had been treated as an opaque "program" to be "implemented," and had not gotten far. But the more recent and far more successful effort had been quite different, with the top leaders getting a hands-on understanding of it (as described earlier), and themselves carrying it, explaining the logic and discussing the concerns and issues throughout the plant.

One apparent result of this openness was that "organization politics" (in the bad sense) were greatly reduced. I have described how in the troubled organizations the retreat to autonomy coincided with the growth of private, back-room deal-making, or at least the widespread perception of such a shift. The picture was again quite different in these four cases.

It was not as simple as saying there was less politics: on the contrary, these four organizations had in a sense brought politics to the forefront. Most decisions were made not in the bureaucratic way of passing it to the responsible official, but by long processes of discussion, and often arguing, among the main players. What was distinctive was that this debate was largely in the open—everyone knew about it and understood the sides. Withdrawing to the back rooms was far less common. A Dest employee remarked,

> For the last nine months there have been no rumors in manufacturing—and this is a rumor-mill company. That's because people have gotten the message about the business goals.

The most impressive demonstration of this shift for me was the outcome of the dispute between the two high-level managers at Apex which I have already sketched in the context of the leadership role. One of these managers was clearly playing an old-fashioned power game—lining up his allies in private, fighting for his turf. When I first became aware of the issue, he had already consolidated a strong position. The division leader, as I mentioned, did not take him on directly, but in various ways made sure that the issue was aired openly, that the main people involved heard for themselves what the dispute was about and expressed their views in open groups. Over the next few months, the turf-oriented manager became gradually more isolated: as he was forced to argue publicly for his views, it became apparent that there was not much behind them besides personal aggrandizement, and his most powerful allies began to pull back. Fairly quickly he was forced to revise his position to one that could be publicly justified in terms of the purposes and norms of the division, and a positive resolution was reached.

OPENNESS TO DIVERSITY

These organizations were notably open to outsiders. The two leaders of Barclay had come from outside rather than up through the system, which caused none of the problems of the outside leadership at, say, Nadir. All four organizations employed many people who had come from other companies without passing through the steps of internal promotion. Unlike in the troubled companies, here these people seemed comfortable and clearly accepted.

In terms of more traditional definitions of diversity—women and minorities—the evidence is less overwhelming, but still positive. There were only five blacks and thirty-five women[4] in my interviews. From this relatively small sample I cannot see clear differences between the dynamic and the troubled companies. But there are some suggestive points.

First, in my sample as a whole, almost all the blacks and about a third of the women complained passionately about discrimination and exclusion. Of these, a couple were in the dynamic companies; these immediately qualified their complaints by saying that things were much better here than elsewhere. Those in the troubled companies were sometimes bitter without qualification.

Second, there was a strong subset of women who had adopted an aggressively independent position—refusing to give loyalty to any company, focusing on building their careers. These were clearly more comfortable in the dynamic companies than in the troubled ones.

The same is true of another group of women who were trying to balance family and career commitments. Almost none in the traditional companies found it possible to do this effectively,[5] while in Apex at least there were several who praised the company for its help in balancing those demands.

It appears, overall, that none of the organizations I studied is a rousing success in managing diversity of race and sex, but the edge goes fairly clearly to the dynamic group. And this group was also unequivocally better at dealing with people entering from the outside, which is another form of diversity.

CHANGING FUNCTIONS OF MIDDLE MANAGEMENT

Middle managers have traditionally had two general roles in the organization (apart from their specific job duties). They have developed the implementation plans for the designs of top management, and they have mentored and managed their subordinates.[6]

In the dynamic organizations such as at Apex, the job looks quite different:

> In a traditional situation you manage people. Here you manage tasks and lead people.

"Tasks" becomes separated from the "people" one leads because managers no longer work primarily with their subordinates. They are working to accomplish projects, which generally involves a huge amount of time in meetings with people from other functions and areas. Their subordinates are similarly working with multiple groups. The boss is far from the sole point of contact; in fact, direct contact with her is often infrequent.

For a loyalist like Sam Lax (chapter 6), this growing distance between superiors and subordinates is a grave problem. Not so for the professionals: they reframe their relation to their reports. Rather than taking on the heavy burden of paternalistic protection of their part of the "family," they encourage those under them to be independent and to develop their own networks:

> I encourage people to diversify. I don't want to hire narrow, world-class experts. When people come in I take them out of their comfort zone to let them flounder, show them failure is OK and we'll get support. People get tremendous confidence from it.

Like the top leaders at Barclay, managers down the line see their role as one of teaching and stimulating change.

In the same pattern, they are no longer the primary evaluators of performance for their subordinates: they coordinate evaluations from all the teams and people that their people work with. Most of these organizations, though they are still experimenting with the details, are moving toward a system in which everyone gets multiple evaluations from quite varied areas, which are then put together into some coherent form by the nominal boss.

So the paternalist power to protect, to control, to reward and punish, is greatly reduced; that is why the job is no longer one of "managing people." The focus shifts to "managing tasks" by working with teams to accomplish projects. "Leading people" becomes a matter of providing the environment for those in a formal reporting relation to develop their own abilities.

The "Professional" Manager

There was a distinctive type of manager, most common in these organizations, who felt at home in the changing environment. Instead of feeling the fear, loss, paralysis, and sense of betrayal I have described so far, these were positive about the future. Their orientation was far from loyalist dependency—they did not expect permanent jobs from their companies, nor were they willing to do whatever they were asked.

Though this relationship is not fully captured by any single word or phrase, I will call it a "professional" type. The term captures a key point: that these managers are not tied to any one organization. At Nadir, it may be recalled,[7] the loyalists were bitterly critical of the new group they characterized as "professionals"; at the four dynamic companies, the same word became a compliment, as in these two statements by employees of Apex and Dest:

"This is a professional environment. . . . The system works because of the extremely high quality of people. There's tremendous ownership and pride because you actually manage your part of the program, you have a responsibility."

"[The president] did a super job of professionalizing the assets management group."

Let me note right away, however, that the relationship is different from that of many traditional professionals such as lawyers and doctors; the word is a shorthand that is only partially accurate.[8] I have tried a lot of alternatives: at times I admit to thinking of these managers as "nouveau," in the sense of new and emergent, but also (like nouveau riche or nouveau wines) in the sense of a little brash, astringent—though, like the wines, they are generally good for their purposes.

I found some examples of this "professional" (or "nouveau") orientation in almost every case, which suggests that in part it comes from individual motivation. But it is also greatly affected by the surrounding organization. In the troubled companies these managers were rare and felt out of place; in the four dynamic organizations they were common, and they felt very much at home.

I will try to deal more theoretically with this type in the next chapter. Here let me just try to capture some of the flavor of what I heard.

John Hall is in some ways unusual, but the unusualness highlights a frequent pattern. When I talked to him he was working in a midlevel job at Apex, but he was an employee of Honeywell.[9] Throughout his career he had moved from company to company, even internationally, helping each company to work with and refine a technology that he had originally developed at Honeywell. He expected to be at Apex for perhaps four or five years.

What is his motivation? He began the interview this way: "I'm committed to a particular technology and I have been for the past twenty-five years." At this point, I assumed that his emotional focus was on the technology, and that he was a kind of hired gun doing a very specific technical job, not caring much whom he was actually working for. He quickly countered that notion, saying, "This company also fits with my personal philosophy and my personal vision of how a company should be run." From there he spoke for most of an hour, with passion and intelligence, about the organizational strengths and weaknesses of Apex, and of what he was doing to try to improve the company.

I am little by little trying to bring manufacturing and product engineering together into simultaneous engineering. What they did at first was simultaneous engineering separately.

There's a real split in culture between the two groups. The early vision was of a self-directed organization with not enough of a reality check. Now the manufacturing people are being told that's a long-term vision, a goal, and we need to work to get there. The product engineering people thought they were already there five years ago, so they're disillusioned and negative. So the two groups don't work well together and the product has suffered.

The teams who understand the goal and how to get there are very sophisticated. There are shop-floor workers talking about return on investment and business concepts. There's only one other company I've seen on four continents that has that kind of sophistication and that's one in Japan.

Clearly he cared about and was deeply involved with the organization of Apex, and he wanted to help the company succeed. I asked him about his role and motives; he told me:

My role is really as an integrator, but I should work myself out of that job. If I can establish an organization which will work together and not throw things over the wall, then we won't need an integrator. When that's done it's time to go do something else.

I've probably never put in as many hours as I have in this program. I put in almost eighty hours a week. This project is very important to the industry.

The most valuable thing I can gain from this is personal growth. And also establishing my credentials in this technology.

Hall's view of careers and relations to the company was not, he said, a personal idiosyncracy; it was applicable to managers throughout the company:

There are four people in my group that I think are really good and on target that I use as role models; but of those four only one is actively looking for a promotion, although their ages are 28 to 34. I've tried to maintain the focus on the task because without task completion there will be no opportunity for any of them. When the task is done the best leaders can take leadership roles in the next project, and others will market their skills to other companies.

There were not many who had lived this type of career as thoroughly as Hall: not many companies are open to people as mobile and un-loyal as this, and almost none would have encouraged such a person a decade ago. Even at Apex there was some uncertainty:

Some people question my allegiance, especially when I make decisions on companies which are competitors of Honeywell and I'm still working officially for Honeywell. A small part of the organization doesn't like this, sees me as a Honeywell person. But for the most part it has been OK.

Apex was unusual in only having "a small part of the organization" resistant to this outsider; at Nadir and others, as we have seen, it is the vast majority.

Given the widespread resistance to outsiders in most companies, the people who had actually moved through multiple companies were rare: they had to be remarkably focused and tough to pull it off.[10] Those of this rare breed who had landed in the dynamic group of companies, like Hall, felt that they had found a haven; those in the troubled group were frustrated and at odds with the environment. All, however, shared a distinctive set of perspectives.

First, they were highly focused on the task and the business. Those in the troubled companies were the *only* ones who had any deep understanding of the competitive environment, and they stood out sharply from their peers. They constantly brought issues back to the essential tasks that needed to be done for the business.

In comparison with the dominant ethic at the troubled companies, they seemed "hard-nosed." They believed strongly that task accomplishment was the key measure of quality, and tended to reject "relationship-building" for its own sake. For example, they were impatient with "participatory teams" that aimed to discuss and deal with job satisfaction.[11]

Second, they balanced two seemingly contradictory impulses. On one hand, they believed strongly in individual responsibility for the construction of their careers, as opposed to the belief of loyalists that the company owed them career stability. On the other, they clearly and strongly rejected the individualistic, "free agent" model in which money replaces loyalty. They were deeply committed to the success of the company, they were enthusiastic about the mission, and they were believers in teamwork to achieve the corporate goals—at the same time that they remained focused on their own independent careers.

I have illustrated this balance in Hall's case; it defines what I am calling a "professional" orientation. The others of this type spoke, like him, of the importance of building teams; they enjoyed working with multiple functions, integrating across boundaries. In the dynamic companies they were leaders of the general enthusiasm for teamwork, and those in troubled companies were intensely frustrated by the "politics" and individual isolation. They were also critical of excessive individualism. Said one "professional" at Dest:

> One mistake I made earlier in my career was focusing on the superstars; then they expected to move too far and there was lots of turnover. You need, in a business, bricklayers as well as architects.

Third, they were the only managers who were enthusiastic about professional commitments and training outside the company. I have mentioned before that I gave up one of my original questions, about outside involvements, because so few managers had real interest in groups beyond the company borders; earlier writers have also noted how much outside activities were traditionally subordinated to company needs. But this group of "professional" managers raised the issue spontaneously.

The conflict with the traditional culture is clearest in the cases of professional managers in troubled companies, as heard in these comments from managers at Marks and Nadir:

> "The top team is good, they are good people, we work well together, they are well trained and intelligent, but they are not up to speed on the new techniques. They are not doing what they could do to train themselves on the new techniques. They haven't read books. I have given them books, they haven't read them. They showed up for training but left after half a day."

> "I do a lot of training and arrange for a lot of training, much more than the others. We have internal professional development seminars. And my managers share the responsibility for hosting it. I drive that. If I didn't drive it, it would fade out. I encouraged the professionals here to join associations like the Society for Quality Control, to improve their professional mileage. I encourage them to go through certification programs."

Finally, they had a view of the mutual obligation between employee and company which centered on the notion of challenge:

> If the challenges continue to be here, I'll stay. But I've always followed interesting projects—I like new projects, I like intellectual stimulation. The key for me is, "What am I interested in doing?"

They generally viewed the time frame of the commitment in terms of completing the project—most frequently a few years. The frequent refrain was, "When that's done, it's time to move onto something else."

> I'm here for the duration. The duration is as long as I'm necessary and useful. . . . I think after a certain point, three years, four years, you've shot all your bullets, you've done all you can do in my kind of job, and it's time to move on to something else. What I expect for that is support for the work that I'm doing. I know that this organization has really wanted me.
>
> When you hear about people who say they are so loyal to the organization, so tied to it, that they'll hang on for twelve years until retirement, I can't relate to that. I couldn't hang on for twelve months in a place that didn't want me.

Unlike the other cases, it was seen as entirely legitimate to talk about managers' individual needs. In Lyco (to refer back to chapter 5) we saw how people avoided raising issues of job quality or personal needs. In the more successful companies, it was expected. Leaders quickly recognized the legitimacy of family demands, as well as requests for professional development through outside experience. They treated very seriously any complaints about excess pressure.

While there was still some reticence, middle managers told me they were generally willing and able to voice these issues.

In the dynamic organizations, this ethic—of flexibility in careers, of not staying when the challenge is gone, of open dialogue—was not isolated but widespread: it was part of the culture, not just of individual personalities. What struck me in particular was that it was even shared by many people who had long been career loyalists. It seemed that these organizations had the power to convert people rapidly to a "professional" orientation.

Most of these dynamic organizations, it will be recalled, were divisions or plants within a corporate parent; in each case most of the managers had spent fifteen to twenty years with the parent, with the same expectations of security as in all of the examples in the past chapters. Yet while the veterans in the troubled companies felt lost and betrayed, those who had shifted to the dynamic companies were caught by the enthusiasm for the professional ethic. A lifelong traditionalist at Apex, for example, used almost exactly the same words as those who had moved through multiple companies:

> We're doing things differently here. We've gotten away from a lot of the traditional givens. . . . The pileup at the top doesn't bother me: I'm looking for my next challenge, not my next promotion.[12]

Conclusion

The four organizations that best succeeded in maintaining the *enthusiasm* of their middle managers—as opposed to a stubborn, "head-down" attachment—were those who most thoroughly transformed their roles. Clearly what is going on in these cases is not a matter of treating people nicely, not a matter of "communicating" well or being clear, in a bureaucratic manner, about responsibilities. The companies and their managers were not holding on to the hope that things would "settle down," or that a "blueprint" would soon emerge.

Instead, they had moved far more extensively than any in the troubled group toward an organization based on shifting teams, expecting constant change. The managers, in turn, conceived of their commitments as temporary and task-focused—based on challenges rather than permanent loyalties.

These examples, incomplete as they are, raise the possibility of a new model—a possibility that, however, requires a great deal more to make it a reality.

8

The Emerging Employment Relation

IN THE LAST CHAPTER we saw four examples of apparently successful organizations that did not rely on stability and loyalty. These companies seemed to have overcome the pain and stagnation characteristic of the other ten in my sample by solving some very difficult problems: they gained the enthusiastic support of their managers, and built a real sense of cooperation, without the promise of long-term security.

This violates the traditional image of the employment relation, still prevalent in most of my sample, which favors a dominant organization that supplies both security and direction. In this long-standing conception employees are expected conscientiously to do whatever their jobs demand; in return the company is expected to take care of them permanently. It is the forced breakdown of this compact that causes the pain and paralysis of the troubled group.

Faced with the pain of the destruction of their relation to the company, loyalists sometimes jump to an opposite extreme. They see no alternative but to become "free agents," selling their services to the highest bidder, focusing only on money. Yet *no one* in all the people I interviewed saw this as a good solution either for themselves or for the company.

The ideal image in the dynamic companies is different from either of these: it is of a voluntary coming together of *individuals with commitments* and an *organization with a mission*. This is the relationship that I have referred to as a "professional" one, forming a community of purpose. It is not a full reality anywhere, but it is in some places an ideal shaping definitions of who owes what to whom.

In this conception, to sketch its ideal form, individuals are committed not to any company as such, but to a personal set of skills, goals, interests, and affiliations. The company offers them not permanent employment, but challenges that give them an opportunity to develop their interests, and a promise of mutual dialogue and openness to manage the two sets of needs. When the two are synchronized, the employees become dedicated to accomplishing the current mission, working with others who are similarly dedicated. They offer not obedience, but intelligence: they will not do whatever they are asked, but they *will* do whatever they can to further the mission. The relationship lasts as long as the organizational vision and the individual commitments are close enough to lead to a sense of mutual contribution. After that, as several said to me in almost identical words, it is "time to move on to something else."

This seems, to use some modern jargon, like a "win-win" for everyone. If the whole organization is sharply focused on the mission, the professional relation can effectively bring together people who care about and are committed to that particular direction, who *want* to be there. When the mission changes, for whatever reasons, the company should be able to shift its focus; when individuals change, they should be better prepared to pursue their goals. Indeed, for the four dynamic companies I studied, the promise seemed largely fulfilled: most of the managers were enthusiastic, and at least three of the four organizations were clearly performing at very high levels.

Of course the solution is not so simple. There are many obstacles to making this ideal work, and much to be done to make it viable beyond a few special cases. Later I will look at some of the ways in which even the best examples fall short, and the difficulty of solving the problems.

Nevertheless, despite these difficulties, I believe that the "community of purpose" prefigured in these best cases could be an effective model for the future. It solves (at least conceptually) some problems central to modern corporations and even to the broader society. It does what all forms of community must do: it lays the moral basis for mutual obligations and stable relationships, and therefore for effective cooperation. But it does so in a way that avoids the limitations and the major oppressive aspects of traditional communities, including the familiar loyalty bargain in corporations: their inescapable, permanent nature, and their pressure for conformity and homogeneity. The evidence from the best organizations I studied suggests that it is possible, at least in some circumstances, to build such a community.

The Key Elements

Let me give more detail on the key elements of this ethic.

INDIVIDUALS WITH COMMITMENTS

The most positive individuals I spoke to were not those wholly devoted to the company, but those with independent interests. The ones who oriented themselves to the company, like "the organization man," quite naturally felt betrayed and confused by the sudden shifts in strategy and expectations. Those who had independent bases, by contrast, could be (and often were) very critical of their companies—especially when they were in troubled organizations—but they seemed to know where they stood. They had their own compass to steer them through what to others seemed like incomprehensible events.

The independent interests were of several sorts. A few people, like John Hall in the last chapter, were focused especially on the development of a particular technology or technique. A larger group identified with a profession, especially engineers and accountants. This was not automatic: many engineers—those who considered themselves loyalists—did not feel an independent identity as professionals, and rarely engaged in outside conferences or seminars. But a subset did emphasize the importance of maintaining contacts with the wider profession and keeping in touch with the latest developments in the field, whether their company expressed a need for it or not.

Another interesting group—about a dozen—saw themselves as change agents, able to move from organization to organization while bringing a special ability to mobilize people around projects. Note, for example, this person's use of the language of passion:

> I know what I want to do with my own career. I'm focused. I have a burning passion to be a turnaround specialist. It doesn't matter whether inside or outside of Crown.
>
> With my last group I got it working so well that I could let them run themselves and then I could do what I like best, which is developing new programs. Middle management needs to be . . . visionary.

This group often spoke of outside training programs in organization development, leadership, team building, and so on. They attended these themselves, and they encouraged their subordinates to attend, because they saw these skills as generalizable ones that could help build a career across companies.

Still another group defined their focus in terms of the industry—"I'm a car nut"—and imagined moving to another company to better realize their vision of what a car company should be. Some people had actually done it: besides Hall, who had some elements of this focus, I was struck by a person from Saturn:

> I came to Saturn three and a half years ago from Ford because of the opportunity and excitement of starting something new, something that hasn't been done since the days of Henry Ford and probably will never be done again. I was a manufacturing engineer in the Taurus Sable program, which was exciting. . . . Here there are so many things that need to be done in developing the team and systems.

Like many in the best companies, this man could be critical of his company, and indeed expressed many things he thought needed to be changed, on the basis of his previous experiences and his ideals of how a company should be run.

Professionals also talked about important commitments that were not directly related to work—social groups, politics, communities, and families. For loyalists, these types of concerns are defined as "personal," and therefore not legitimate to raise at work. The professionals were open about them.

This was especially true of women and minorities. There was, for example, a particularly impressive and clearly successful black woman at Glover. She was the *only* one in the more than thirty I spoke to in that organization who had a sophisticated understanding of the business and the competitive reality, and who recognized the serious problems that were being denied by her peers. Yet she also spent considerable time talking about her family and the tensions she felt with her job, especially at crucial moments of her daughter's adolescence. This never happened among the loyalists: it seemed that they accepted an unspoken code that to speak of family commitments was to put in question the seriousness of their loyalty to the company.

Other commitments besides family matters were important to the professionals. As I have indicated, they were far more involved than the loyalists in outside associations that provided skills and relations beyond the company. Some of them were also committed to social movements, like those of women and minorities, and brought those into the workplace. This was rare in my sample, so I don't want to overstate it, but it was noticeable that it was far more legitimate to express issues about black or female identity for the professionals than for the loyalists. Occasionally this led to the beginnings of caucuses to pursue these issues.

These commitments often required difficult judgments. For loyalists, the demands of the corporation come first, and all others are subordinate; even their families would have to pick up and move if the company demanded it. For professionals, the mix was far more even. Promotions and career moves were explicitly weighed against family needs, and sometimes against the sense of allegiance to communities or social groups. I heard several stories of promotions foregone or transfers resisted for these reasons, and others of minorities taking their courage in both hands to express to their bosses a sense that they, not as individuals but as social groups, were being wronged. This was never an easy proposition, even in the most enlightened companies; people often had to work themselves up to a pitch of anger in order to take such a "disloyal" step. Challenges of this sort were possible solely due to developed commitments to legitimate social groups. And clearly some companies are struggling to adapt to these pressures. A woman at Emon noted, "Ten years ago you really couldn't turn down a transfer; now, if you have good family reasons, you can, without destroying your career."

For professionals, then, there is no easy calculus, and the company does not always come first.

ORGANIZATIONS WITH A MISSION

The successful organizations had also defined a sense of mission that clarified and limited their commitment to their employees.

"Missions," like "teams," have become something of a fad in the recent years: almost all large companies have issued solemn documents that hang on walls throughout the organization. But just as there are teams that mean something and ones that don't, so missions come in several flavors.

In the dynamic companies, unlike the rest, missions are complex and time-limited. They are not eternal general values, nor are they specific yearly performance goals. They specify a course for the organization for a particular phase, usually over a time frame of two to five years.

This is different from the orientation to very long-term values or culture characteristic of loyalist organizations. The organizations with the highest loyalty are those with the strongest "cultures." Here is a typical value statement of this type:[1]

> Everyone will work together to achieve Mazda's corporate goals through management policies; "everlasting effort for everlasting cooperation."

At the other extreme is the very short-term, goal-focused approach advocated by "tough-minded" consultants and managers. This has some conceptual appeal for dealing with rapid change: it is a radical break with the paternalist past. But this was not the way the dynamic organizations in my study worked. They rejected an environment of rapid turnover and short-term focus because it disrupts people's ability to work together.

Instead, the dynamic groups sought something in the middle: a general sense of enthusiasm and sharing, but for a limited time and a particular project. There was a general definition of the *challenges faced by the organization* in the current period.

This kind of mission is positive and complex. It is not a matter of generalities, nor is it a matter of "beating the competition." It is a rich picture of the basic issues faced by the organization and what is needed to deal with them. It involves multiple purposes that are often in tension but are intertwined, such as cost reduction and quality improvement.

Given this level of complexity, missions were generally not written up on the walls of the dynamic organizations; but middle managers could define in a consistent way the key priorities and issues in the current phase. And this then became the frame within which everyone focuses together. At Barclay it was implementing the just-in-time system and reducing costs below the competition; at Apex it was establishing a new market; at Dest, an employee explained,

> The president has put a challenge out. He's put out five things that we want to accomplish, including be number one in customer satisfaction and be one of the top three players in the industry, and the result was that everyone stepped back and said what can we do to achieve those goals.
>
> We got together and zeroed in on those goals and figured out what we could do. We focused on customer satisfaction which included getting better coordination with research and development and we also focused on the profit goal. I myself offered to put myself under research and development, because I know that in our competitors R&D and manufacturing are one department. We need better coordination there. That hasn't happened yet, but that offer certainly reduced the turf issues.

SHARED PURPOSE: "NEGOTIATING" THE IMPLICIT CONTRACT

The coming together of individual and organization in the professional organization is a kind of balancing act, or negotiation. This was not in any of the cases a formal negotiation, but rather a constant process of open communication about the relationship.

These managers spoke a language of balance: an Apex manager said,

> I have a tremendous amount of loyalty to this company because I have a lot of myself in it. But at the same time I have my own personal career objectives and my own values and I don't consider myself a lifelong employee.

One important difference from the loyalist ethic is that in these organizations it was legitimate to talk publicly about individual purposes as well as corporate ones. Complaints about working conditions, which were essentially taboo in loyalist organizations,[2] were far more common in the dynamic group. Because these organizations were not promising permanent security, they had to pay more attention to other needs and commitments of their employees.

For loyalists the idea that corporate purpose could change, and that their particular skills and interests could no longer be needed by the corporation, is a basic violation of the moral contract. They believe that if they have put in time and good-faith effort, the corporation has an obligation to find a way to use them:

> They send you along and you are swimming along and then all of a sudden one day they say you don't fit the mold anymore. But I've been here for twenty years. Bang. You send the guy forty-five years old out on the street who's making $60,000, where is he going to get another job?

For the professionals, by contrast, the assumption is that the match between individual and organization is a temporary one, defined by the frame of the project or mission. The fact that you have done your best for twenty years is not the point, and entails no obligation on the part of the company; contributing to the current direction of the firm is what matters.

The relationship requires a sense from both sides that it is productive. Therefore the main *moral* obligation on both sides is to be aboveboard in discussing interests and commitments. This is essential to the functioning of a system in which both sides are trying to reach an accommodation of purpose: as an Apex "professional" put it,

> What's the psychological contract? The main thing is to keep things open. We have agreed to have open agendas, nothing hidden, no hidden agendas, to be open and honest with each other.

On one side, honesty requires managers to talk about their own needs and plans. In the troubled companies these were suppressed: at Lyco, to refer back to chapter 5, we saw how people avoided raising issues of job quality or personal needs. Among professionals, such expression was encouraged. Leaders quickly recognized the legitimacy of family demands, as well as requests for professional development through outside experience. They treated very seriously any complaints about excess pressure. While there was still some reticence, middle managers told me they were generally willing and able to voice these issues.

On the other side, honesty requires "full disclosure" by the company of its plans and prospects. Again, those struggling in the troubled organizations frequently found the task complicated by a systematic lack of openness. A major reason for this is that it is part of the paternalistic aspect of the culture of loyalty to protect subordinates. With the best of intentions, higher managers (as we saw in the case of Lyco)[3] typically pull punches, disguise the extent of the problems, try to take the burdens on themselves rather than "worrying" those dependent on them.

But such an attitude makes impossible a genuine accommodation between individual and organization: it puts power in the hands of the latter, which then has to take on the responsibility to use it wisely. For the more successful companies, it was a central principle to be fully honest about the future—not making promises which could not be kept, not softening or shading the extent of potential changes.

The central point of reference for the "negotiation" process is the company's mission—its direction over the next few years:

> I think one of the best things that a company must do is to set clearly what the goals are, in order for everybody to know if those goals fit with your personal goals. Because if you have that information in advance and they don't fit, you better not go in. I always say what I perceive my personal success in doing this is that my personal goals and the goals of the company are positive ones, and they don't conflict.

Though the professional view is more conditional, less embracing than the paternalist community, it is not entirely "cold"; not is it amoral. The relationship does involve moral obligations for both parties. The "negotiation" between individual and organizational interests, if both sides are honest, establishes *commitments* for the duration of the project or phase.

These commitments are not absolute, but they are still binding. If things change—if business gets drastically worse than expected, or the employee finds a hot new career opportunity—there is an obligation to make the other party whole as much as possible for that period. The company does not have an obligation to guarantee employment, but it does have one to help employees cope with changes that were not predicted and are beyond their control: sudden layoffs, for instance, should entail significant help in finding something else. Employees do not have an obligation to stay forever, but if they want to leave suddenly they do need to help make sure the project gets done: by staying long enough to find a replacement, by helping to train new people, and so on.

It is clear that the balance, the coming together of commitments and missions, is much more complex than the implied contract of loyalty. While loyalty is simple and permanent, the professional relationship is mixed and temporary. It requires constant attention and care from all parties.

The Potential Strengths of a Community of Purpose

The traditional corporate community, as we saw in chapter 4, is fundamentally unable to manage the growing challenges of diversity and continuous change. In order to build the needed level of trust it makes long-term promises to individuals, and expects in return subordination of personal needs. But this bargain leads both to suppression of claims of diversity and to inflexibility in the face of outside pressures.

One alternative is the "free agent" ethic espoused by many economists. This renounces the search for community and sets individuals free to sink or swim on their own. But that is not what the "professionals" have in mind: they believe in the need for deliberate cooperation. What they represent is an attempt, however imperfect, to find a way of working together that does not involve dependence on an organization.

THE INADEQUACY OF A "FREE-AGENT" ETHIC

The ethic of the marketplace gained greatly during the 1980s. As an ethic, it is extremely meager: the obligations of employees and companies are limited to specific legally binding contracts. In this view there is nothing wrong with leaving for a little more money somewhere else, and there is nothing wrong with laying off people on short notice.

This attitude is the polar opposite of the ethic of loyalty, and it is therefore one dramatic way of breaking free of the past. It is not purely a coincidence that the 1980s, which marked the downfall of old corporate loyalties, also saw the Reaganite celebration of individualism.

But in the context of corporations, the market approach is less useful for building the new than for breaking down the old. Virtually no one in my interviews embraced a free-agent ethic. The loyalists, quite naturally, viewed it with intense contempt, almost horror. But the professionals were also critical of pure individualism and pursuit of personal gain. Though they were open about their personal needs, they always stressed the element of challenge. For them, to leave without completing the task that drew them is both wrong and an admission of defeat.

They also argued strongly that the free-agent approach was bad for a business. Even those who had moved through several companies in their careers did not support a "superstar" mentality: people who were only interested in their own advancement, they said, break up the teamwork necessary to get things done. A Dest manager told me, "When I first started I tried to hire superstars. I was thinking of a company like the Dallas Cowboys, where everybody was a star. But I found that they would work for six months and then want to do something else. So now we have a more diverse group." Again, the touchstone was the project: people had to stay together long enough to get the project done, to meet the challenge, and then they could move on to other things.

One popular policy that reflects the assumptions of free agency is the move to link pay more tightly with performance. This idea seems so logical, and had such currency in the 1980s, that most of the companies in my sample had introduced or enlarged variable-pay schemes. This seems like a promising way to distinguish those who are performing well from those who are not, and to encourage the former to stay and the latter to go.

But very few managers I spoke to liked pay-for-performance plans much or thought they were effective. Among loyalists, not surprisingly, the reaction was fiercely negative. Indeed, at GM, a bastion of loyalism, a 1986 attempt to force managers to give differential rewards to their subordinates met with such resistance that it was withdrawn a year later. Such schemes attack a fundamental assumption of loyalty: that all employees will be protected if they do their best.[4]

What is significant is that most *professionals* were also critical, though more mildly, of pay-for-performance plans. They too stressed the importance of maintaining teamwork and avoiding a pure dog-eat-dog environment. In keeping with their general approach, they sought a balance—somehow recognizing individual contribution without denying the importance of the group. They were not satisfied with the pay system in any of the organizations in my study. The problem of balancing individual versus group contribution, and short-term versus long-term performance, still seems too complex to have produced a good system, in their eyes.

Overall, my evidence on the effectiveness of the free-agent relationship is almost entirely negative: nobody and no organization I studied really practiced it. This in itself certainly suggests there is something wrong with it. Rejection of free agency was just as characteristic of those who embraced change in general as of those who resisted it. I can't prove that they are right, but I can make an argument about why I think they are.

The problem is that business organizations need a higher level of cooperation than can be achieved through market systems. On a broad scale markets can work pretty well to focus collective effort by moving the highest rewards to the areas of highest demand. What Adam Smith meant by "the invisible hand" was that markets lead people to cooperate without being aware of it. But large-scale production requires more than that: it requires conscious cooperation. It would be far too slow and cumbersome to get people to sign contracts for specific services every time you want to adjust your goals. There needs to be some general commitment by a group of people to work together.[5]

Loyalty is one form of general commitment: in exchange for protection, people agree to do what they are told. The professional relation is a different form, in which people agree to work together on a task. The free-agent approach, however, fails to provide any basis for conscious working together.

That is the essence of the practical argument that almost everyone I spoke to made: that if you are dealing with people who put their personal interests too far above those of the organization, you can't work effectively with them and you can't get things done. The moral argument about the value of organizations is another matter, to which I will return.[6]

RESOLVING THE TENSIONS

The first part of this study argued in essence that loyalty is too limited to hold people together in situations of rapid change and diversity. Free agency moves to the other extreme, which creates its own problems. One might say loyalty creates too thick a bond, and free agency a bond too thin.

Professionalism balances the two ends of the continuum. It places neither the organization's needs nor those of the individual in the dominant position, but values them both. It therefore looks for ways to negotiate the relationship and to build common interests.

Faced with the pressures of change, loyalists are lost, bewildered, often angered. They have no good solutions. Many of them feel they are being forced into a free-agent attitude, which they hate. In effect they jump from one extreme to the other: from a focus on the group to a focus on themselves. But they find this so repugnant that they tend to jump right back again. They hang onto loyalty as long as there is any possibility of maintaining it, leading to the defensive conservatism we observed in chapters 4 and 5.

The professionals, however, feel much more confident: they can give up loyalty without feeling lost, and also without embracing the opposite ethic of pure individualism. They hold a balance that maintains both the freedom of the individual and a commitment to cooperation.

Let me illustrate by tracing a discussion I had, centering on this theme, with a mixed group of managers at an executive education program. I started by laying out the three types of responses to corporate restructuring: loyalism, free agency, and professionalism. Most of the group immediately said they *wanted* to be loyalists. But like so many we have already heard in the troubled companies, they felt bewildered. They felt that since their companies had violated the compact they perhaps had no choice but free agency; yet they resisted this alternative mightily:

> I am an extreme loyalist, but because of the pain that I have been put through as a young middle management person for twelve years now, I am heading toward free agency. I work for an organization that was able to get people to be so loyal because ... they don't have a lot of other business experiences, they worked their way up this organization.
>
> But what happened is that we had to implement painful decisions that we were not a part of making—having to sit across the table from somebody and saying, "You don't have a job. Your $80,000 is gone now. Your house payment of $3,200 a month cannot be made."
>
> Then you begin to realize this isn't a family. This is a business. It's like a husband who has an affair on you. What I mean is, you may forgive, but you never forget. So you say, "Maybe I should be a little bit more of a free agent."

In the same group, though, were several people who clearly and strongly identified themselves with the "professional" category.

> I have no intention to be a loyalist to any company, whatever it can do for me. As far as I'm concerned, if you want loyalty go get a dog.

> Today, it's almost impossible in my industry to be a loyalist. You can't do it, because you can walk in on any given morning and your job is gone. It's just a fact of life.
> *So is it basically a free agent?*
> No, I would say professional, ... in the sense that I'm there to do the best I can. I will stay for as long as that relationship remains positive for both of us, for the bank and myself.

What is significant is that as the "professionals" in the group talked, the loyalists started to embrace this ethic as a better alternative. Though they had a hard time grasping it, it seemed more attractive than pure free agency. One professed loyalist responded to my summary of the professional point of view by struggling to adapt his beliefs:

> I think it's a more progressive loyalist view. If you want to have a family-type atmosphere in your business, if you want people to be loyal to you, there are two different ways. One is what my dad had in his job years back: you were loyal, you had a good job, you were going to get a 7 percent cost-of-living increase every year. Now companies have more of an obligation to earn that loyalty. So they earn that loyalty, but we all know it's a business.

This person is trying on the one hand to hold on to the idea of a "family-type atmosphere" like that in his father's day, and on the other hand to deal with the fact that "we all know it's a business." He moves toward thinking of it as a negotiated, "earned" relationship centered on the business, rather than the unconditional acceptance of the past.

Another person who described himself as a former loyalist who has been pushed away from that attitude added:

> I don't think, as a manager, you want loyalty—you don't want blind loyalty, anyway. I think it doesn't do the organization any good to have just total blind loyalists on everything you want to do. The organization doesn't grow, because everybody is just following the line of what is being said instead of bringing new ideas to the organization.
>
> That's the balance. Again, I think we are groping for something in the middle. That's what I feel.

This discussion captures in microcosm the pattern of this study: the loss of loyalty, the rejection of free agency, and the effort to construct the balance I have called "professional." The fundamental strength of the professional ethic as I have described it is that it balances the sense of meeting one's own needs with that of contributing to something larger, in a way that allows for dynamic change. It enables people to deal with the loss of a "family" atmosphere without falling into cynicism and it allows companies to adapt to new circumstances without falling into a cold "sink or swim" philosophy.

Problems and Cautions:
The Limitations of the Best Cases

The suggestion that mobility is a good thing and that loyalty is not troubles most people I have tried it on, whether corporate managers or just interested observers. It violates their basic perceptions of how people work together, and contradicts basic moral definitions of good relationships. It seems to lead toward loss of caring and community and to open the door to unhealthy selfishness rather than cooperation.

That skepticism must be taken seriously. I have a few cases that seem to go against the accepted wisdom, but that does not make them right. The leap from cases to general principles is often made far too easily, which produces a lot of fads. In moving from an example (or even four examples) to a model, it is necessary to think about the underlying logic, and to examine closely the weaknesses, limitations, and long-term prospects of the examples used.

I believe, as I have just argued, that the professional ethic and the community of purpose offer the best way out of the problems posed for middle managers by continuous change and increased diversity. I also believe we can outline the things that have to be done to make it work. But the truth is that there remain many serious problems to overcome. Even the most successful organizations in my study have major limitations.

The first problem is obvious, and I have not forgotten it: the issue of career security is not really resolved in these companies. What happens to people who can't get jobs when they need to "move on to something else"?

I did not interview people who were currently unemployed, but I know it is a desperate circumstance.[7] For the purposes of this study, which is about the employment relationship, the question is whether the fear of unemployment will eventually corrode the links of shared purpose between organization and employees.

Aside from the few who had actually demonstrated an ability to market their skills, most of the professional types I spoke to remained uneasy about the future. They were, to be sure, far more optimistic than their loyalist counterparts, believing that the experience they were gaining would serve them well if they needed to go into the outside market, but they were not fully sure it would work.

What appears to be happening is that people have simply not confronted the issue yet. Career aspirations are relatively long-term and can be somewhat delayed, especially in a crisis, without major readjustment. But no one in my sample had an answer for the longer term, and most agreed that the piper would have to be paid in the end.

In short, the ethic of career mobility had for most people not really been tested. Only a small minority had actually proved their ability to move from company to company.

This leads to the second limitation: none of the examples I have been using has survived long enough or succeeded thoroughly enough to prove that it is possible permanently to run an organization in the shifting, open, flexible way that characterized the dynamic group. None of them had institutionalized a professional community on a wide scale for a long period of time. Though they had succeeded in some instances in building flexible teamwork, they all showed shortcomings and signs of fragility. They were, at best, partway along the road.

Some people in Apex were particularly conscious of their distance from the target. They stressed that most effective "teaming" still took place within the restricted community of the small work group. The cooperation beyond that scope was, by all indications, better than most, but still far below what was sought:

> The camaraderie has not spilled over into other business units. There are so many things that need to be done in developing the team and systems within the business units, but [there is] not enough opportunity to get out and interface with other divisions.

Decision making therefore fell short of the ideal in most parts of the organization, especially when problems went beyond the scope of the small team. There was a tendency to blur responsibility and to avoid clear commitments:

> I have trouble finding people to make decisions. In theory it allows you to get in touch with the actual end-users and get people with ownership involved in decision-making processes. In actuality often someone has responsibility but not authority, so the decision doesn't stick, or more people want to get in later.

The other "dynamic" cases had their problems as well. In the case of Dest, the culture I have been describing was well-developed only in parts of the organization, and only at a relatively high level—within three or four levels of the CEO. Though this was far enough to move beyond the scope of immediate personal relationships, it left a great deal of resistance and confusion at crucial levels of management. The organization was still in big trouble overall. Barclay was a small organization—a single plant—so the problem of working out an extended impersonal network was not really put to the test. Yet even in this context many noted a continuing tendency for subparts of the organization to assert autonomy rather than interdependence.

Most interesting of all, from this perspective, was Crown. This division, it seemed, had gone a long way toward a professional community about three years previously. There had been a remarkable change process spurred by new competition, culminating in a complex set of task forces and committees that, according to most sources, had worked quite well. But this "Quality Improvement Process" (QIP) had fallen on hard times. Although there had been no layoffs, the new mechanisms of cooperation had been put under a series of intense pressures: the parent company had acquired another company with a traditional culture that had taken away much of Crown's work; they had moved to a new location; and at the time of my interviews they were in the middle of a very stressful shift to a new information management system.

These pressures appear to have been too much for the cooperative commu-

nity that had existed previously, forcing most people back toward individualistic autonomy. There were many remnants of the professional perspective:
a sense of pride in the mission, a very sharp business focus, a sense of commitment rather than loyalty. Clearly a good deal of spontaneous cross-functional coordination was continuing in the framework of the QIP network: Yet
the predominant mood was one of exhaustion and an inability to sustain the
new connections:

> "The organization's having a tough time, it's really just this overload of
> things so you turn off for a while. People just feel left alone with little sup-
> port."

> "QIP is going through a valley now. We haven't had time recently to go
> through the process. It's true that people feel alone. We don't have the oppor-
> tunity to sit down very often and talk about our problems."

In short, the professional structure had not yet proved itself anywhere in
this sample to be deeply institutionalized or robust. Though its level of teamwork was clearly higher than the troubled organizations, it had not consistently solved the essential problem: how to put together teams as needed for
problem solving without the lengthy process of personal trust building.
"Teamwork" tended to get stuck within small and stable teams, rather than
framing a flexible problem-solving approach throughout the larger organization. In one case where the larger community was put under pressure, it
tended to fragment.

Finally, I would note some evidence that not everyone could make the move
to a professional orientation. I was impressed, on the whole, by how thoroughly
lifetime loyalists, when moved into one of the dynamic organizations, seemed to
convert to the new values and to feel liberated by them. Most said that they
were growing and learning more than ever before, and that their work was
more interesting, even less stressful. But a few I spoke to didn't seem to be
making it. By all accounts (besides the ones I met myself, I heard stories of others) such outright failures were a small minority, perhaps on the order of 10
percent. But that is certainly enough to pose an ethical problem, and to bring
into focus the fact that we don't know much about what it takes for people to
make this transition.

These difficulties tell us that none of the actual cases, even the most positive,
has yet solved the problem: none has achieved a stable form of unity without
loyalty. Both moral and practical problems remain. The system does not treat
everyone fairly—indeed, it may increase the gap between the fortunate and the
unfortunate. And it has not produced the kind of reliable large-scale cooperation that was characteristic of loyal bureaucracies at their best. These companies have only indicated a possibility.

What Is Still Needed for It to Work?

There remain, then, two big problems.

1. Organizing firms so that they can function effectively with less hierarchy and more discourse, freedom of movement, and acceptance of employee needs.
2. Opening labor markets so that mobility is a real option for more employees—including providing support for those caught by circumstances.

This study has paid a good deal of attention to the first of these—the transformation of organizations, since my data come from managers within companies. The second level, "above" the firm, has received a lot less attention here and elsewhere, but it is equally important. The transformation of the employment contract does not only happen inside individual firms; it also changes the whole labor market among firms.

These two areas are crucial for the development of the community of purpose. A third issue, I think, is less central for practice, though important for understanding: that is the psychological changes involved for managers in making the transition. I treat it as less important because I don't see much need for intervention on this level. Most managers do not need to be psychoanalyzed to deal with the current changes. My evidence is that, on the contrary, an effective organization can help most people change their orientation from loyalist to professional in a very positive way. But there are some individuals who have more trouble with it, and it is still important to think about how to make this move less painful for individuals.

TEAM-BASED ORGANIZATIONS

The organizational issues touch on a large body of current practice and literature. Professionals fit best in organizations that do most of their work in project teams put together from multiple levels, functional specialties, and stakes to accomplish a task. The community of purpose matches challenges with interests; temporary teams are the natural organizational form for it.

This is why the companies who had moved furthest in the "team" direction were also those who had most developed the professional ethic. But we also saw that none of them had really stabilized the system. Team-based systems are not easy to build: they are not just a modification of bureaucracy, but a fundamentally different type of organization that is now being invented, undoing a century's experience in the construction of stable hierarchies.[8]

There are at least two major problems which remain for making this new form work.

Large-Scale Consensus Building

The first problem is how to build shared understanding and purpose in a large group. Bureaucracy doesn't really require this: as we have seen, few middle managers have traditionally had any real understanding of strategy beyond their own narrow slice of the business. It is held together not by shared understanding in all parts, but by a kind of blind faith in the authority of the top. The professional form, however, demands that everyone orient to the overall purpose and think independently, breaking out of the bureaucratic box. It requires a more open level of discussion, including a willingness to challenge superiors and to cross functional lines. We have seen how uncomfortable this makes those used to the rules of bureaucracy: they see a danger of fragmentation, faction, and general confusion.

The four most successful companies nevertheless show that it can be done, at least sometimes. They, along with many others, have pioneered the developent of "organizational process": systematic consensus-building discussions throughout large organizations bringing together groups of people based on their relation to a problem rather than their position in an organization. Apex and Crown in particular conducted elaborate processes with representative multilevel groups to develop new organizational structures.

Let me recall two perspectives already discussed to show the contrast between old and new ways of acting. Sam Lax, quoted at length in chapter 6, believed that bureaucracy was necessary in order to "arbitrate" disputes among people at the same level of an organization. But Apex, when faced with a dispute between two high-level managers, explicitly avoided referring it to higher levels for arbitration. Instead it created a group including the two in question, and also the representatives of the major groups they dealt with or affected. This "stakeholder group" then worked on the issue until a consensus was reached. In this situation, a turf battle, the process avoided the bitterness typically caused by higher-level arbitration, which often pleases no one. Furthermore, by involving people with interests in the solution, it came up with something that better met everyone's needs than anything that either side proposed at first.

These processes are very hard to do. I heard about several failures at Apex as well as successes. Frequent obstacles include people who seek to play old-style "politics" and who undermine trust, and simple lack of understanding among many participants. But this is also an area of tremendous innovation. Public consensus-building dialogues were unknown in traditional organizations;

today there are many successes.[9] Thus, though it is still not possible to *reliably* build shared purpose in an organization, it is increasingly possible to do it some of the time.

Accountability Without Bureaucracy

A second problem I see frequently is accountability. When individuals move frequently among teams, when they work with many different people, when they may have many supervisors or (in the case of "autonomous" teams) none at all, how can they be held accountable?

This, too, is an area of great ferment. I think the basic path is clear, though the implementation is difficult. In bureaucracy, accountability is built into the structure—it is, in effect, automatic and doesn't have to be thought about much. In a team-based organization, accountability has to be constructed, or negotiated, for each project, and it may look different for each.

Many aspects of tasks have to have some individual to make them happen. In that case those working on a project need to agree who will take it on and what the milestones will be. So it is common, in these organizations, for teams to spend a lot of time negotiating who will take on specific projects: some volunteer, some are jokingly shamed into taking things on, others do it because they are the only ones who know a given task. Then they discuss when reports will be given and what the expectations are for each stage. When the process works well, these review points are actually remembered and held to. But it takes new habits and skills to pull off those negotiations effectively and to keep people accountable in such a varied and flexible environment, and in the early stages it can easily break down.

It is also important to have accountability and rewards for teams. Companies I am familiar with are experimenting with an enormous array of practices for dividing pay among teams and individuals, and getting assessments from all those affected by a project or an individual. Sometimes it seems that more energy is being spent in measuring performance than in actually performing. Though no clear system or answer is yet visible, many companies are managing to do it well enough to keep functioning effectively without the clarity of simple bureaucratic accountability.

There remains much to be learned in these two areas. The point I would stress, however, is that the partial successes of the dynamic companies are already the result of a great deal of learning during the last twenty years or so. This gives me faith that remaining hurdles can be worked through in time. Many companies are continuing to extend the principles of team-based organization, especially in "Total Quality" efforts, which rebuild organizations around processes—major tasks—rather than functional specialties. Much of the most popular management writing of the past decade has tried to preach this gospel or to codify the learnings.[10] The further development of these efforts is the first condition for the extension of the professional model.

OPEN LABOR MARKETS

While the development of flexible organizations has gotten a lot of attention, there is a second major problem that has gotten much less: how to improve labor markets so that movement across companies is a real option for more people. This issue can't be solved by individual firms. It lies "above" that level, involving ways of connecting firms to each other.[11]

The United States is already better in this respect than many countries. In Japan, most notably, it is apparently virtually impossible for middle managers to change companies: the internal focus of large companies is so strong that people cannot pick up in a new organization in midcareer. Still, the barriers to movement in this country, too, are substantial. We have reviewed the degree to which outsiders are treated with suspicion in most of the corporations in my study. Benefits have also been systematically structured since the early years of this century to discourage movement, especially by making pensions dependent on years of service within one company. Other common policies with the same effect include highly company-specific training programs and strong emphasis on particular corporate "cultures." Finally, since most benefits— including health insurance—are tied to employment, the risks involved in moving between companies are much higher than in countries where these benefits are provided by governments.

In order to build a professional culture, major changes are needed to make movement more feasible. These include better information for managers about opportunities and conditions of work in different companies; better access to skill training and development; and security of income and benefits during the transitions. A basic sense of security is especially important: if leaving a company carries high penalties and risks, it is impossible to have an open labor market.

The direction of change is less charted here than at the level of the organization. A natural solution might be to look to the government to provide these mechanisms—through expanded unemployment insurance, national health care and improved pensions, and skills training. But government has been caught up, too, in the rebellion against paternalism: the idea that it should "take care" of people is accepted much less than twenty years ago. The difficulty of getting even modest health care reform through a Democratic Congress is a current measure of how deep the suspicion runs.

So far, then, not much innovation has yet occurred at this trans-firm level. In thinking about how to manage this critical area, one has to build off fragmentary efforts. My view is that a solution will need to combine three key elements: a strong network of private service and insurance providers; governmental coordination and oversight; and national associations of managers.

Market Mechanisms for Security and Mobility

Some of the most important developments so far have been in private systems to help managers deal with transitions. I am especially struck by the growing role of "headhunting" organizations, which are employed by companies to help them hire managers. They have penetrated far in a short time: a great many of the people I interviewed had been contacted by headhunters. These firms have formed, on an entirely private basis, a substantial network that cuts across firms and spreads some information about opportunities. A second growth area has been in associations for laid-off managers, which have also proliferated for the same purpose.

This is hardly enough. These networks are still extremely limited compared to the extent of the labor market: they certainly do not reliably get news of openings to the right people, and they deal only with one of the needs—information about job opportunities. They do nothing about income security, health coverage, and so on. In combination with other innovations, though, they could contribute to a more effective system than we have now.

One piece of a more complete system would be an extensive development of private insurance and services. There is no essential reason managers could not buy unemployment insurance for themselves, for example. The idea has not developed yet, in part, I think, because most managers and employers still cling to the image of traditional career tracks within one company. But if current trends continue for much longer, there will have to be a large-scale recognition of the need to protect oneself. Other forms of security—health insurance and pensions, for example—could similarly be provided by insurance mechanisms.

Insurance companies are not very popular at the moment, as their role in health care is hotly debated. There are serious problems, from preventing fraud to guaranteeing that those at high risk will be covered. To meet the needs of managers private insurance would have to be mediated by government and intermediate associations.

The Role of Government

Government could almost certainly not, in the current political environment, provide security on its own. But it still has a role, though a changing one: it has been shifting away from being a provider of security to coordinating private efforts. There are certainly things it could do to develop labor markets which would fit this image, and therefore be politically feasible.

- It could organize data banks of managers and jobs to improve the ability to get matches—several states have already begun to do this, though they tend to focus so far at the blue-collar level.
- Through tax incentives, it could encourage savings to cover transitional periods. Individual Retirement Accounts, Keoughs, 401(K)s, and so on are existing ways to encourage people to save for retirement. The government would do well to encourage similar accounts to be drawn on in periods of unemployment.
- It could provide back-up support and a regulatory framework for private insurance networks—a "safety net," to use a much-abused term.

The role of government in relation to markets and insurance companies is much debated now; I won't try to canvass that issue here. The essential point is that the change in the employment relation requires mechanisms that cut across many firms, rather than the single-firm benefit systems we have now. Government is one such higher-level mechanism, and markets are another. The nation seems to be groping for a new relation between the two in many spheres, and this is one where it is greatly needed.

Another area much in need of development is the law of the employment relationship. The traditional doctrine of "employment at will," dating to the 1880s, is based on old master-servant codes. It supports a crude version of personal loyalty, placing heavy obligations of loyalty on employees, but allowing employers to dismiss people without notice or justification.

Clearly a professional employment relation does not fit with such a conception of law. There needs to be some recognition of the mutual nature of the relationship, balancing the commitments of employees with the requirements of employers for the completion of particular tasks.

Significant movement has been made in this direction in the past few decades, though without overall coherence. The employment at will doctrine has been deeply eroded by both legislation and court rulings. "Personal" needs of employees, viewed as illegitimate in a loyalist conception, have gained some protection: employers are now required to respect such demands as (depending on the jurisidiction) family obligations, religious convictions, sexual orientation, political beliefs, and physical disabilities.

But we are still a long way from a coherent doctrine defining the rights and obligations of a professional relationship. Some in the legal community—most notably Ian MacNeil—have begun to sketch the norms underlying such an employment contract.[12] Without getting too far into alien terrain, I would note a few basic principles of the ethic sketched above that might well form a basis for lawyerly elaboration:

1. The obligation of both parties to full disclosure of all information that might affect the mutual commitment, including business prospects on the part of the employer and personal obligations on the part of the employee.
2. The right of employees to voice personal concerns, with a corresponding obligation of employers to make "reasonable accommodations" (to use the existing language of the Americans with Disabilities Act).
3. The right of employers to commitment from employees for the term of given projects; with a corresponding obligation for the employee, if seeking to leave in the middle of the task, to help find a replacement or other means of completing it.
4. The obligation of the employer to provide predictability and security for the term of the project, including a duty, if unforeseen crises arise, to make the employee whole as much as possible through job placement, severance, or other means.

Intermediate Bodies: Managerial Associations

Part of the answer is that markets and government are not enough: there needs to be a third set of institutions between them, pulling together groups with common interests. Government regulation is appropriate for things that must be uniform on a large scale; markets are appropriate for things that are truly individual choices. But when there are concerns that touch on social groups, something needs to organize those interests.

In the case of middle managers this would mean managerial associations. They are needed for two major purposes: to make sure that benefit systems (whether coming from government or the private market, or in combination) meet the needs of this group, and to help individual managers make sense of the choices.

An obvious role is in organizing an insurance market for unemployment and benefits. If this remains a purely individual matter, the same thing will happen here as in health care: those who really need it won't get it. The people at greatest risk—those in troubled companies or shrinking industries, or with outdated skills—will be left out. The solution is to pull together the whole class, high- and low-risk, to negotiate pooled agreements. This, of course, is the approach long ago developed by the American Association of Retired Persons for its members, and adopted by health care groups, unions, and other membership associations.

A second function of managerial groups would be to give members the information they need to choose among all the options in planning their careers. Few people have the knowledge to do effective financial planning, to prepare for the inevitable risks of shifting jobs, or to structure themselves a good package of retirement and health benefits. This lack of knowledge can be a powerful force keeping people anchored in jobs they don't like, with employers who don't really want them.

A third function would be to give managers information about different companies, so that they have a basis for the negotiation process I have described as central to the professional relationship. Some professional associations have been doing this, circulating summaries of wages and working conditions at corporations where their members work. Some have even published standards they expect employers to meet, which gives individuals a little more leverage in the discussion.

A fourth role would be to help members develop the generalizable skills needed for flexible careers. This is a service that professional associations have increasingly provided for their members: classically, groups like the Institute of Electrical and Electronics Engineers (IEEE) have offered courses and certification programs so that members could gain knowledge beyond company-specific training programs. A good managerial association might provide education in "general management" skills like strategy, organization change, team-based management, and the use of advanced information systems; such knowledge would greatly increase most people's mobility.[13]

So far managers, unlike professionals, have not organized effectively in this way. Very few in my interviews referred to any kinds of associations at all (even though this was a question I asked regularly). Those who did referred to two types: professional associations of the kind just described—of engineers or accountants; or internal "caucuses" around social identity—women, gays, and blacks, and the disabled.

Caucuses remain a largely hidden phenomenon, and it is hard to know how widespread they are. I ran across a number among my interviewees. Two of them, at Emon, were encouraged by company management and were brand-new. One, a black group at Karet, was highly adversarial and underground, and had recently surfaced to file a suit against the company. (I did not manage to track down any of its members.) I heard references to groups of women and blacks, at Apex and Dest, that met independently to discuss career opportunities and skill development.

Some recent research has uncovered similar caucuses at many companies. One of the best-documented is the black caucus at Xerox, which in over more than a decade of life has had a huge impact in increasing the number of blacks at high levels of the company. The computer industry is apparently full of electronic bulletin-board discussion groups around social identities. Many companies in this industry, being new, stress loyalty less than most, and they also have developed the technology of network communication to a high degree.[14]

In general, the members of caucuses I spoke to saw them not as adversarial bodies, but as ways of helping members balance their personal interests with the company needs. These associations often do offer courses in general management skills, and occasionally organize private benefit pools. But they tend to be single-company organizations, and therefore don't go far in helping people think beyond their current career horizons.

Caucuses and professional groups do some things, but not the most important things: they do not provide *cross-company* support *for managers*. At the moment, there is very little activity in this area. For example, involvement with national groups of women or minorities, among the managers I interviewed, was rare—or at least they didn't relate it to their work lives. And no one mentioned the American Management Association, which would seem to be a natural to play the kinds of roles I have described but apparently has failed to do so.

The reason, I think, is that most companies still strongly oppose any kind of managerial association. Within the logic of loyalty, which most companies and managers still hold to, getting involved in something that encourages looking beyond the firm is tantamount to treason. It is a career-killer within the company, even though it might be a career-saver beyond it. Few are willing to risk their current positions, fragile though they may be, for an alternative that doesn't even exist yet.

But this is a short-sighted view. If companies want to move beyond the limitations of loyalty and bureaucratic stability, they must accept that their employees will constantly explore opportunities. Management associations are essential to giving managers anchors of skills, security, and information outside the firm. This is a third crucial piece in the development of open labor markets.[15]

THE PSYCHOLOGY OF ADAPTABILITY

I will add only a few words about the psychological perspective. The evidence from my interviews clearly supports that of other studies that have stressed the trauma and pain caused by the managerial layoffs.[16] This pain involves not only the obvious loss of income and standard of living but also the moral upheaval of losing a community, of trust betrayed. While other studies have documented it among the laid-off, I found it as strongly among those who remained employed. Among the latter, it produced a set of defensive reactions, including the "retreat to autonomy" described in chapter 4.

Does the adoption of a professional orientation involve a fundamental psychological transformation? The people I spoke to implied that it was relatively easy. I observed managers who were lifelong loyalists who, when transplanted into Apex or one of the other dynamic organizations, quickly felt rejuvenated and enthusiastic about the idea of increased independence and mobility.

This seems to me to speak for the enormous power of community in defining individual orientations. Community is the boundary between the group and the individual: it defines whom individuals want to please, or whose standards they feel are important. Communities are powerful because their standards (as Freud would say) are internalized in individuals and become personal motivations. Thus when individuals are put into a context where the people they care about and respect are enthusiastically adopting a new set of standards, they can very quickly join in. This is perhaps especially easy in cases like Apex or Crown, where the top leaders were also lifetime loyalists who had converted.

But there may be more to it than my interviews showed. Most of those I talked to had not been put to the test yet—they hadn't really had to face the pain of detaching their own identity from the company. And I didn't explore the psychological learning process of those who had in fact built careers across multiple companies. This may be a harder process than they let on or the others expect.

There is one very impressive study, by Paul Leinberger and Bruce Tucker, which complements this one by looking more deeply at the psychological angle, focusing on managers who had been laid off. Their evidence suggests that building a personality which is tough enough and flexible enough to avoid dependence on an organization is a difficult process.[17]

Their description of managers who have successfully coped with layoffs has much in common with what I have called a "professional" orientation: their word is "subject-directed." These managers have constructed their own identities, not from any single social role, but from many influences. They are not primarily "managers" or "General Motors men" or any other particular role; they have put together an individual pattern that combines the identity of manager with social attachments, families, and so on. These authors come, in other words, to the same place as I have in stressing the *complexity* of commitments among managers who can cope with change.

Getting to this orientation, they find, involves a process of mourning: it is this that keeps complexity from just falling apart into depression or narcissism. People who have negotiated the trauma of change pass through a period of loss that leaves them less fixed on a single goal, more humble, and more open to discussion and dialogue with others. They become not radically individualist, but interactive; they shape their sense of right and wrong not from the absolutes of a single social group, but from discourse. Again, there is overlap between the psychological mechanisms they describe and the process of "negotiated" relationships that I outlined at the organizational level.

The managers studied by Leinberger and Tucker are not "can-do" individualists who love risk. They are people who accept the reality of constant change through a psychology of *reluctant* risk taking. Again, this connects to my own finding that the most successful managers are not "free agents," but rather people who make commitments for limited times, and who are prepared to move on when necessary.

In my terms, Leinberger and Tucker trace the psychodynamics of the professional orientation, and one crucial trajectory that brings people there from loyalism. For the people they looked at, who had been laid off, the process was a long and difficult one. But because their interviews centered on people outside of organizations, they do not answer the question of whether people can make this transition without going through actual layoffs: whether organization change of the type I have described in the dynamic companies can enable people to stretch their identity and goals in this way, and what are the marks of the passage. This is an area that needs further study.

Conclusion

The professional employment relation is a complicated balance between independent individuals and mission-focused companies. The expectations are sharply different from those built into loyalty. Rather than requiring employees to subordinate their needs to the corporation, it expects them to build their own identities and careers. From the company it demands not protection but honesty. This relation is in principle flexible enough to meet the needs of rapid change, and open enough to adapt to the demands of diverse employees.

But there is danger in this image. It can easily become an excuse for companies to reject all responsibility; it can be destructive for managers who don't have the skills or the strength to separate themselves from a paternalistic organization. There is a great deal that must still be done, within companies and in the wider society, to prepare both sides of the relationship for their new roles. I have suggested a substantial list of innovations that will be needed to make the system work; if they are left incomplete the result may be worse distress than we have now.

9

Conclusion: Managers as Professionals

T HE ETHIC of corporations has traditionally been a paternalistic one, in which a powerful organization provides security and in return demands obedience. The downsizing of middle management and the restructuring of corporations has broken the promise that corporations will take care of their managers. What are the consequences?

My research doesn't lead me to predict an uprising or even a "strike" by managers: one strong finding is the strength of the attachments that keep them loyal even while their world is being overturned.[1] But it does lead me to anticipate an extremely difficult road ahead, for managers and for corporations.

The most successful companies so far—those that have best maintained enthusiasm and a positive outlook among their managers—are those that have made the biggest changes. They have dismantled many of the structures of bureaucratic hierarchy and replaced them with flexible teams; they have opened their boundaries wide to the outside. They demand far less unconditional loyalty from their managers, encouraging independence and mobility.

But they haven't gone nearly far enough: though they are doing better than the organizations that have tried to hang on to the past, these dynamic companies still have serious problems. More thoroughgoing innovations in the structure of corporations and surrounding institutions—including new government policies—will be needed to build a system that works for the long run. In particular, we need to increase the ability to organize effective teams, especially on a large scale; we need to find ways to open labor markets to make mobility a real option for everyone; and we need to find ways to help those who find themselves in the wrong place at the wrong time in the process of change.

Let me reemphasize the difficulty of the task. The professional ethic has nothing in common with the simple nostrums of Social Darwinism: it does not suggest that companies should feel guiltless about laying people off, or that strong people shouldn't mind being laid off. Such attitudes do break the restraints of loyalty, but they put in its place a code of cynicism and one-sided competitiveness which, attractive as it may be to some economic theorists, is rejected by nearly everybody with whom I spoke.

Professionals instead seek a new form of cooperation, and they shoulder a new set of obligations. This task of reconstruction is large and only partially understood. There is much resistance and uncertainty about the path. The movement toward what I have called a "professional" orientation can very easily be derailed by resistance and uncertainty. If it is to move forward, it must be backed by compelling reasons that appeal to the interests of both corporate leadership and employees.

Why Change?

The basic reason for change is that people can no longer count on companies to structure their careers and their identities, so they have to take responsibility for themselves. If they continue to attach to and depend on a single corporation, they will get hurt; their only responses at that point will be defensive withdrawal or cynical individualism.

There are three ways for managers to make sense of the sudden wave of layoffs; two of them have destructive effects. First, they can interpret the events as a result of a temporary crisis, brought on by international competition and perhaps unfair trade practices. This would imply that once the emergency is past things will go back to normal, and that they should just wait it out. Many of those I spoke to had adopted just this passive attitude.

Second, they can see layoffs as a result of corporate selfishness, the degeneration of social bonds, the decline of morality, the replacement of caring and civility by naked financial self-interest—"the crumbling of everything." That leads people, reluctantly, toward a cold ethic of free agency, forgetting about duty and obligation, going wherever the deal is best. But most of them don't like it.

The managers I interviewed, especially those in the ten troubled organizations, generally held a discouraged combination of these two views: they hoped that loyalty could be restored, and they feared that it couldn't. Many felt themselves being driven from a community they cared for deeply, leaving them only the abhorrent option of cynical game-playing. Caught between these two choices, they tried to downplay the problems, becoming defensive and withdrawn.

There remains just one constructive way to make sense of the current upheaval: to see it as part of a larger transformation, not just a crumbling of an old order, but the construction of a new one.

That is what the more successful organizations and individuals are doing. The dynamic companies are not simply cutting heads to save money and get through a crisis: they are rejecting bureaucratic principles of organization and seeking to build flexible team-based systems. They are moving from an inward focus on building capacity to an outward focus on meeting the needs of markets and customers. Managers with a professional orientation as opposed to a loyalist stance, similarly, are not trying to wait things out or figure out what their bosses want: they are developing their own sense of what is important and the skills to back it up. On both levels there is not merely a crisis reaction to outside pressure, but the beginnings of a reordering of the employment relation.

FORCES UNDERMINING LOYALTY

I have sketched key catalysts in this transformation: continuous flexibility and diversity of values. Both of these undercut key requirements of loyalty.

Loyalty requires *stability,* and is at odds with continuous flexibility, because it is based on long-term promises of security. Loyal employees count on the company to provide for them down the road. They are willing to wait, and they are willing to give their superiors the benefit of the doubt; they are even willing, to an astonishing degree, to accept that short-term crises may require temporary suspension of the promise of security. But they cannot accept that the days of security are over for good.

Large corporations offered high stability until the 1970s; they did not expect to change fundamentally over the course of an individual's career. But that time is past, and there is no prospect that it will return. Virtually all of the companies in my study were publicly assuming that they would look very different in five years, for reasons of technology and market shifts, and that they would probably again look very different five years after that. And, as one person put it pithily,

How loyal can I be to an organization that is constantly changing?

Loyalty also requires *homogeneity* in a crucial sense: employees must subordinate their personal needs to those of the corporation. What they think, do, or value in private must not interfere with their work. Now, this may sound all right at first blush, until one realizes how much of "private" life can affect work. If you wear your hair long, it may reflect badly on the corporate image. If you are a political activist in radical causes, corporations have said (and courts have agreed) that it may undermine the corporate culture. If your children want to stay in one place, it may interfere with the need to place you in another part of the country. You may feel that women have been discriminated against, but you should never suggest that women in any way have special claims; you should just put your head down and do your best like everyone else. Violations of these

codes may not get you fired, but they are certain career-killers: the career path
is the ultimate reward and the ultimate sanction enforcing the dominance of
organizational needs.[2]

More and more employees, however, are insisting precisely on the right to
assert personal interests that do affect their jobs. They want to be able to
respond to family needs without being seen as disloyal; they want to publicly
assert their identity as women, minorities, gays, or disabled, and they want the
workplace to accommodate that identity. Those claims compete with the traditional loyalty demanded of managers, and they require a kind of negotiation in
place of automatic subordination to the organization.

The pressures for continuous flexibility and for the recognition of diverse
interests have grown stronger over the past two decades, and there is no sign
that things will settle down. At this point, corporations and individuals are
increasingly shifting gears, accepting the fact that they can no longer expect
things to return to "normal."

WHY "PROFESSIONALISM" IS BETTER

Companies now don't need loyalty. Loyalty motivates people to do their jobs
as well as possible, to work hard, to do whatever the job requires. But in a situation of continual change, obedience is not enough. What is needed now is a way
to motivate people to do *more* than their jobs—to contribute creatively to the
purpose of the whole, and to transform their jobs when necessary.

That takes an ethic in which the individual can push back against the company, rather than be dominated by it. The ideal of a loyal organization is of people responding quickly to new demands from above. The ideal of a community
of purpose is of everyone responding quickly to demands from the outside,
whether or not they are formally part of the individual's job. It requires people
to pull together quickly across functions and across levels, arguing through to
agreements rather than waiting for "arbitration" from above.

In chapter 5 I described the strict limits to legitimate "pushing back" in a
traditional organization. Loyalists essentially define a domain that is theirs:
the domain of their job assignments. They have a right, even an obligation, to
resist encroachment. So if a decree from higher up is seen as "micro-managing," trying to tell them in detail what to do—especially if it seems wrong—
they feel entirely justified in rejecting it and even fighting openly against it.
But by the same token they avoid like the plague any hint of stepping into
other's turf. They don't challenge their superiors about strategy (however
much they may complain in private!), and they don't criticize peers in their
area of functional expertise. So the terrain is neatly divided up, and conflict is
for the most part avoided.

This order, however, suppresses creativity, and it hinders responsiveness. It depends on a clear "road map" from higher levels of the organization, so that all employees know their places and their jobs. That is why the current period of transformation is so profoundly disorienting to loyalists:

> Most of us are willing to be molded and bent in any direction that is a part of Karet middle management. But we did not know what direction they wanted us to be bent.

A community of purpose is certainly messier: there is a far wider range of legitimate debate. People can argue over almost anything, including strategy and the way other functions are working. It is out of this widespread argument that responsiveness and innovation arise. The value of individuals is not that they "are willing to be molded and bent," but that they are willing to think for themselves.

What prevents it from degenerating into bickering and anarchy is the universal understanding of and commitment to the purposes of the organization: as an Apex manager put it, "The discipline of the business will pull us together." That in a sense replaces deference to superiors as the unifying force. The collective purpose is a *moral* force above the individual—which leads us to the ethical issues.

THE MORAL QUESTION

On the level of values, I for one, after the conversations reported in this book, will not mourn the loss of the paternalistic ethic of dependence and protection. But it cannot simply be abandoned. Without a shared ethic, groups fragment and individuals feel lost. Most of the managers I spoke to held fiercely to loyalty, despite company violations of its side of the bargain, because they had no alternative vision to move to.

While I hesitate to make sweeping statements about "human nature," most people appear to have a powerful need to feel that they are part of and contributing to something larger than themselves. Pure egocentrism is the negation of moral fulfillment. In any case, as I have indicated, a primary reason so many managers lament the destruction of loyalty is the sense that this will cast them and others into the abyss of asocial cynicism. So the point I would stress is that the professional ethic is in fact an *ethic:* that is, it has a definition of obligations among people in the pursuit of something beyond individual interest.

One focus of the obligations is the mission—not the company as an entity, but what it is currently trying to accomplish. It led John Hall (chapter 7) to go far beyond his technical mandate to try to improve coordination among units. It led a manufacturing manager cited earlier to offer to place himself under research and development, because he felt that that was the key driver of what needed to be done. It enables teams to work together without excessive battling over turf. It weighs in the balance in career decisions, preventing people from simply taking the best deal offered.

I cannot elaborate a philosophical argument for why this complex is better than loyalty; I can only reflect on my own responses. I feel that there is something *wrong* when a loyalist manager says, "Most of us are willing to be molded and bent in any direction," or, in another's words,

> You owe them a day's work, a hard day's work, but they owe you that grooming and that process of making you, or developing you. That's perfect. They owe you that.

What seems to me wrong is that this expectation gives too much power to the employer to "make you, develop you"; it sounds like Gepetto's relation to Pinocchio. Loyalty leaves the employee essentially in a passive position, working hard but waiting to be "molded" and "bent." It violates the essential right of the individual to shape an identity. This is what I mean by a paternalist bargain.

In the loyalist relationship the employee has no moral independence. Lest that seem too strong a statement, let me point out that it has for a century been literally true in employment law; only recently has it been challenged. Until the 1970s, for example—and in some jurisdictions down to the present day— employees got no protection from the law if they refused an order to perform an illegal act. The theory was that the illegality was the responsibility of the employer, so the employee should not take the initiative to object. This is one of the more extreme manifestations of a long-term tendency of courts to treat the burden of loyalty as almost completely unqualified. The employee must (in this view) follow the lead of the employer.[3]

As long as the company can fulfill its side of the deal by providing protection and security, loyal dependence can seem satisfying. But when security begins to break down, the underside of this ethic is revealed. I saw in these downsizing companies too many loyalist managers in their late fifties whom I can only describe as pitiable—who had hitched their entire lives and identities to a company, and who now felt lost and deeply hurt. These were, it should be remembered, *not* the people who had been laid off: these were survivors, but so dependent that they had no sense of self. A Nadir manager protested,

> I don't know what my motivation is anymore. Am I working just to retire? Why doesn't the company make use of all my knowledge and skill? Older people are still useful. We can teach the younger people. We are dedicated. Use me. I'm here. I'm willing and able.

No one should be that powerless. Yet that is a natural result of the expectation that the company will take care of one's career, that the company will provide development and security.

"Professional" managers refuse to put themselves in such a position—they have a different sense of right:

> I don't expect the company to come to me and say, "This is how we are going to help you get better." It's my obligation to say what I need in this position, and also to give the people who are underneath me . . . what we have agreed that they need. I don't believe that the company has to come down to me.

Note that this person doesn't say, "I have to take care of myself": this is not a cynical statement that you can't trust anyone. Disappointed loyalists are the ones most likely to take that attitude. What professionals say is that they have an obligation to *say* what they need, and (in their capacity as representative of the company to subordinates) to stick by *agreements*.

This aspect of the professional ethic essentially values good-faith negotiation. There is an obligation on the part of both the employer and the employee to speak honestly, to express their real interests; and then there is an obligation to live up to whatever bargain they strike. The employment relation is not a "market" contract of specific fees for specific services, but rather an agreement to work together for a time to meet broad mutual interests. The company, in addition to money, provides challenges and opportunities; the employee provides intelligence in the pursuit of the mission.

Fundamentally, then, there are two values in this professional ethic: to negotiate in good faith, and to work to accomplish the common purpose. This leaves the obligation for the development of people not on the company, but on the individual. The employee is seen as an independent moral being with multiple commitments, of which the job is only one: "private" claims can be publicly brought forward, criticisms can be voiced, without the stigma of disloyalty. For my money that is morally better than the dependent ethic of loyalty.

THE REEVALUATION OF VALUES

The shift in values involves breaking long-standing corporate taboos. Companies must first of all support independence. They must respect the personal needs of their employees. They must accept the legitimacy of "third-party" associations. They must encourage talking back to superiors. Most counterintuitive of all, they must help people to gain the skills and knowledge to move out of the company.

These are all very difficult to accept for those raised in the ethic of loyalty. The fact is that almost all the companies I studied resisted these moves, at least part of the time. In some cases the objections are explicit, in others implicit. Most business leaders accept the premise that security is no longer possible, but they have accepted only some of the consequences.

One of the easier ones for leaders to buy into rhetorically is the need for open dialogue across levels. This was a public goal at most of the companies I studied, but none of the troubled ones had effectively achieved it. The resistance often seems to come from the middle managers, not from the top. But it is really a subtle symbiosis. Since managers have been dependent on companies for their security and their future, it doesn't take much to snuff out signs of independence. It is all too easy for companies to bring the move toward a professional orientation to a halt.

Middle managers themselves *expect* any move toward openness to fail. They rarely even try to test the limits, backing off from opportunities to voice their doubts in public. Partly this is for fear of retaliation, especially in their career prospects. But there is also a more complicated, ambivalent motivation. Managers don't entirely *want* to be able to confront their superiors or to assert their independence; if they can do these things, it puts into question the stability and security of the system that they are relying on to protect them.[4]

The emerging employment contract requires "personal" issues to be treated as legitimate. There has been some movement in this area, but so far little clarity from the top about which claims are acceptable and which are "career-killers." Those who push the boundaries run grave risks. Some managers feel it is fine for a parent to leave suddenly to deal with a sick child, but many see it as a violation of the loyalty due the company. There is generally an increasing acceptance that employees have legitimate independent lives, but it is an acceptance fraught with ambivalence and mixed messages.

The tension increases with pressure from independent and diverse outside forces. The family isn't too threatening, since everyone has a family and the demands are reasonably controllable; but the idea of managers openly preparing for careers that may go outside the company raises hackles higher. And the idea of their joining outside associations—or even unions—to represent their interests and help with their choices is still completely outside the limits of acceptability.

My claim is that it is in the interests of companies to help their employees build outside connections. This is so counter to existing values that I need to elaborate it once more. In a loyalist organization, motivation is based to a very high degree on career prospects in the company. People are rarely punished immediately for failures, and there is very little pay difference; failure to live up to company standards shows up at promotion times. There is no greater source of terror for loyalist managers, no more powerful motivator, than the fear that some action will have career-damaging consequences.

But if the company can no longer promise internal career opportunity, what is the basis for motivation? If good performance doesn't guarantee rewards even in the long run, why should people try to satisfy their bosses? The logic was succinctly put by a manager at Lyco:

The lack of opportunity has really started to affect younger people. They say, "What the hell, what's the use? Why should I continue to get involved in all these quality programs? I'm not going anywhere."

Most managers are still trying to deny or ignore the fact that careers are closing within their company, but they admit it when I put the issue directly. Surely this awareness, now centered among "the younger people," will spread with time. At that point there is only one way to motivate people: to convince them that good performance *now* will help their careers *wherever they go.* The company interest, to avoid the passivity just described, is to persuade people that they have a good chance to construct a continuing career *outside* the company as things change inside.

If companies can no longer be responsible for "molding" employees, if they can no longer play the parental role, caring for them throughout their careers, then they must accept that employees have to develop motivations and connections that go outside, and in fact encourage them to do it. This takes a deep reexamination of values, but it is inescapable on the course that has been set.

Practical Implications

I have been taking the long view so far. Let me briefly sketch some more immediate implications of the argument—things that can be done now.

COMPANY POLICIES

The first implication of these examples for personnel management is that company policies should encourage employees to be mobile—freely bringing in people from the outside and actively helping their existing employees to develop marketable skills. In place of fostering obedience, they should foster independence.

On the other hand, it would be neither right nor effective for corporations to leap suddenly to a professional view of the employment relation. It would be wrong because employees, who have the most to lose, are generally not ready for the shift in terms of their skills and expectations. It would be ineffective because companies aren't ready either: they haven't mastered the organizational problems of achieving flexibility without chaos.

There are steps that have already been taken by the dynamic companies in my study, and by others, which move in the right direction.

1. *Clarify the company mission,* in the sense I have outlined: a two- to five-year direction or focus. This is a piece that has not been widely stressed

in management "how-to"s: most recommend either a sharp set of short-term goals and measures, or a long-range "vision." These are important pieces, but the thing that most distinguishes the more successful companies is a midrange shared purpose.

The mission is what defines the business—not in the financial sense, but what it is as a collective project. It answers the question, What are we trying to do together? And it therefore serves as the force that pulls people into a working relation for a period of time. The company then becomes in effect not an entity to which one swears allegiance, but a project to which one contributes.

2. *Organize around the mission.* Build projects, tasks, and teams around the accomplishment of the purpose. If this happens effectively, it will not be *possible* for managers to focus only on their piece, and to ignore the rest of what makes a business successful. It then should go without saying that there needs to be effective education and information sharing.

The cause-and-effect relation does not work in reverse: pushing education and information sharing does not lead to a shared understanding of the business. Many troubled companies have conducted education blitzes without effect, because managers didn't have to *use* the knowledge. If individuals can continue with "business as usual," they don't need to know about the business.

3. *Encourage the development of general skills and business knowledge*—abilities that can potentially help managers get jobs outside the company.

It doesn't help just to act when a crisis hits, by providing "outplacement" help in a downsizing. Outplacement may help a few people, but it does nothing to reduce the disorientation in the general culture. When constant change becomes a way of life, it is essential that everyone be thinking about careers independently and taking responsibility for his or her own development.

Companies can help in ways that are obvious but traditionally rare: by supporting time spent in general professional development and business education through tuition benefits, time allowances, and referral services.

4. *Develop flexible approaches to "personal" needs of employees.*

There has been a great deal of debate about how corporate policies can adapt to the needs of parents with young children, or other private demands—religious, political, and so on. There is no clear single solution, but it is clear that these claims have to be treated seriously by employers rather than simply subordinated to company needs, as was the custom in the past.

Work at home, flexible schedules, work sharing, and "cafeteria" benefits are among the approaches that are being tried in many companies.

These are only beginnings, and they can still be career-killers in companies with a loyalist orientation. Leaders need to make it very clear that claims from outside the workplace are legitimate subjects of discussion and do not indicate a "bad" employee.

5. *Establish regular dialogues around career prospects, commitments, and performance.*

Even the best policies will be ineffective if they are simply decreed from on high. The essence of the emerging employment relation, as I have stressed, is an open and continuing dialogue between employer and employee about challenges, commitments, goals, and support needed to do the job.

Professionals do not expect the company to "come down to" them, and they don't expect it to plan their development; but they do expect that when they take on a task, the expectations will be cleared and the commitments carried through. They also expect to be able to discuss their personal needs and to try to work out mutual accommodations.

In some ways it has become harder to conduct these kinds of discussions in the dynamic companies because people no longer have a single boss who watches over them. It takes more deliberate organizing to make sure that everyone has points of contact who can make commitments for the company and discuss the employee's performance, on the one hand, and his or her needs, on the other.

The best solution I have seen so far is that the formal superior in the chain of command takes on a kind of "mentoring" responsibility, gathering feedback from all the people that an individual works with and discussing plans for the future. This superior may have very little "bossing" responsibility, as formal subordinates will spend increasing time working on projects and teams outside the superior's scope. In such cases a key role of the "boss" becomes that of point person for bringing together the needs of the company and the employee.

6. *Establish portable benefits.*

If companies recognize the need for a trans-firm approach to security and benefits, they can play a constructive role in promoting a shift toward wider and more flexible benefit networks. There are signs of movement already: the growth of personal retirement accounts has been greatly aided by the support of companies for Keough and other government plans. Another model, not used in industry to my knowledge, is the benefit plan for university faculty (TIAA/CREF): this is a single private insurance network to which almost all universities subscribe, so that someone moving between institutions does not lose retirement contributions.

HOW INDIVIDUALS CAN PREPARE THEMSELVES

On the side of the individual the professional employment relation requires a new level of responsibility for one's own career. There are three things that seem to me necessary to prepare oneself in the short run:

1. *Develop general skills.*

     This is the flip side of the suggestion above that the company should encourage such learning. The true professionals were distinctive in seeking out opportunities for learning outside the company, and defining interests apart from their immediate jobs. One talked of taking courses in negotiation, another in strategy, several in general management skills and organization change, and so on.

     In addition to portable skills, they also worked to develop a general awareness of the business world beyond what their company told them. They read the business sections of the daily papers avidly and spoke knowledgeably about the competitive environment; several also subscribed to trade publications. In these ways they developed an independent view of the prospects for the company in which they worked, and the basis for a constructively critical perspective.

2. *Build outside networks and associations.*

     The traditional way to build a career was to find the right connections (or mentor) within the company. A primary source of distress for loyalists in a restructuring company is the disruption of these internal networks. But if the career is no longer expected to stay in a single company, people need to have connections beyond it. They need to build, through a network of relationships, an identity or set of interests that can guide them steadily across a number of specific organizations. This is a matter of building an identity through involvement in multiple networks, rather than hitching one's wagon to a single star. It is more than skill development: it is developing a sense of self, and a corresponding reputation, which has breadth and flexibility.

     One crucial dimension is a set of relationships that can provide knowledge and contacts for potential job searches. For many managers, active involvement in a professional association can be an effective channel. For others, there are general courses and programs increasingly available from universities and business schools.

     Another important dimension is social-interest groups or communities—religious groups, women's networks, neighborhoods, and so on—which can help one develop a feeling of "groundedness" outside the corporation. If your sense of worth is tied solely to the success of your company, you are in a vulnerable position in this fluctuating age. Traditional policies systematically discouraged developed independent value bases, because the company's values were supposed to be paramount; they can no longer serve as such a primary reference point.[5]

Finally, it is worth developing some collective security base. Professional associations are more and more playing the role of supporting managers who have been wrongly treated, and of advocating (through publicity and other forms of pressure) fairness in the employment relation. The professional ethic I have described gives the individual a greater legitimate voice in negotiating the employment relation, rather than just accepting what the company wants; but it is always hard for individuals to make good on these rights without some independent support.[6]

3. *Save for transitions.*

This, like many of the other suggestions, is obvious once one makes the mental shift to an expectation of multicompany careers. But it is rarely done in a systematic way. People save for their children's college education, and they may raid that fund if they are laid off; they rarely create a fund specifically for periods of unemployment. Yet increasingly the latter is almost as inevitable as the former.

I am not suggesting that individual saving is a permanent solution to the problem. This is an ideal area for sharing the risk: some managers during their careers will be unemployed much more than others, often through no fault of their own. Private insurance pools and government backup will be essential to stabilizing a truly mobile labor market. In the short run, however—until these systems are in place—it pays to prepare on one's own.

Expectations of the future shape action in the present. If managers expect to stay with their companies for the rest of their careers—and most I spoke to still do—then the possibility of layoffs is terrifying and disorienting. If companies expect their employees to be loyal—and most still do—then managers who prepare themselves sensibly for an uncertain future are viewed with suspicion.

The proposals I have made follow from the expectation that people will *not* follow careers within a single company. In that case it only makes sense they should take steps to establish identities, values, interests, affiliations, and security outside the company. And since corporations are no longer prepared to offer their managers lifetime security, they should encourage them to establish these outside bases.

Close

The starting point of this essay was the observation, among the fourteen organizations I studied, that those who clung to loyalty weren't doing well. Loyal individuals, faced with downsizing and restructuring, were bewildered and lost; companies in which loyalty remained dominant were stuck, inward-looking, and resistant to change.

But it is hard to give it up. The idea of an ordered hierarchy that keeps things working smoothly by assigning everyone a place, and which protects its members in exchange for their undivided loyalty, is fundamental to our culture. Plato's Republic was one of the earliest images of this paternalistic form of human cooperation.

The capitalist revolution of the past few centuries has been driven in part by the desire of people to break free of the oppressive aspects of these communities—to express an individual identity apart from one's place in an order, to move around, to escape stultifying pressures for conformity. In that sense markets are tremendously liberating, and for that reason they always eat away at traditional communities.

Markets, however, have not provided a replacement for the sense of involvement in a larger moral order, for trust and good fellowship. As the great economist Joseph Schumpeter pointed out long ago, capitalism lives in part off the remnants of communal values which it is constantly obliterating.[7]

So in corporations the need for community continues to emerge in essentially regressive ways: I have called it "paternalistic," and several of the most insightful observers of traditional corporate culture have described it as "tribalistic" or "feudal."[8] It recreates the age-old trade of protection for loyalty.

The desire for a sense of belonging is so strong that managers and corporate leaders have great difficulty in accepting that the old community is gone—shattered by the need for rapid flexibility and for the accommodation of diverse interests. Too often they hang on to old images, hoping that downsizing and layoffs are a temporary hardship, blocking out the magnitude of the changes around them. The result is that they fail to prepare themselves for the future.

The more successful companies are adopting an ethic that seeks a more equal relationship, respecting the independence of individual identity and the responsibility of the individual for developing it. This transforms the image of the corporation from a group of people serving an organization to a group of professionals coming together to accomplish a mission or project. There is still much to do to make this image real, but it offers a path forward from the morass in which most middle managers are lost.

APPENDIX

The following is a summary of the main themes of the interviews at each of the companies studied.

Apex

SITE STUDIED
- Division headquarters and plant

SIZE OF UNIT
- Medium

INDUSTRY TYPE
- Heavy manufacturing

PARENT ORGANIZATION
- Large conglomerate

HISTORY
- 5 years old, innovative by design

INTERVIEWS
- Middle managers:
  - 13 in 1989 (5 individual, 8 group)
  - 10 in 1991
- Leadership: Human Resources

DOWNSIZINGS
- No—still in growth phase

STRUCTURAL CHANGES
- Very team-based, matrixed, few formal titles

CULTURAL CHANGES
- Informal, egalitarian, much pride and enthusiasm

COMPENSATION
- Still being revised; aim 20 percent performance-based

VOICE
- Many channels and forums, formal and informal

ORGANIZATION PERFORMANCE
- Excellent by all accounts

MORALE
- Excellent

BUSINESS UNDERSTANDING (AMONG MIDDLE MANAGERS)
- Excellent—remarkable grasp of industry and trends

LOYALTY
- Low—people like the company but do not look beyond next few years

RELATIONS TO TOP MANAGEMENT
- Distant but respected

Barclay

SITE STUDIED
- Plant

SIZE OF UNIT
- Medium

INDUSTRY TYPE
- Heavy manufacturing

PARENT ORGANIZATION
- Large, single-product category

HISTORY
- Old plant, serious trouble 2 years before

INTERVIEWS
- Middle managers:
  - 9 in 1991 (2 individual, 7 group)
  - 5 in 1993
- Leadership:
  - Plant manager and production manager in 1991
  - Brief discussion with plant manager in 1993

DOWNSIZINGS
- Significant reduction through layoffs and attrition

STRUCTURAL CHANGES
- From functional to focus factory organization based on major customers

CULTURAL CHANGES
- Big shift from paternalist to business orientation

COMPENSATION
- More performance focus, some tension around forced-curve

VOICE
- Strong informal communication, poor formal recourse

ORGANIZATION PERFORMANCE
- Excellent—turnaround

MORALE
- Excellent
- Excitement, optimism, some stress

BUSINESS UNDERSTANDING (AMONG MIDDLE MANAGERS)
- Excellent

LOYALTY
- Low—most like this plant, but no unwillingness to move

RELATIONS TO TOP MANAGEMENT
- Plant manager and assistant drove initial change
- They remain respected, but distant; much delegation

Crown

SITE STUDIED
- Division headquarters

SIZE OF UNIT
- Medium

INDUSTRY TYPE
- Complex design and manufacturing

PARENT ORGANIZATION
- Large multi-product category

HISTORY
- Old bureaucracy, turned around by involving charismatic manager in early 1980s
- Current manager much lower-key, but continues basic policies

INTERVIEWS
- Middle managers: 8, 2 to 4 levels below division leader
- Leadership: Human Resources director

DOWNSIZINGS
- Not recent—layoffs in 1970s, maintained lean structure since then

STRUCTURAL CHANGES
- Lean bureaucracy, many project groups

CULTURAL CHANGES
- Highly participative and involved

COMPENSATION
- Little merit distinction; forced-curve imposed by corporate, resisted

VOICE
- Elaborate system of committees and teams, losing energy

ORGANIZATION PERFORMANCE
- Excellent

MORALE
- Good, some feelings of isolation, stress, overwork

BUSINESS UNDERSTANDING (AMONG MIDDLE MANAGERS)
- Excellent: clear understanding of strategy and competition

LOYALTY
- Medium—many see opportunities in parent company, others oriented to professions
- Generally not "stuck" on staying in organization

RELATIONS TO TOP MANAGEMENT
- Feeling of being cut off from corporation
- Respect for division manager

Dest

SITE STUDIED
- Corporate headquarters

SIZE OF UNIT
- Large

INDUSTRY TYPE
- High-technology production

PARENT ORGANIZATION
- (independent)

HISTORY
- 30 years, new CEO 4 years before, business crises began at same time

INTERVIEWS
- Middle managers: 10—mostly vice presidents (one level below CEO's staff)

DOWNSIZINGS
- First layoffs in 1985, sizeable and continuing layoffs since

STRUCTURAL CHANGES
- Moving from functional to business units

CULTURAL CHANGES
- Move from highly paternalist, technology-driven to more business-focused

COMPENSATION
- Management by Objectives, increasing performance focus

VOICE
- Historically very poor, now improving
- Task forces, many recently created communication mechanisms

ORGANIZATION PERFORMANCE
- Overall very poor: losing market share
- Managers blame product decisions made years earlier
- Managers claim operations have greatly improved, still much more needed

MORALE
- Very good: concern, understanding of serious business problems, but feeling of moving in right direction
- High level of cooperation

BUSINESS UNDERSTANDING (AMONG MIDDLE MANAGERS)
- Excellent: clear sense of competitive environment and long-term strategy

LOYALTY
- Among old guard, loyalty shaken but still high. At same time, rapidly increasing focus on "professionalization" of business widely supported by middle managers, leading most to think about possibility of outside careers
- Many "outsiders" recently brought into middle and higher management

RELATIONS TO TOP MANAGEMENT
- General respect, but concern about conflicts at top

Emon

SITE STUDIED
- Division headquarters, plants

SIZE OF UNIT
- Large

INDUSTRY TYPE
- Manufacturing, mostly continuous-process

PARENT ORGANIZATION
- Large, single-product category

HISTORY
- Old oligopolist bureaucracy

INTERVIEWS
- Middle managers: 19 (6 individual, 13 group)—including a few supervisors and plant managers
- Leadership: division manager

DOWNSIZINGS
- Recent forced 5 percent layoff, voluntary 5 percent retirement—unprecedented

STRUCTURAL CHANGES
- Cutting some layers, lean structure, more task forces

CULTURAL CHANGES
- Five year sequence of programs, including "The Right Way to Manage" quality initiatives, and so on
- Left most managers with confused sense of change, but no clear direction

COMPENSATION
- Increased pay-for-performance emphasis. Complaints that this created competitive atmosphere, lowered cooperation

VOICE
- Little fear, but few effective channels of voice other than immediate boss

ORGANIZATION PERFORMANCE
- Generally good, some downturns

MORALE
- Mixed, overall moderately positive: good will, some confusion, resignation
- Reports that supervisors very unhappy

BUSINESS UNDERSTANDING (AMONG MIDDLE MANAGERS)
- Poor data

LOYALTY
- Shaken, previously extremely high

RELATIONS TO TOP MANAGEMENT
- Distant, random

Fixx

SITE STUDIED
- Corporate headquarters

SIZE OF UNIT
- Large

INDUSTRY TYPE
- Manufacturing, mostly continuous-process

PARENT ORGANIZATION
- Large, single-product category

HISTORY
- Old oligopolist bureaucracy

INTERVIEWS
- Middle managers: 6 (3 individual, 3 group)—business managers, one OD person

DOWNSIZINGS
- 3 early-retirement waves with heavy pressure. Major headcount reductions
- Strong sense that downsizing would continue

STRUCTURAL CHANGES
- Move from functional to business unit structure underway
- Removal of some layers, general "cutting fat"
- In a few areas, increasing use of matrices and project teams

CULTURAL CHANGES
- Heavy paternalism, loosening up. More outsiders at top levels

COMPENSATION
- Loose forced curve, somewhat increasing performance focus

VOICE
- Through immediate supervisor only—no formal mechanisms

ORGANIZATION PERFORMANCE
- Generally good in both operational and financial terms, but not outstanding—much pressure to improve

MORALE
- Mixed to good
- Embattled, hopeful, lonely

BUSINESS UNDERSTANDING (AMONG MIDDLE MANAGERS)
- Improving, but still heavy focus on past performance rather than competition

LOYALTY
- Much concern, recognition of change, but no new model

RELATIONS TO TOP MANAGEMENT
- Changing, distant—waiting to see what "they" will do
- Reasonable confidence in abilities of top

Glover

SITE STUDIED
- Division headquarters, one plant

SIZE OF UNIT
- Large

INDUSTRY TYPE
- Heavy manufacturing

PARENT ORGANIZATION
- Large, single-product category

HISTORY
- Old oligopolist bureaucracy facing competitive crisis

INTERVIEWS
- Middle managers:
  - 11 in 1988, including manufacturing managers, a Public Relations person, 2 engineering managers; 9 in headquarters, 2 in a plant
  - Another 10 in 1991; similar mix
- Leadership: Interview with Human Resources manager in 1988; meeting with top team of division in 1991 to discuss findings and their responses

DOWNSIZINGS
- 25 percent in last few years by attrition and strong retirement incentives

STRUCTURAL CHANGES
- Reorganization some years previously around product lines
- In 1991, just before my second visit, another realignment whose rationale was not clear to middle managers

CULTURAL CHANGES
- Confused—much rhetoric about product focus, empowerment, teamwork, but managers were very unclear about meaning of these initiatives or long-term direction
- Only clear item: increased quality focus

COMPENSATION
- Increased emphasis on pay-for-performance system caused much discontent

VOICE
- Based on personal relations—some felt they could talk to their supervisors, others not Two had personal friendships higher up in organization and could "short-circuit" the hierarchy. Otherwise, people avoided making waves

ORGANIZATION PERFORMANCE
- Extremely poor by any measure

MORALE
- Mixed: short-term turmoil, isolation; long-term hope
- Worse at lower levels

BUSINESS UNDERSTANDING (AMONG MIDDLE MANAGERS)
- Generally poor. Strong focus on quality, but little knowledge of what competition was doing or of other strategic factors besides quality

LOYALTY
- High, sense that "this too shall pass"

RELATIONS TO TOP MANAGEMENT
- Very low respect for corporate leadership
- In division, general respect for division leader but increasing puzzlement about his direction

Hardin

SITE STUDIED
- Plant

SIZE OF UNIT
- Medium

INDUSTRY TYPE
- Heavy manufacturing

PARENT ORGANIZATION
- Large, single-product category

HISTORY
- Old plant, long one of the worst in division, recent modest improvement
- Previous plant manager a highly directive and controlling type; recent replacement an old (near retirement), paternalist, "caring" manager

INTERVIEWS
- Middle managers: 14 (4 individual, 10 group)
- Leadership: plant manager; personnel director

DOWNSIZINGS
- Some attrition, a few recent layoffs
- Widespread sense that layoffs just beginning

STRUCTURAL CHANGES
- Recent focused factories, but weakly implemented—haven't changed most people's jobs much

CULTURAL CHANGES
- Current plant manager has shifted tone from highly autocratic toward more delegation and risk, informal teamwork

COMPENSATION
- Forced curve pay for performance, very unpopular

VOICE
- Generally very poor, despite some recent efforts at personal communication Most say they cannot speak out for fear of being "labeled"

ORGANIZATION PERFORMANCE
- Poor, improving slightly (according to both managers on site and headquarters representatives)

MORALE
- Mixed: very poor two levels down from plant manager, intense bitterness and anger. Fair one level down

BUSINESS UNDERSTANDING (AMONG MIDDLE MANAGERS)
- Improving at top, very poor lower

LOYALTY
- Still high—most say they are very loyal to company, though they also say that loyalty is declining among other people

RELATIONS TO TOP MANAGEMENT
- New plant manager gets some respect
- Deep alienation from parent corporation

Isony

SITE STUDIED
- Plant

SIZE OF UNIT
- Medium

INDUSTRY TYPE
- Manufacturing

PARENT ORGANIZATION
- Large, single-product category

HISTORY
- Old oligopolistic bureaucracy, recent increase in competition

INTERVIEWS
- Middle managers: 9—1 to 2 levels above supervisor including senior engineers and one ombudsperson
- Leadership: Plant manager

DOWNSIZINGS
- 50 percent reduction by retirement, a few "pressured"—unprecedented

STRUCTURAL CHANGES
- Cut one layer, switched from functional to product-line organization

COMPENSATION
- New team award focus; changes in job ratings caused anger, sense of unfairness

CULTURAL CHANGES
- Slightly increasing business focus

VOICE
- Elaborate council system established 1983, moderate effectiveness

ORGANIZATION PERFORMANCE
- Fair to poor

MORALE
- Mixed-poor; much confusion, some anger, low trust

BUSINESS UNDERSTANDING (AMONG MIDDLE MANAGERS)
- Poor; pure product focus, no awareness of strategy or competitors

LOYALTY
- Poor data: this was my first research site, before I had honed in on concept of loyalty

RELATIONS TO TOP MANAGEMENT
- Low-key, improved communication with plant superintendent
- Major gulf with corporate level

JVC

SITE STUDIED
- Division headquarters/plant (sole location of division)

SIZE OF UNIT
- Medium

INDUSTRY TYPE
- Manufacturing

PARENT ORGANIZATION
- Large old-line paternalist oligopoly

HISTORY
- Still a near-monopoly of product area, but a declining market. Need to move to new types of product lines
- A family-owned business until 1969; autocratic management till mid-1980s; then an enthusiastic participatory head, and now a tight controlling one

INTERVIEWS
- Middle managers: 19 (7 individual, 6 group)—2 to 4 levels from division manager
- Leadership: one member of president's immediate line reports

DOWNSIZINGS
- 50 exempt layoffs, first ever, 4 years before; continuing dismissals of poor performers

CULTURAL CHANGES
- In last 7 years, from paternalism to loose, informal enthusiasm to tight financial orientation
- Current president seen as ruling by fear. Confronts, belittles, attacks subordinates

STRUCTURAL CHANGES
- Shift from functional to business-unit structure 6 years before, but functions still dominant

VOICE
- Very poor, much fear
- People told me of coverups (poor products shipped for fear of telling the boss, and so on)

COMPENSATION
- Management by Objectives, moderate performance variation, no complaints

ORGANIZATION PERFORMANCE
- Operations very poor, according to middle managers: missing targets, loss of quality, some major errors resulting from lack of open communication

MORALE
- Very poor: fear, confusion, anger; mostly personal at division manager

BUSINESS UNDERSTANDING (AMONG MIDDLE MANAGERS)
- Very poor: focus on internal politics, almost none on competition or business
- Little agreement among managers about even basic numbers or results

LOYALTY
- High tension—some thinking of jumping ship

- But most feel pendulum has swung, they can wait till it swings back—no serious loss of loyalty

RELATIONS TO TOP MANAGEMENT
- Great and widespread anger at division manager

Karet

SITE STUDIED
- Division headquarters, one plant

SIZE OF UNIT
- Large

INDUSTRY TYPE
- Heavy manufacturing

PARENT ORGANIZATION
- Large, single-product category

HISTORY
- Old oligopolist bureaucracy, still somewhat protected from competition by import quotas

INTERVIEWS
- Middle managers: 13, mostly 3 to 4 levels below division manager, including a project manager and a plant manager
- Leadership: presentation to top division managers, including division head, heads of line organizations, and Human Resources director. Also several interviews with Human Resources director

DOWNSIZINGS
- 20 percent over previous three years by attrition and incentives

STRUCTURAL CHANGES
- Continued dominance of functional structure
- Some effort to create cross-functional teams and matrices, widely seen as weak and ineffective

CULTURAL CHANGES
- Confused, no clear image
- Much rhetoric about participation and teamwork
- Reports of increased "politics," infighting

COMPENSATION
- Recent performance push, widely resented

VOICE
- Generally poor
- Recent formal system established by division manager: two who were directly involved praised it, but most were skeptical

ORGANIZATION PERFORMANCE
- Excellent financial, but according to the managers, poor operations—much confusion, slow product development, conflict among units

MORALE
- Poor: much anger and frustration, especially from project managers

BUSINESS UNDERSTANDING (AMONG MIDDLE MANAGERS)
- Poor: focus entirely on product, little or no understanding of competitive position

LOYALTY
- Declining, but still strong

RELATIONS TO TOP MANAGEMENT
- Little faith in division and functional managers, less in corporate

Lyco

SITE STUDIED
- New laboratory

SIZE OF UNIT
- Small (growing from 0 to 600)

INDUSTRY TYPE
- Research and product development

PARENT ORGANIZATION
- Large, single-product category

HISTORY
- Division of old, large, stable company; recent deregulation

INTERVIEWS
- Middle managers: 21 in 1989, 8 in 1992
- Technicians, technical supervisors, three levels of middle management, location managers
- Leadership: Business Unit head, BU Human Resources director

DOWNSIZINGS
- Some pressured early retirements, rumors of more to come—all this unprecedented

CULTURAL CHANGES
- Conscious effort to build state-of-the-art participatory culture, with openness across functions and levels. Attempt to "empower" managers, technicians, and occupationals
- Deliberately "informal" culture—no coats and ties, open offices, and so on

STRUCTURAL CHANGES
- Recent move to business units cross-cutting functional units; confusion

VOICE
- Concerted efforts to increase voice—"Congress" of representatives from different areas and levels, much preaching of participation
- Heavy self-censorship, fear, little real openness

COMPENSATION
- Small variations based on performance; no recent changes

ORGANIZATION PERFORMANCE
- Undeterminable: standards not clearly set or widely understood. Depended on who you asked, what political winds were blowing
- Managers thought unit was doing adequately but not well

MORALE
- Very poor: changes seen as random, frightening

BUSINESS UNDERSTANDING (AMONG MIDDLE MANAGERS)
- Very poor: no understanding of strategy or competitive environment

LOYALTY
- Badly shaken, but still strong

RELATIONS TO TOP MANAGEMENT
- Not respected, many decisions seen as incomprehensible

Marks

SITE STUDIED
- Company headquarters / plant (sole location of subsidiary)

SIZE OF UNIT
- Small

INDUSTRY TYPE
- Machining

PARENT ORGANIZATION
- Large conglomerate

HISTORY
- An old company at the core, acquired by larger conglomerate in 1962. Two recent acquisitions had expanded it

INTERVIEWS
- Middle managers: 6 interviews transcribed (about 20 interviewed in all by me and a colleague)
- Plant manager, Human Resources head, president
- Leadership: president, Human Resources director
- Additional survey taken of about 30 managers

DOWNSIZINGS
- Frequent firings, low security, known plan to reduce force significantly

STRUCTURAL CHANGES
- Two acquisitions folded in

CULTURAL CHANGES
- Heavy technology focus, computers becoming central

COMPENSATION
- Heavy performance component based essentially on president's opinion

VOICE
- No one feeds back to president
- Some feedback possible informally within some departments

ORGANIZATION PERFORMANCE
- Very poor operationally—poor service quality, deadlines commonly missed by months
- OK financially—little direct competition for major customers

MORALE
- Very poor: widespread anger, frustration

BUSINESS UNDERSTANDING (AMONG MIDDLE MANAGERS)
- Very poor understanding of strategy—managers had given up trying to make sense of it

LOYALTY
- High: people expect and want to stay

RELATIONS TO TOP MANAGEMENT
- No honest communication; sense that president "very smart" but "has his feet off the ground"; many apparently arbitrary interventions by the president, "micromanaging"

Nadir

SITE STUDIED
- Division headquarters

SIZE OF UNIT
- Large

INDUSTRY TYPE
- Manufacturing

PARENT ORGANIZATION
- Large multi-product company

HISTORY
- Old near-monopoly, highly paternalist, growing competition

INTERVIEWS
- Middle managers: 20 (6 individual, 14 group)—headquarters managers, line and staff
- Leadership: Human Resources director of division and Human Resources Vice president of corporation

DOWNSIZINGS
- Small layoff in 1985, continued slimming by attrition & individual separations

STRUCTURAL CHANGES
- Move from centralized functional organization to decentralized business units, then recentralization—much shuffling
- Many task forces, but widely seen as poorly organized, ineffective

CULTURAL CHANGES
- Concerted effort by top leader (brought in from outside) to move culture in direction of "In Search of Excellence" principles—decentralized, informal, focused on customers. Not seen as effective, dismissed as a fad by most managers. New top leader brought in a year before, moved in the direction of tightening the organization, reasserting traditional control

COMPENSATION
- Traditional Management by Objectives. Ratings had become inflated—everyone rated high. Recent attempt to reestablish curve had caused tension
- Most managers did not like link of evaluation to compensation—said that prevented honest feedback, created political maneuvering

VOICE
- Excellent for hourlies, poor for middle managers—dissidence seen as bad, no outlet for concerns

ORGANIZATION PERFORMANCE
- Poor—improving financially, mixed operationally

MORALE
- Poor: much anger, confusion, bitterness

BUSINESS UNDERSTANDING (AMONG MIDDLE MANAGERS)
- Poor: virtually no understanding of competitive pressures or strategy

LOYALTY
- High: people love the company

RELATIONS TO TOP MANAGEMENT
- Very great alienation: top seen as outsiders who don't understand

NOTES

Chapter 1: The Assault on Middle Management

1. American Management Association (1993).
2. The data on overall trends in middle-management numbers are confusing. It is possible to make a case that the middle ranks have continued to grow down to the present day—because of increases in middle management at smaller and midsized firms. In *large* firms, on which this study focuses, there was some controversy until the late 1980s whether there was a real decline in management numbers, but that dispute seems to have died away now—the evidence of downsizing is too consistent.

   There is much evidence of a rapid growth in middle management between 1900 and about 1960, though as usual the evidence is weakened by lack of a consistent definition of "middle management." Nevertheless:

   - According to the Census Bureau, numbers of "salaried administrators" in the United States grew from 1.3 percent of the labor force in 1900 to 3.0 percent in 1930—from 352,000 to 1.35 million (U.S. Department of Commerce, 1971).
   - White-collar workers went from 12 percent of the work force in 1900 to 22 percent in 1930, 24 percent in 1940, and 60 percent in 1983 (Jurgen Kocka 1980, 19).
   - Porat's remarkably careful data shows a surge in "private bureaucracy" in the 1940s and 1950s, leveling off since about 1960 (Marc Uri Porat 1977, 166 ff.).

   My comment that middle managers "built the suburbs" relies primarily on William H. Whyte (1956), Part VII.

   Evidence for the high contentment of middle managers historically can be found in C. Wright Mills (1951) and William H. Whyte (1956). Research indicating that they worked fairly normal hours (9 to 5) in the 1950s and 1960s is summarized in Mintzberg (1973) and supported by the other studies in the 1950s.

3. Alfred D. Chandler, Jr. (1977); Peter F. Drucker (1946); Olivier Zunz (1990).

4. For a review of the downsizing phenomenon internationally, see Myron J. Roomkin (ed.) (1989).

5. Different countries, and even different companies, have very different ideas of what constitutes a "middle manager." I wasted (I will say in retrospect) a good deal of time trying to come up with an index that would allow a reliable comparison across organizations with existing data, but was unable to do so.

6. American Management Association (1993).

7. See Shoshana Zuboff (1988).

8. Accounts of managerial expectations before the recent upheavals have stressed the importance of stability, loyalty, cooperation, and steady career advancement. William Whyte's "organization man" remains the best-known crystallization of this image, and it has been echoed in a series of studies since that time.

9. The number of interviews is not exact because there are a few cases in which I had an ongoing relationship with a manager, or a series of informal conversations, which on reflection gave me the answer to most of my questions, but which did not involve formal interviewing. There are also some early interviews that missed some questions that later became important. The total number of interviews for which I have written notes is 245.

10. There are few attempts even to develop an operational definition of middle management, and still fewer that make sense conceptually. For example, J. H. Horne and Tom Lupton (1965) define their focus without justification as from one to four levels below the CEO. This presents a number of problems. My interviews and experience suggest a sharp difference between those in the CEO's working team—those who meet with him or her regularly—and those below or outside that circle. Furthermore, four levels down means very different things in organizations of different sizes. Finally, the counting of levels is a very uncertain business, as I quickly discovered when trying to do something like Horne and Lupton: every organization (nowadays, at least) is rife with half-levels, skip-levels, and simply vague levels. The two markers I have placed—outside the general manager's direct team, and above first-level supervision—are not ideal, but they are both relatively easy to operationalize and do seem to mark off a group with a distinctive relation to the organization.

11. The most negative organizations were Lyco, Marks, and Nadir; the mixed ones were Hardin, Isony, JVC, and Karet; the more hopeful ones were Emon, Fixx, and Glover; and the highly positive group were Apex, Barclay, Crown, and Dest.

Chapter 2: The Meaning of Loyalty

1. See, for instance, the text by Michael Beer et al. (1985).

2. Max Weber (1947): 330.

3. For a summary of this early management literature, see Claude S. George (1968).

4. There is, of course, an important tradition within sociology that notes the irrational aspects of bureaucracy: see, for example, Michel Crozier (1964); Alvin W. Gouldner (1954); Peter M. Blau (1963).

5. The "Hawthorne study" was documented in F. J. Roethlisberger and William J. Dickson (1939). On the continuing resistance to Taylorist motivation, see also Stanley B. Mathewson, (1931) and Richard Edwards (1979).

6. On the importance of "working knowledge" see Ken Kusterer (1978); Tony Manwaring and Stephen Wood (1984).

7. Agency theory tends to identify the interests of the whole with those of the shareholders. That raises a set of issues that I will skirt here: it may be that shareholders can do well *at the expense of* the health of a company, by taking short-term gains and sacrificing underlying strength. In that case short-term individual incentives may be the best way to manage, because you are not aiming at strengthening the organization as a whole. In this entire essay, however, I will assume that the objective is a strong and healthy (profitable, effective) organization.

8. See George P. Baker; Michael C. Jensen; and Kevin J. Murphy (1988). Other applications of agency theory to managerial practice include Michael C. Jensen and William H. Meckling (1991).

9. Max Weber did not make the third, rationalist assumption: he was in fact a great critic of utilitarian thought. Still, he saw bureaucracy as the apotheosis of rational-legal evolution, and therefore underestimated many of the "nonrational" forces which later analysts have revealed within the structure.

10. Chester I. Barnard (1938): 220.

11. Lewis A. Coser (1974).

12. For other examples of loyalty to an autocratic CEO, see Robert Jackall (1988), esp. p. 27; Rosemary Stewart (1970), pp. 131–32; and Graeme Salaman (1977).

13. See, for example, J. Patrick Wright (1980).

14. Robert K. Merton (1940).

15. Peter Drucker (1988) describes such a case in the British rule of India. But while Drucker believes he is describing a radically new form of organization, he has really found just an unusually clear example of an effectively decentralized bureaucracy, with jobs neatly segmented. That is possible because of the geographic segmentation of the system

16. James Burnham (1941).

17. For example, Peter M. Blau (1963).

18. The following description of managers in traditional firms is drawn primarily from the following "observational" studies: C. Wright Mills (1951); William H. Whyte, Jr. (1956); Rosabeth Moss Kanter (1977); Diane Rothbard Margolis (1979); and Robert Jackall (1988). See also William G. Ouchi (1981).

19. On employment law and the obligation of loyalty, see James B. Atleson (1983); Karl E. Klare (1983).

20. See Olivier Zunz (1990).

21. On the institutional significance of internal labor markets, see Suzanne Berger and Michael J. Piore (1980). On the motivational importance of career advance-

ment, see, for example, Robert F. Pearse (1977); Rosabeth Moss Kanter (1977); Myron J. Roomkin (ed.) (1989).

22. There is no general data that I can find about how much stock middle managers own in their companies. I can say that many of those interviewed—especially at the higher levels, but even lower down—saw it as a significant part of their financial planning.

23. See Robert E. Hall (1982).

24. The word *man* is here used advisedly: these cultural patterns are an important source of resistance to the advancement of women, as Rosabeth Kanter (1977) has demonstrated.

25. *NLRB v. Local 1229, IBEW,* 346 U.S. 464, 472 (1953). See also James B. Atleson (1983), esp. chap. 5.

26. *NLRB v. Yeshiva University,* 444 U.S. 672, 100 S. Ct. 856 (1980).

27. See especially Ken C. Kusterer (1978).

28. For general reviews of this literature on middle-management jobs, see Rosemary Stewart (1981 and 1982); Colin Hales (1986); John Machin, Rosemary Stewart, and Colin Hales (1981); Henry Mintzberg (1973).

29. For a sample of the consistent findings about the considerable time spent by middle managers on lateral relations, see Harvey Mintzberg (1973): 45ff, 204. On the nature of organizational politics, see Robert W. Allen and Lyman W. Porter (eds.) (1983); George Strauss (1962); Robert Jackall (1988); John P. Kotter (1982); Gideon Kunda (1986).

30. The "political" function of middle management has been underplayed in research, at least until recently: see, for example, a 1970 review article by Rosemary Stewart, or the compendium by Robert W. Allen and Lyman W. Porter (eds.) (1983), which spends a great deal of time lamenting the lack of knowledge about organizational influence processes. The picture has not much improved since.

   Of the few exceptions to this picture, a classic in the field is the unusual participant-observer study by Andrew M. Pettigrew (1973). Recently the subject has received some attention from an "organizational behavior" perspective—see especially John Kotter (1982); also Ted Stephenson (1985). But these do not answer the organizational question.

31. This phenomenon—managers' inability to describe their own managerial work—has also been noted by Derek Torrington and Jane Weightman (1987).

32. It is not generally recognized that Management by Objectives, or MBO, is not a new phenomenon: it was introduced in the mid-1920s by that great inventor of classical corporate bureaucracy, Alfred Sloan.

33. I did not in fact ask this of *everyone* in my sample; but this was a topic I explored in most interviews, and I found no disagreement on the point.

34. For formal discussions of the problem of "learning systems," see Stafford Beer (1981); Mario Bunge (1969); H. H. Pattee (1973); Clifford Grobstein (1973); Richard Levins (1973). Burgelman's (1983) study of internal corporate processes, unusually rich in detail, seems to me the closest to capturing this essential learning function of middle management.

35. Some organizations have recently begun to deny the importance of loyalty—for example, GE under Jack Welch, who has explicitly renounced that value, and

some of my sample, who have done so less explicitly. But all have had a culture of loyalty in their "classic" period.

36. For a classic description of such informal conflict management, see Andrew M. Pettigrew (1973).

37. Adam Smith (1751).

38. David Riesman (1950); Robert N. Bellah, Richard Madsen, William M. Sullivan, Ann Swidler, and Steven Tipton (1985).

39. Of course, the creator of Lake Wobegon, Garrison Keillor, is fully aware of this ambivalence and draws much of his comedy from it: his is far from a one-dimensional nostalgia for the past! See Garrison Keillor (1985).

40. Not all middle managers want to be loyal, of course. To prevent too much dithering in the text I keep some qualifications in footnotes. Though my questions evolved as I conducted the interviews, I estimate that over 75 percent of my sample would agree that they *want* to be loyal; perhaps a quarter of these are cynical and believe they can no longer afford the luxury of being loyal; and less than 5 percent actively embrace free-agent values.

Chapter 3: The First Shock

1. Nadir and Marks were the only cases in which anger was widely expressed in the organization. Marks was unusual in that it was a kind of "pre-corporate" organization, heavily dependent on the personality of one man. For that reason I use Nadir as the best example of the "worst case" scenario. In addition, I found pockets of major turmoil in Lyco, Karet, JVC, Isony, and Hardin. But these organizations were more widely characterized by successful defensiveness.

2. Thomas J. Peters and Robert H. Waterman, Jr. (1982).

3. Although I interviewed from the top group in this company only the human relations director, his point of view was totally consistent with written documents, and also with the attributions of lower-level managers. He was, in addition, one of the more "business-oriented" of the HR managers I spoke to. There is no reason to doubt that he accurately represented top management's definition of the situation.

4. This included most of my sample. The companies that were closest to the moment of trauma were, in addition to Nadir, Lyco, Hardin, Fixx, and Emon.

5. For evidence on hours of work, see Juliet B. Schor (1991).

6. Almost without exception, in this case.

7. See, for instance, Talcott Parsons (1969), chaps. 4 and 7; Mark Gould (1990); G. Goethals and J. Darley (1987).

8. The only clear example of blaming affirmative action was, once again, from Nadir: "Reverse discrimination is a problem. My position has been terminated as of January 1 and I'm blocked from moving anywhere else by all this affirmative action stuff."

9. See Roger Brown (1986), Part VI.

Chapter 4: The Retreat to Autonomy

1. The better explorations of management "deal-making" include Andrew M. Pettigrew (1973); Melville Dalton (1959); Peter M. Blau (1963); Edward J. Lawler and Samuel B. Bacharach (1983); George Strauss (1962).
2. Though polls of middle managers are few, inconsistent, and rarely of good quality, they broadly support some of my findings. In particular, many find a surprising amount of support for cuts (Mark L. Goldstein, 1986) and a general lack of rebelliousness; some even find an upturn in satisfaction during the 1980s (Brian S. Morgan and William A. Schiemann, 1986). At the same time, they pick up a lot of "grumbling" about top management and the general direction of companies. Career security is almost always found to be on the decline. See, for example, Amanda Bennett (1990), p. 215 et passim; B. Z. Posner and W. H. Schmidt (1984); Robert F. Pearse (1977); Ron Zemke (1986); Emmanuel Kay (1974); Robert M. Tomasko (1987), p. 49.
3. See especially Rosabeth Moss Kanter (1977).
4. I will qualify this only a little bit. There were a very few cases in which people had personal friendships with people several levels above them and could talk freely to them. The other more intriguing exception was that some women and minorities felt relatively able to break through the hierarchy. I interpret this as due in part to the fact that they were not "insiders" to the traditional organization anyway, but had necessarily made their way by going against the grain; they were not bound by the norms of the old community.
5. More often I heard claims that *despite* the increased pressures people were continuing to work surprisingly well together. But even in these claims there was an implied sense that competition was starting to drive out cooperation.
6. I could not get hard numbers on changes in the span of control. The complexity of organizational structures—the use of matrix reporting, and so on—is such that no one, including top Human Relations leaders, could give numbers with any confidence. In general the best estimate in a range of companies was that spans had increased from about 5 to 8 to about 8 to 10.

Chapter 5: The Walls of the Box

1. Albert O. Hirschman (1970).
2. For a small sampling of this literature, see Laura J. Spencer (1989); Len Schlesinger, Todd Jick, Amy B. Johnson, and Lori Ann MacIsaac (1991); Tom Peters (1987); Thomas J. Peters and Robert H. Waterman, Jr. (1982); D. Yankelovich et al. (1983); Daniel R. Denison (1984); New York Stock Exchange (1982); US News & World Report (1981); Rosabeth Moss Kanter (1986); Richard E. Walton (1985); Edward E. Lawler, Gerald E. Ledford, and Susan A. Mohrman (1989); Edward E. Lawler (1986, 1988); Richard E. Wal-

ton (1982); Richard E. Walton and Paul R. Lawrence (1985).

3. See chapter 4.

4. Lewis A. Coser (1974).

5. On the greediness of corporations in relation to families, see esp. Lilian Breslow Rubin (1976).

6. Of course, the ability to describe the company's business strategy became more common as one moved higher, but even at fairly rarified levels knowledge remained remarkably thin.

7. Recall that the top leaders at Glover made much the same kind of argument about their fears of being completely honest about the business prospects.

Chapter 6: The Loyalty Trap

1. Cannings (1989), building on Hirschman (1970), draws a distiction between attachment deriving from voice and attachment deriving from difficulty of exit. The latter is a "rational" economistic motive, and generally (she argues) harmful to companies; the former has emotional components that keep good performers in place even when this is not in their best interests.

2. I did not explicitly ask everyone about outside professional associations; this was a regular part of my interview for the first three companies, and then began to drop the question because it produced blank stares and little response. After that, I made sure to ask at least a few people in each organization about this, just so I would pick up if there were any dramatic exceptions to the pattern set in the first three.

3. For a very interesting treatment of the dynamics of corporate ideology and morality, see Robert Jackall (1988).

4. A distinction: though they almost never oriented their loyalty to an individual, many managers did long for strong leadership, and they often constructed visions in which a particular leader would rescue the company from the new forces overwhelming it. (I have referred to this response in the case of Nadir in chapter 3, and it appeared in some form in many of the other "loyalist" companies.) The distinction is that the leader in this structure was not personally the object of loyalty (as was, for example, the leader at Marks), but was an (imagined) embodiment of the best values of the company. The attachment was not to the leader for his own sake, no matter what he might do, but to his ability to make the true nature of the company live again.

5. In the other companies one should be more cautious about saying they are defensive. Not because managers had a different view of the world: everywhere in the "bottom 10" the views were similar—we need to change, but we are already making the changes, and we will be all right. Caution is called for only because the "objective" evidence of trouble was in these cases somewhat less overwhelming. It is at least possible that they were just right, rather than defensive.

6. In the end the question of whether the "incrementalist" approach is defensive or right—or both—depends on one's own judgment of whether fundamental change is necessary. I believe that events are daily demonstrating the need for more than tinkering with, or "cleaning up," existing structures, and that more limited responses are therefore defensive.

7. See Thomas J. Peters, and Robert H. Waterman, Jr. (1982): 75, 258 ff. et passim.

8. The only companies in which "empowerment" or "teamwork" was *not* a major rhetorical theme of top management were Marks, which was the one example of a company in a "pre-bureaucratic" phase, dominated by an individual; and JVC, where a tough manager had recently replaced one who was an enthusiast of empowerment.

9. I have reduced this interview by about 50 percent, in part by cutting a long attempt by Lax to draw a picture of the organization which is impossible to put down on paper. I have also cut a great deal of repetition and meandering to make it read "tighter" than it was spoken. In one or two instances I have grouped comments that actually occurred at different places, but which were a single logical thought—in other words, when he returned to an earlier theme.

Chapter 7: Breaking Through

1. The only exceptions to the emphasis on sharing of business information and clarification of the mission were Marks and (at least until shortly before my visit) Hardin.

2. To avoid too much elaboration in the text, let me add here that the leadership role at Dest seems to have been quite similar; and at Crown, while I did not interview the division manager and I am less clear about his role, the data I do have are consistent with this picture of "intermittent" management—far more than any of the ten troubled companies.

3. This process of hidden decision making in "the vault," incidentally, was only a more intense version of what had been done earlier at the very top levels of the organization. Other companies had not carried the symbolism of isolated decision making to quite this extreme, but the basic pattern was widespread.

4. As usual, these numbers are approximate because there are quite a few people whom I did not formally interview but whom I sometimes have used as evidence. It depends on whether you count them or not. In addition, I often did not note whether interviewees were minorities or not—this was not in my original focus—and therefore have had to reconstruct this point from memory.

5. The only person in the troubled companies who talked openly of the balance between family and work, and who claimed to have reached reasonable balance, was in Marks. This, it will be recalled, was an old-time organization with few formal systems, focused entirely around the personality of the leader. He favored this woman and took her interests to heart.

6. These themes have been addressed at length elsewhere: the "political" func-

tions of middle managers in traditional organizations in chapter 2; the "protective" role toward subordinates in chapter 4.

7. See chapter 3.

8. Traditionally, "professionals" are defined, for example, by a shared educational base (law school or medical school) and by autonomous mechanisms of self-governance (ethics boards, etc.). See, for example, Robert Dingwall and Philip Lewis (eds.) (1983); Margali S. Larson (1977); Talcott Parsons (1968). None of these apply to the management case.

Indeed, many writers have seen tension and contradiction in the relation between managers and professionals, with the latter being by nature resistant to bureaucratic control. See, for example, Mark Abrahamson (ed.) (1967); G. Harries-Jenkins (1970).

My view is that in bureaucratic organizations, managers are indeed in tension with professionals, but that currently the two are coming together—the key similarity being that both traditional professionals and successful managers today are more oriented to abstract commitments than to any particular organization. This argument was made many years ago on a theoretical level by Talcott Parsons (1960 and 1971).

9. "Honeywell" is a substitute for the real company.

10. I count about a dozen people in my sample who had moved through two or more companies besides their current employer after the age of thirty. It is not uncommon for people to work for several companies at the start of their careers, but very uncommon once they begin to progress through the hierarchy of one company. I have this information for most, but not all, of the people I interviewed.

The following remarks about mobile managers are based primarily on this dozen. There were also a number of others who had moved once in midcareer, or who had moved unusually widely within their company, and who shared many of the same perspectives.

11. There was one identifiable "professional" manager at Lyco; he, consistent with this view, was scornful of the "quality of life" orientation of the employee Congress.

12. The Barclay-Hardin pairing provides further evidence. At Hardin, as we saw, there was at best complacent, inward-looking satisfaction, and at worst bitter frustration. Barclay's middle managers had come from the same environment, yet they were caught up in the widespread enthusiasm for the changing business and focused strongly on the outside.

Chapter 8: The Emerging Employment Relation

1. I take this statement from a public source so as not to break confidentality in my sample.

2. See the discussion on the taboo on discussion of working conditions in Lyco in chapter 5, pp. 87–93.

3. Chapter 5, p. 92.

4. Loyalists often express abstract support for the idea of paying people for their performance—it is an idea deeply rooted in American ideology. But when confronted with it in practice in their organizations, they uniformly hated it, arguing that it causes unnecessary divisions and bitterness within the community.

5. The need for cooperation beyond market mechanisms has been accepted even by many economists, especially those in the stream carved by Oliver Williamson (1975 and 1985). Williamson puts it in terms of the "transaction costs" incurred when trying to accomplish certain tasks through market contracting when these costs are too high it is more efficient to use a stable organization. From this perspective I am extending the argument to say that there are conditions in which the costs of maintaining a permanent organization are too high, and it is more efficient to build a mission-focused system.

6. I have argued elsewhere (Heckscher, 1991) that importing the free-agent ethic into a business organization simply produces a distorted hierarchy, in which the orders of the higher levels replace market demand. This just makes the reasons for business decisions even more confusing and opaque and leads to increased "politics."

7. All my interviewees were currently employed by large companies. A few had been laid off but then had found new jobs, and one person was on the way out the door.

   For evidence of the desperation of unemployment—if evidence is needed—see Katherine S. Newman (1988). She, incidentally, offers evidence that even those who have been laid off remain loyal to their companies and justify the layoffs, very much like the managers I quoted in chapter 4. They justify the company's actions in terms of the kind of bureaucratic/loyalist ethic I have described. She quotes one man: "A policy is a policy and a procedure is a procedure. That's the way you operate. If you're part of the corporate world you understand. . . . If I got back into the game, I'd play it the same way. And I'd expect the same things to happen to me again" (p. 77).

8. For a more detailed treatments of the rise of "post-bureaucratic organization," see Charles Heckscher and Anne Donnellon (eds.) (1994); Walter W. Powell (1990); Tom Burns and G. M. Stalker (1961).

9. "Search conferences," a technique drawn from long experience among the Tavistock School of organization theory, are growing increasingly commonplace; these are public explorations of possible directions and opportunities for the future. See Marvin R. Weisbord (1987); and Barbara Gray (1989). For a more extensive discussion of the issues in this section, see Charles Heckscher, Russell A. Eisenstat, and Thomas J. Rice (1994).

10. The most popular work advocating alternatives to bureaucratic management is still *In Search of Excellence* by Thomas J. Peters and Robert H. Waterman, Jr. (1982). Too many works to mention have followed in its wake, but I will nevertheless mention Robert H. Waterman, Jr. (1990); Rosabeth Moss Kanter (1990); Gifford Pinchot (1994); Meg Wheatley (1992); George P. Huber (1984); Peter Drucker (1988).

11. Economists have of course written a great deal about labor markets, but I am not aware of any significant literature about how to make them more open. The question certainly has not been addressed in the management literature, nor, I think, in general policy analyses.

12. The employment at will doctrine, and its roots in master-servant law, is masterfully dissected by James B. Atleson (1983). See also Paul Weiler (1987) and B. Heshizer (1985), and my own exploration of the incursions on the employment at will doctrine in Heckscher (1988): chap. 7.

    Ian MacNeil's theory of "relational contracting" is the most thorough attempt I know of to explore the norms underlying ongoing relationships, including employment; see Ian MacNeil (1980).

13. For further discussion of the emerging role of associations, see Charles C. Heckscher (1988), esp. chap. 9.

14. On caucus groups, see Ray Friedman and Donna Carter (1993); Caitlin Deinard and Raymond Friedman (1990); Elizabeth L. Bishop and David I. Levine (1993).

15. In some European countries management associations have progressed beyond our own. Though they have drawn encouragement from labor laws and the union movement, they have remained separate from traditional unions and have taken on a distinct character. They put much less emphasis on traditional adversarial tactics such as the strike, and much more on pressure through publicity. They also provide services for career development and training.

    Europe is as big on loyalty as the United States, so for the most part management unions have not overcome the barriers. The exception is Sweden, where they have become part of the corporatist equilibrium and have focused on maintaining pay differentials from blue-collar workers. In Britain and Germany less than 10 percent of managers are unionized, and that mostly in the public sector; in France and Japan it is even smaller.

    For general discussions of managerial unionism in Europe, see European Association for Personnel Management (1979); Yves Delamotte (1985); Myron J. Roomkin (ed.) (1989); and Paul Frost (1980).

16. For explorations of the psychology or personal experience of managers under downsizing, see Paul Leinberger and Bruce Tucker (1991); Katherine S. Newman (1988).

17. Paul Leinberger and Bruce Tucker (1991).

Chapter 9: Conclusion

1. Predictions are, of course, risky. Defensive patterns can easily produce explosions when they are finally broken, as any psychiatrist can attest.

    It would not be too surprising if there were an abrupt shift of mood among managers. If layoffs and restructuring continue to a point where denial is no longer possible, and if no satisfactory alternative has developed, there could be a mass reaction. My sense, though, is that elements of the "professional" ethic are already widespread enough that people will increasingly latch onto it, as did the group described in the last chapter. I have always kept in mind, to avoid hubris in prediction, the experience of a group of French social scientists who in April 1968 published a report on the quiescent mood of the population, asserting that uprisings like those then under way in the United States or Germany would not happen in France. The explosive *évènements de mai,* which engulfed the country in furious conflict, occurred barely a month later.

2. Traditionally many corporations demanded an even higher level of conformity than this. Melville Dalton's (1959) classic study of managers in the 1950s, for instance, detailed how pressure was put on them to join the right clubs (the Masons). This type of pressure, though, is not really a test of *loyalty.* It is a way of assuring that people who enter into the higher circles of power are similar enough to those already there that they can feel "comfortable" with them in an informal sense. Such "clubbiness" acts as a very effective bar to the advancement of women and minorities, but the dynamics are not exactly the same as those of loyalty.

3. See James B. Atleson (1983).

4. For further discussion of the managers' own resistance to greater voice, see chap. 5, pp. 87–93.

5. The set of "observational" studies on traditional management referred to in chapter 2, *n.* 18, all stress the systematic dominance of company values over outside connections.

6. For an elaboration of the changing role of professional associations, and a more developed argument about their potential role in representing employee rights in professional ranks, see Charles C. Heckscher (1988), esp. chaps. 8–10.

7. Joseph A. Schumpeter (1942).

8. Writers who have referred to traditional corporate culture as "feudal" or "tribalistic" include Rosabeth Moss Kanter (1977); Elton Mayo (1949); Robert Jackall (1988); Diane Rothbard Margolis (1979); William H. Whyte, Jr. (1956).

BIBLIOGRAPHY

Abrahamson, Mark (ed.). 1967. *The Professional in the Organization.* Chicago: Rand McNally.

Allen, Robert W., and Lyman W. Porter (eds.). 1983. *Organizational Influence Processes.* Glenview, Ill.: Scott Foresman.

American Management Association. 1993. "1993 AMA Survey on Downsizing: Summary of the Key Findings." New York: American Management Association.

Atleson, James B. 1983. *Values & Assumptions in American Labor Law.* Amherst: University of Massachusetts Press.

Baker, George P., Michael C. Jensen, and Kevin J. Murphy. 1988. "Compensation and Incentives: Practice vs. Theory." *Journal of Finance,* May.

Barnard, Chester I. 1938. *The Functions of the Executive.* Cambridge, Mass.: Harvard University Press.

Beer, Michael, et al. 1985. *Managing Human Assets: The Groundbreaking Harvard Business School Program.* New York: Free Press.

Beer, Stafford. 1981. *Brain of the Firm.* Chichester: John Wiley & Sons (2d ed.).

Bellah, Robert N., Richard Madsen, William M. Sullivan, Ann Swidler, and Steven Tipton. 1985. *Habits of the Heart: Individualism and Commitment in American Life.* Berkeley: University of California Press.

Bennett, Amanda. 1990. *The Death of the Organization Man.* New York: William Morrow.

Berger, Suzanne, and Michael J. Piore. 1980. *Dualism and Discontinuity in Industrial Societies.* Cambridge and New York: Cambridge University Press.

Bishop, Elizabeth L., and David I. Levine. 1993. "Computer-Mediated Communication as Employee Voice: A Case Study." Mimeo draft. Berkeley, Calif.: Haas School of Business Administration.

Blau, Peter M. 1963. *The Dynamics of Bureaucracy.* Chicago: University of Chicago Press.

Brown, Roger. 1986. *Social Psychology: The Second Edition.* New York: Free Press.

Bunge, Mario. 1969. "The Metaphysics, Epistemology, and Methodology of Levels." In L. L. Whyte and A. G. Wilson et al. (eds.): 17–28.

Burgelman, Robert A. 1983. "A Process Model of Internal Corporate Venturing in the Diversified Major Firm." *Administrative Science Quarterly* 28: 223–24.

Burns, Tom, and G. M. Stalker. 1961. *The Management of Innovation*. London: Tavistock.

Cannings, Kathy. 1989. "An Exit-Voice Model of Managerial Attachment." *Journal of Economic Behavior and Organization* 12: 107–29.

Chandler, Alfred D., Jr. 1977. *The Visible Hand: The Managerial Revolution in American Business*. Cambridge, Mass.: Harvard University Press.

Coser, Lewis A. 1974. *Greedy Institutions: Patterns of Undivided Commitment*. New York: Free Press.

Crozier, Michel. 1964. *The Bureaucratic Phenomenon*. Chicago: University of Chicago Press. Original French ed. 1963.

Dalton, Melville. 1959. *Men Who Manage: Fusions of Feeling and Theory in Administration*. New York: John Wiley & Sons.

DeMaria, Alfred T., Dale Tarnowiewski, and Richard Gurman. 1985. *Manager Unions? An AMA Research Report*. New York: American Management Association.

Deinard, Caitlin, and Raymond Friedman. 1990. "Black Caucus Groups at Xerox Corporation (A) and (B)." Boston: Harvard Business School.

Delamotte, Yves. 1985. "Managerial and Supervisory Staff in a Changing World." *International Labour Review* 124, 1 (Jan.–Feb.): 1–16.

Denison, Daniel R. 1984. "Bringing Corporate Culture to the Bottom Line." *Organizational Dynamics* 13, 2: 4–22.

Dingwall, Robert, and Philip Lewis (eds.). 1983. *The Sociology of the Professions: Lawyers, Doctors, and Others*. London: Macmillan.

Drucker, Peter. 1988. "The Coming of the New Organization." *Harvard Business Review* 88, 1 (Jan.–Feb.): 45–53.

———. 1946. *Concept of the Corporation*. New York: John Day.

———. 1985. "Playing the Information-Based Orchestra." *New York Times*, June 4, p. 32.

Edwards, R. 1979. *Contested Terrain: The Transformation of the Workplace in the Twentieth Century*. New York: Basic Books.

European Association for Personnel Management. 1979. *Management Unionization in Western Europe*. European Association for Personnel Management.

Friedman, Ray, and Donna Carter. 1993. "African-American Network Groups: Their Impact and Effectiveness." Boston: Harvard Business School Working Paper 93-069, May.

Frost, Paul. 1980. "The Representation of Managerial Interests." In M. Poole and R. Mansfield: chap. 11.

Galbraith, John Kenneth. 1980. *American Capitalism: the Concept of Countervailing power*.

George, Claude S. 1968. *The History of Management Thought*. Englewood Cliffs, N.J.: Prentice-Hall.

Goethals, G., and J. Darley. 1987. "Social Comparison Theory: Self-Evaluation and Group Life." In B. Mullen and G. Goethals (eds.): 21–47.

Gouldner, Alvin W. 1954. *Patterns of Industrial Bureaucracy: A Case Study of Modern Factory Administration*. New York: Free Press.

Gray, Barbara. 1989. *Collaborating: Finding Common Ground for Multiparty Problems*. San Francisco: Jossey-Bass.

Grobstein, Clifford. 1973. "Hierarchical Order and Neogenesis." In H. H. Pattee: chap. 2.

Hales, Colin. 1986. "What Do Managers Do? A Critical Review of the Evidence." *Journal of Management Studies* 23, 1 (January).

Hall, Robert E. 1982. "The Importance of Lifetime Jobs in the U.S. Economy." *American*

Economic Review 72, 4 (September): 716–24.

Harries-Jenkins, G. 1970. "Professionals in Organizations." In J. A. Jackson (ed.): chap. 3.

Heckscher, Charles. 1988. *The New Unionism: Employee Involvement in the Changing Corporation.* New York: Basic Books.

———, and Anne Donnellon (eds.). 1994. *The Post-Bureaucratic Organization: New Perspectives on Organizational Change.* Thousand Oaks, Calif.: Sage Publications.

———, Russell A. Eisenstat, and Thomas J. Rice. 1994. "Transformational Processes." In C. Heckscher and A. Donnellon (eds.): chap. 6.

Heshizer, Brian. 1985. "New Common Law of Employment: Changes in the Concept of Employment at Will." *Labor Law Journal* (February): 95–107.

Hirschman, Albert O. 1970. *Exit, Voice, and Loyalty: Responses to Decline in Firms, Organizations, and States.* Cambridge, Mass.: Harvard University Press.

Horne, J. H., and Tom Lupton. 1965. "The Work Activities of Middle Managers: An Exploratory Study." *Journal of Management Studies* 2, 1: 14–33.

Horton, Thomas R., and Peter C. Reid. 1991. *Beyond the Trust Gap: Forging a New Partnership Between Managers and Their Employers.* Homewood, Ill.: Business One Irwin.

Huber, George P. 1984. "The Nature and Design of Post-Industrial Organizations." *Management Science* 30, 8 (August): 928–51.

Jackall, Robert. 1988. *Moral Mazes: The World of Corporate Managers.* New York: Oxford University Press.

Jackson, J. A. (ed.). 1970. *Professions and Professionalization.* Cambridge, Eng.: Cambridge University Press.

Jensen, Michael C., and William H. Meckling. 1991. "Specific and General Knowledge, and Organizational Structure." In Lars Werin and Hans Wijkander (eds.).

———, and Kevin J. Murphy. 1990. "CEO Incentives: It's Not How Much You Pay, but How." *Harvard Business Review* (May–June): 138–53.

———, and W. H. Meckling. 1987. "The Nature of Man." Draft. Boston: Harvard Business School.

Kanter, Rosabeth Moss. 1977. *Men and Women of the Corporation.* New York: Basic Books.

———. 1986. "The New Workforce Meets the Changing Workplace: Strains, Dilemmas and Contradictions in Attempts to Implement Participative and Entrepreneurial Management." *Human Resource Management* 25, 4 (Winter): 515–37.

———. 1990. *When Giants Learn to Dance.* New York: Simon & Schuster.

Kay, Emmanuel. 1974. *The Crisis in Middle Management.* New York: Amacom.

Keillor, Garrison. 1985. *Lake Wobegon Days.* New York: Viking.

Klare, K. E. 1983. "The Bitter and the Sweet: Reflections on the Supreme Court's *Yeshiva* Decision." *Socialist Review* 71 (Sept.–Oct.): 99–129.

Kocka, Jurgen. 1980. *White-Collar Workers in America, 1890–1940: A Socio-Political History in International Perspective.* Beverly Hills: Sage.

Kotter, John. 1982. *The General Managers.* New York: Free Press.

Kunda, Gideon. 1986. "Engineering Culture: Control in a High-Tech Organization." Ph.D. diss. Cambridge, Mass.: MIT.

Kusterer, Ken C. 1978. *Know-How on the Job: The Important Working Knowledge of "Unskilled" Workers.* Boulder, Colo.: Westview Press.

Larson, Margali Sarfatti. 1977. *The Rise of Professionalism: a Sociological Analysis.* Berkeley: University of California Press.

Lawler, Edward E., Gerald E. Ledford, and Susan A. Mohrman. 1989. *Employee Involve-*

ment in America: A Study of Contemporary Practice. Houston: American Productivity and Quality Center.

———, and Samuel B. Bacharach. 1983. "Political Action and Alignments in Organizations." *Research in the Sociology of Organizations* 2: 83–107.

Leibenstein, Harvey. 1987. *Inside the Firm: The Inefficiencies of Hierarchy.* Cambridge, Mass.: Harvard University Press.

Leinberger, Paul, and Bruce Tucker. 1991. *The New Individualists: The Generation After the Organization Man.* New York: HarperCollins.

Levins, Richard. 1973. "The Limits of Complexity." In H. H. Pattee: chap. 5.

Machin, John, Rosemary Stewart, and Colin Hales. 1981. *Toward Managerial Effectiveness: Applied Research Perspectives on the Managerial Task.* Westmead: Gower.

MacNeil, Ian R. 1980. *The New Social Contract: an Inquiry into Modern Contractual Relations.* New Haven: Yale University Press.

Manwaring, Tony, and Stephen Wood. 1984. "The Ghost in the Machine: Tacit Skills in the Labor Process." *Socialist Review* 14, 2 (March–April): 55–83.

Margolis, Diane Rothbard. 1979. *The Managers: Corporate Life in America.* New York: William Morrow.

Mathewson, Stanley B. 1931. *Restriction of Output Among Unorganized Workers.* New York: Viking Press.

Mayo, Elton. 1949. *The Social Problems of an Industrial Civilization.* London: Routledge & Kegan Paul.

Meyer, Marshall W. 1985. *Limits to Bureaucratic Growth.* Berlin: deGruyter.

Mills, C. Wright. 1951. *White Collar: The American Middle Classes.* London: Oxford University Press.

Mintzberg, Henry. 1973. *The Nature of Managerial Work.* New York: Harper & Row.

Morgan, Brian S., and William A. Schiemann. 1986. "Employee Attitudes: Then and Now." *Personnel Journal* (Oct.).

Mullen, B., and G. Goethals (eds.). 1987. *Theories of Group Behavior.* New York: Springer Verlag.

New York Stock Exchange Office of Economic Research. 1982. *People & Productivity: A Challenge to Corporate America.* New York: New York Stock Exchange Office of Economic Research.

Newman, Katherine S. 1988. *Falling from Grace: The Experience of Downward Mobility in the American Middle Class.* New York: Free Press.

Olson, Mancur. 1971. *The Logic of Collective Action: Public Goods and the Theory of Group.* Cambridge, Mass.: Harvard University Press.

Ouchi, William G. 1980. "Markets, Bureaucracies, and Clans." *Administrative Science Quarterly* 25 (March): 129–41.

———. 1981. *Theory Z: How American Business Can Meet the Japanese Challenge.* Reading, Mass.: Addison-Wesley.

Parsons, Talcott. 1969. "On the Concept of Political Power." In T. Parsons: chap. 14.

———. 1969. *Politics and Social Structure.* New York: Free Press.

———. 1968. "Professions." In David L. Sills (ed.), *International Encyclopedia of the Social Sciences.* Vol. 12 (536–47). New York: Crowell Collier and Macmillan.

———. 1960. "Some Ingredients of General Theory of Formal Organization." In Talcott Parsons, *Structure and Process in Modern Society* (59–96). New York: Free Press.

———. 1971. *The System of Modern Societies.* Englewood Cliffs, N. J.: Prentice-Hall.

Pattee, Howard H. 1973. *Hierarchy Theory: The Challenge of Complex Systems.* New York: George Braziller.

Pearse, Robert F. 1977. *Manager to Manager II: What Managers Think of Their Managerial Careers.* New York: Amacom.

Peters, Thomas J., and Robert H. Waterman, Jr. 1982. *In Search of Excellence: Lessons from America's Best-Run Companies.* New York: Harper & Row.

Peters, Tom. 1987. *Thriving on Chaos: Handbook for a Management Revolution.* New York: Knopf.

Pettigrew, Andrew M. 1973. *The Politics of Organizational Decisionmaking.* London: Tavistock.

Pinchot, Gifford, and Elizabeth Pinchot. 1993. *The End of Bureaucracy and the Rise of the Intelligent Organization.* San Francisco: Berrett-Koehler.

Porat, Marc Uri. 1977. *The Information Economy: Definition and Measurement.* Vol. 1. Washington, D.C.: U.S. Dept. of Commerce, Office of Telecommunications.

Posner, B. Z., and W. H. Schmidt. 1984. "Values and the American Manager: An Update." *California Management Review* 26, 3 (Spring).

Powell, Walter W. 1990. "Neither Market nor Hierarchy: Network Forms of Organization." *Research in Organizational Behavior* 12: 295–336.

Riesman, David. 1950. *The Lonely Crowd: A Study of the Changing American Character.* New Haven: Yale University Press.

Roethlisberger, E. J., and W. J. Dickson. 1939. *Management & the Worker.* Cambridge, Mass.: Harvard University Press.

Roomkin, Myron J. (ed.). 1989. *Managers as Employees: An International Comparison of the Changing Character of Managerial Employment.* New York: Oxford University Press.

Rubin, Lilian Breslow. 1976. *Worlds of Pain: Life in the Working-Class Family.* New York: Basic Books.

Salaman, Graeme. 1977. "An Historical Discontinuity: From Charisma to Routinization." *Human Relations* 30, 4: 373–88.

Schlesinger, Len, Todd Jick, Amy B. Johnson, and Lori Ann MacIsaac. 1991. "Xerox Corporation: Leadership Through Quality (A) & (B)." Harvard Business School Case 9-490-008 (rev.).

Schor, Juliet B. 1991. *The Overworked American: The Unexpected Decline of Leisure.* New York: Basic Books.

Schumpeter, Joseph A. 1942. *Capitalism, Socialism, and Democracy.* New York: Harper.

Simon, Herbert. 1991. "Organizations and Markets." *Journal of Economic Perspectives* 5, 2 (Spring): 34.

Sloan, Alfred P. 1964. *My Years with General Motors.* Garden City, N.Y.: Doubleday.

Smith, Adam. 1751. *The Theory of Moral Sentiments.* London: Millar.

Spencer, Laura J. 1989. *Winning Through Participation: Meeting the Challenge of Corporate Change with the Technology of Participation.* Dubuque, Iowa: Kendall/Hunt.

Stewart, Rosemary. 1982. *Choices for the Manager.* Englewood Cliffs, N.J.: Prentice-Hall.

———. 1972. *The Reality of Organizations.* London: Macmillan. Reprint. Garden City, New York: Doubleday.

———. 1981. "The Relevance for Managerial Effectiveness of My Studies of Managerial Work and Behavior." In J. Machin, R. Stewart, and C. Hales (eds.): chap. 2.

Stephenson, Ted. 1985. *Management: A Political Activity.* London: Macmillan.

Strauss, George. 1962. "Tactics of Lateral Relationship: The Purchasing Agent." *Administrative Science Quarterly* 7, 2 (Sept.).

Tomasko, Robert M. 1987. *Downsizing: Reshaping the Corporation for the Future.* New York: Amacom.

Torrington, Derek, and Jane Weightman. 1987. "Middle Management Work." *Journal of General Management* 13, 2 (Winter): 74–89.

U.S. Department of Commerce, Bureau of the Census. 1971. *Historical Statistics of the U.S.* Washington, D.C.: Government Printing Office.

US News & World Report. 1981. "The Coming Industrial Miracle."

Walton, Richard E. 1985. "From Control to Commitment in the Workplace." *Harvard Business Review* (March–April): 76–84.

Waterman, Robert H., Jr. 1990. *Adhocracy: the Power to Change.* Whittle Direct Books.

Weiler, Paul. 1987. "Employment and Its Termination: The Uses of the Market, Legal Regulation, and Collective Bargaining." Mimeo draft. Cambridge, Mass.: Harvard Law School.

Weisbord, Marvin R. 1987. *Productive Workplaces: Organizing and Managing for Meaning, Dignity, and Community.* San Francisco: Jossey-Bass.

Werin, Lars, and Hans Wijkander (eds.). 1991. *Main Currents in Contract Economics.* Oxford: Blackwell.

Wheatley, Meg. 1992. *Leadership and the New Science.* San Francisco: Berrett-Kohler.

Whyte, L. L., A. G. Wilson, and D. Wilson (eds.). 1969. *Hierarchical Structures.* New York: Elsevier.

Whyte, William H., Jr. 1956. *The Organization Man.* New York: Simon & Schuster.

Williamson, Oliver E. 1985. *Economic Institutions of Capitalism.* New York: Free Press.

———. 1975. *Markets and Hierarchies: Analysis and Antitrust Implications.* New York: Free Press.

Wright, J. Patrick. 1980. *On a Clear Day You Can See General Motors.* New York: Avon.

Yankelovich, D., et al. 1983. "Work and Human Values: An International Report on Jobs in the 1980s and 1990s." Queenstown, Md.: Aspen Institute for Humanistic Studies.

Zemke, Ron. 1986. "Delayed Effects of Corporate Downsizing." *Training* (November): 67–74.

Zunz, Olivier. 1990. *Making America Corporate.* Chicago: University of Chicago Press.

INDEX

Accountability, 73, 162–63

Agency theory, 13–14, 16–18, 21, 24, 203n7

Ambivalence, 59–60

American Management Association, 3, 5

Anger, of middle managers: extent of, 205n1; projection of, 51, 52; toward peers, 51–52; toward top management, 40–41, 44–45, 47–53

Apex (corporate pseudonym), 9, 122, 123, 126, 128–29, 131–40, 143, 150, 151, 158, 161, 185–86

Associations, 166–68, 177, 211n15

AT&T, 9, 103, 109

Attrition, 54, 58, 62

Autonomy: in bureaucracies, 20–21; desire for, 66, 98, 99; and feudal dependency, 19–20, 31; retreat to, 53, 73–75, 107–8, 124. *See also* Free agents; Individualism

Barclay (corporate pseudonym), 9, 122, 123, 124–30, 132, 133–36, 138, 158, 186–87

Blue-collar workers, 3, 4; as expendable, 28; in Japan, 5, 27; motivation of, 14–18; rationalism and, 14–18

Bureaucracy: advantages of, 14–15; continuation of, 98–99; corporate loyalty and, 27, 115–16; decentralized, 4; disadvantages of, 21, 27; increase in, 58, 69–72; incremental improvement and, 107–8, 208n6; key aspect of, 17–18; loyalty patterns in, 20–21; moving away from, 57; participatory management versus, 78–79, 80; and paternalism, 6–7; rationalism and, 14–15, 17; team-based organizations versus, 161–63

Bureaucratic capitalism, 7

Business strategy, 90–93, 122, 127–29, 134, 207n6

Business understanding: of competition, 127–28; of corporate strategy and mission, 90–93, 122, 127–29, 134, 207n6; customer focus and, 57, 74, 102; lack of, in troubled companies, 61–64, 67–68, 90–93, 207n6; quality focus and, 63–64, 74, 104, 127, 158–59; strength of, in dynamic companies, 122, 127–29, 134, 149–50

Capitalism: bureaucratic, 7; and community breakdown, 8; criticisms of, 33

Career advancement, 4, 178–79; and corporate loyalty, 23–24, 25

Caucuses, 167–68

Change: continuous, 97–100; limits to, 108–11; need for, 172–79; resistance to, 84, 85–87, 95–96, 104–8; as threat to corporate community, 97–100, 173–74

Change agents, 147

Chrysler, 5

Coaching, as manager role, 71, 79, 80, 86

Commitments, individual, 146–49, 151, 178–79, 182–83, 207n2, 208n5

Communication, 67; business strategy discussions, 90–93, 207n6; changing rules of, 87–93; honesty in, 151, 166; open patterns of, 127–29, 131–33, 178

Community: attitudes toward, 33–34; criticism of, 33; loss of, 8, 41–42, 59, 64–66, 75, 97–99; love of, 41–42; loyalty toward, 34–35

Community of purpose, 9, 11, 32. 175; change and diversity as threats to, 97–100, 173–74; described, 145–46; individuals with commitments in, 146–49; limitations of, 156–59; moving toward, 121–43; open labor markets and, 163–68; organization with a mission in, 145, 149–50, 151–52; potential strengths of, 152–56; psychology of adaptability and, 168–70; shared purpose and, 145, 150–52; team-based organizations and, 159, 160–63, 173

Compensation incentives, 16, 29, 46, 57, 58, 60, 67, 153–54

Competition, knowledge of, 127–28

Computers, impact of, 5–6

Conflict management, 32, 56, 131–33, 154–56, 161, 205n36

Conformity, 23, 35, 173–74, 212n2

Consensus building, 161–62

Continuous improvement, as threat to corporate community, 97–100, 173–74

Contracting-out, 61, 78

Contribution, desire for, 46

Cooperation, 7; in community of purpose, 150–52, 154–56, 160–63; and corporate loyalty, 28–32, 69–72; difficulty with, 27–28, 42, 44; in dynamic companies,

127–36; in middle manager networks, 25, 28–32, 69–72, 204n29–30

Corporate culture: change in, 57, 60–61; and corporate loyalty, 108–10; as limit to change, 108–10; participatory management and, 77–94

Corporate loyalty, 22–35; benefits to corporation, 27–31; breakdown of, 64–66; bureaucracy and, 27, 115–16; career advancement and, 23, 24–25; community focus in, 28–32, 69–72; continuous change and, 97–100; and cooperation, 28–32, 69–72; and corporate culture, 108–10; described, 22–23; development of, 23–27; diversity and, 97–100, 173–74; employment security and, 24, 26–27; factors in, 25; forces undermining, 173–74; gratitude and, 25; internal career tracks and, 23–24, 25; limitations of, 31–32, 95–118; and organizational identity, 108–10; participatory management and, 77–79, 135–36; problems of, 95–118; and resistance to change, 95–96, 104–8; stock sharing and, 24. See also Loyalty

Cross-functional teams. See Team-based organizations

Crown (corporate pseudonym), 29, 30, 122, 124, 127–28, 129, 131, 135, 158–59, 187–88

Customer focus, 57, 74, 102

Decentralization, 4, 41, 57, 74, 115–16, 125

Decision making, 135–36, 157

Defensiveness, 105–8, 125, 168, 211–12n1; denial, 62–66, 106–7; exclusiveness, 40–41, 48–51, 102–3; incrementalist approach in, 107–8, 208n6; inwardness, 62–66, 102, 105–6; projection of anger, 51, 52; regression, 105–6; resistance to change, 84, 85–87, 95–96, 104–8; scapegoating, 51, 52

Denial, 62–66, 106–7

Dependence: and corporate loyalty, 25, 31, 101–2; moving away from, 169–70; personal, 19–20, 31

Dest (corporate pseudonym), 19, 20, 122, 124, 131, 132, 136, 138–39, 141, 150, 153, 158, 188–89

Diversity: increasing levels of, 97–100; openness to, 136–37; as threat to corporate community, 97–100, 173–74. *See also* Conformity

Dow Chemical, 9

Downsizing: extent of, 3–5; impact of, 11–12; by largest corporations, 3; motivation problems and, 45–49

Dupont, 4, 9, 23

Dynamic companies, 10–11, 122

Early retirement programs, 54, 58, 62

Emon (corporate pseudonym), 29, 50, 71, 148–49, 189–90

Employment at will doctrine, 165, 211*n*12

Employment law, 23, 24–25, 165–66, 176

Empowerment, 7, 57, 110, 208*n*8

Entitlement, attitude of, 44

Entrepreneurship, 3, 7, 57, 58

Ethics, loyalty and, 7–9, 32–35, 150–52, 175–77

Exclusiveness, 40–41, 48–51, 102–3

Family, corporation as, 100–104, 156

Fear, 73; and corporate loyalty, 25; effects of, 45–46; and self-censorship, 88

Feudal dependency, 19–20, 31

Figgie International, 9

Financial planning, for downsizing, 183

Fixx (corporate pseudonym), 9, 132, 190

Ford, Henry, 35

Free agents, 152–54, 155, 156, 210*n*6. *See also* Autonomy; Individualism

Gemeinschaft and *Gesellschaft*, 22, 33

General Electric, 3, 54, 205*n*35

General managers, 10

General Motors, 3, 4, 9, 23, 95, 96, 102, 103, 104, 106, 108, 109–10, 153

General skills, 180, 182

Geographic transfers, 23, 24

Glover (corporate pseudonym), 9, 17, 22, 58–75, 78, 95, 105, 106, 110, 127, 135, 148, 191–92

Government: bureaucracy in, 21; role in open labor markets, 163, 164–66

Habits of the Heart (Bellah et al.), 33

Hall, John (pseudonym), 139–40, 141, 147, 175–76

Hardin (corporate pseudonym), 124–26, 129–30, 192–93

Hawthorne study, 15, 203*n*5

Hierarchy, 4, 6, 7, 32, 101–2, 132–33, 171. *See also* Bureaucracy

Hirschman, Albert, 77, 78, 94

Homogeneity, 23, 35, 173–74, 212*n*2

Honesty, 151, 166

Honeywell, 9

Human relations approach, 53–56, 68; attrition in, 54, 58, 62; early retirement programs in, 54, 58, 62; niceness in, 11–12, 53–56, 68

IBM, 3, 31, 35, 96, 102, 103, 109

Implicit contract, 7–9, 32–35, 150–52, 175–77. *See also* Paternalism; Professionalism

Incentives, 17

Income growth, 4–5

Individualism, 11–12, 53, 99, 141, 152–54

Individuals with commitments, 146–49

In Search of Excellence (Peters and Waterman), 40, 210*n*10

"Insider/outsider" problems, 40–41, 48–51, 102–3

Insurance, 163, 164, 165, 166

International competition, impact on middle managers, 4–5

Inwardness, 62–66, 102, 105–6

Isony (corporate pseudonym), 79, 91, 193

Japan, 4, 5, 163; company loyalty in, 5, 27; employment security in, 24

JVC (corporate pseudonym), 69, 79, 88, 102, 108, 133, 194–95

Karet (corporate pseudonym), 17, 29, 69, 70, 91, 195–96

Labor markets, opening, 163–68; government and, 163, 164–66; insurance in, 163–66; managerial associations and, 166–68, 177, 211*n*15; market mechanisms for, 164; portable benefits in, 181
Lax, Sam (pseudonym), 111–17, 138, 161, 208*n*9
Layoffs. *See* Downsizing
Leadership, by top managers, 4, 114–15, 133–35
Learning systems, 204*n*34
Locke, John, 33
Love for a company, 26–27
"Loyalists," middle managers as, 7–9, 11, 42–44, 55, 57, 59, 100–101, 104, 111–17, 138, 147, 148, 150–51, 153, 155, 156, 178, 184, 207*n*4, 210*n*4
Loyalty: bureaucratic, 20–21; defined, 6–7; ethical dimension of, 7–9, 32–35, 175–77; in Japan, 5, 27; master-servant form of, 23, 27, 165–66; paradoxical effects of, 11–12; patterns of, 18–27; personal dependence and, 19–20, 31. *See also* Corporate loyalty
Lyco (corporate pseudonym), 9, 47, 52–54, 69, 79, 80–87, 89, 90–93, 95, 100–101, 106, 111–17, 128, 132, 142–43, 151, 196–97

Management associations, 166–68, 177, 211*n*15
Management by objectives, 28, 204*n*32
Marks (corporate pseudonym), 19–20, 70, 88, 133, 142, 197–98
Master-servant relationship, 23, 27, 165–66
Matrix management systems, 65–66
Mentoring, 181
Middle managers: associations of, 166–68, 177, 211*n*15; changing functions of, 100–101, 137–38; classic image of, 3, 4, 6, 202*n*8; criticism of, 3; defined, 9–10; and downsizing trend, 3, 4–5, 8; and international competition, 4–5; lateral contacts of, 25, 28–32, 69–72, 204*n*29–30; layoffs of, 3, 5, 40, 41; "loyalists," 7–9, 11, 42–44, 55, 57, 59, 100–101, 104, 111–17, 138, 147, 148, 150–51, 153, 155, 156, 178, 184, 207*n*4, 210*n*4; number of, 201*n*2; outside commitments of, 148–49, 151, 178–79, 182–83, 207*n*2, 208*n*5; "professionals," 7, 43–44, 138–43, 146–49, 151, 153, 155–56; rationalism and, 16, 18; roles, changes in, 100–101, 137–38; and technological change, 4, 5–6; top managers forcing change on, 61, 66–68. *See also* Community of purpose; Corporate loyalty
Mills, C. Wright, 22
Minority groups, 7, 32, 52, 137, 148, 167–68, 206*n*4
Mission. *See* Vision
Mobility, job, 26, 163–68, 209*n*10; company policies and, 179–81
Morale: defined, 10; and downsizing, 45; of middle managers, 125–26
Moral righteousness, 104
Motivation: of blue-collar workers, 14–18; bureaucratic approach to, 20–21; corporate loyalty approach to, 22–35; of middle managers, 16, 18; problems with, and downsizing, 45–49; rationalist approach to, 13–18

Nadir (corporate pseudonym), 9, 34, 39–56, 59, 73, 74, 95, 102, 107–8, 133, 138, 142, 198–99
Networks, middle manager, 25, 28–32, 69–72, 204*n*29–30

"Old boys' networks," 32
Open door policies, 79, 80
Organization Man (Whyte), 24, 202*n*8
Ouchi, William, 22

Participatory management, 15–16, 77–94; business strategy and, 90–93; coaching and, 71, 79, 80, 86; and decision making, 135–36; focus groups and, 79, 80, 85; and lack of voice, 77–80; open door policies and, 79, 80; openness and, 127–29, 131–33, 178; self-censorship by managers in, 87–90, 97–98; self-censorship of managers and, 87–90, 97–98; team-based organization and, 62–63, 81–87, 90–91, 110–13, 129–31, 141, 159, 160–63, 173

Paternalism, 184; decline of, 6–9; defined, 6; and family image of corporation, 100–101, 113; negative aspects of, 8; participatory management versus, 80; and rise of professionalism, 9

Performance appraisals, 46

Performance-based rewards, 16, 46, 57, 58, 60, 67, 153–54

Personal issues, 88–90, 151, 166, 173–74, 178, 180–81

Pitney-Bowes, 9, 96

Plato, 33

Portable benefits, 181

Post-bureaucratic organizations, 210n8

Productivity: growth of, 4–5; and soldiering, 15

Professional associations, 166–68, 177, 211n15

Professional development, 167, 180, 182

Professionalism: advantages of, 174–75; company policies encouraging, 179–81; concept of, 34, 44; ethics of, 175–77; individual preparation for, 182–84; individuals with commitments and, 146–49; as negative concept, 43; psychodynamics of, 168–70; rise of, 9; and team-based organizations, 159, 160–63; traditional, 209n8

"Professionals," middle managers as, 7, 43–44, 138–43, 146–49, 151, 153, 155–56

Promotion, 4, 23–25, 137, 178–79

Psychological responses, to downsizing, 168–70. *See also* Defensiveness

Quality, 63–64, 74, 104, 127, 158–59

Quality circles, 78–79

Rationalism, 13–18; agency theory in, 13–14, 16–18, 21, 24, 203n7; bureaucratic approach to, 14–15, 17; Taylor's approach to, 14–18

Regression, 105–6

Resistance, to change, 84, 85–87, 95–96, 104–8

Risk taking, 169–70

Scapegoating, 51, 52

Scientific management, 15, 16, 18

Search conferences, 210n9

Security, 4; corporate loyalty and, 24, 26–27; and fear, 46; and unemployment, 157, 164, 166, 183, 210n7

Shared purpose, 145, 150–52

Sloan, Alfred, 4, 92

Smith, Adam, 8, 33, 154

Taylor, Frederick, 14, 15, 17

Team-based organizations, 62–63, 81–87, 90–91, 141, 159, 160–63, 173; loyalist resistance to, 110–13; professional support for, 129–31

Technological change, impact on middle managers, 4, 5–6

Top management: anger toward, 40–41, 44–45, 47–53; business strategy and, 90–92, 134, 207n6; forcing change on middle management, 61, 66–68; leadership role of, 4, 114–15, 133–35; low-key approach of, 133–35

Troubled companies, 10–11, 122

Trust: and corporate loyalty, 29, 31–32; shared loyalty and, 69–72

Unemployment, 157, 164, 166, 183, 210n7

Values: sense of shared, 25; shift in, 177–79

Vision: bureaucratic, 62; clarity of, 127–29, 179–80; corporate mission as, 145, 149–50, 151–52; lack of, 41, 46–49; of middle managers, 91–92

Voice: caucuses and, 167–68; and corporate loyalty, 77–79; self-censorship by managers and, 87–90, 97–98. *See also* Participatory management

Wang, 9
Watson, Thomas, 109
Weber, Max, bureaucratic theory of, 14–15, 17, 20, 21, 203n9

Welch, Jack, 54, 55–56, 205n35
Whyte, William H., Jr., 22, 24, 202n8
Women, 7, 52, 137, 148, 167–68, 204n24, 206n4
Worker participation. *See* Participatory management
"Working to rule," 15–16

Xerox, 3, 167